RECOVERING CONVICT LIVES

Studies in Australasian Historical Archaeology

Martin Gibbs and Mary Casey, Series Editors

The Studies in Australasian Historical Archaeology series aims to publish excavation reports and regional syntheses that deal with research into the historical archaeology of Australia, New Zealand and the Asia-Pacific region. The series aims to encourage greater public access to the results of major research and consultancy investigations, and it is co-published with the Australasian Society for Historical Archaeology.

An Archaeology of Institutional Confinement: The Hyde Park Barracks, 1848–1886
Peter Davies, Penny Crook and Tim Murray

Archaeology of the Chinese Fishing Industry in Colonial Victoria
Alister M. Bowen

The Commonwealth Block, Melbourne: A Historical Archaeology
Tim Murray, Kristal Buckley, Sarah Hayes, Geoff Hewitt, Justin McCarthy, Richard Mackay, Barbara Minchinton, Charlotte Smith, Jeremy Smith and Bronwyn Woff

Flashy, Fun and Functional: How Things Helped to Invent Melbourne's Gold Rush Mayor
Sarah Hayes

Good Taste, Fashion, Luxury: A Genteel Melbourne Family and Their Rubbish
Sarah Hayes

Port Essington: The Historical Archaeology of a North Australian 19th-Century Military Outpost
Jim Allen

Recovering Convict Lives: A Historical Archaeology of the Port Arthur Penitentiary
Richard Tuffin, David Roe, Sylvana Szydzik, E. Jeanne Harris and Ashley Matic

The Shore Whalers of Western Australia: Historical Archaeology of a Maritime Frontier
Martin Gibbs

RECOVERING CONVICT LIVES
A Historical Archaeology of the
Port Arthur Penitentiary

Richard Tuffin, David Roe,
Sylvana Szydzik, E. Jeanne Harris
and Ashley Matic

SYDNEY UNIVERSITY PRESS

A catalogue record for this book is available from
the National Library of Australia.

ISBN 9781743327821 paperback
ISBN 9781743327838 epub
ISBN 9781743327845 pdf

Cover photo by Port Arthur Historic Site Management Authority (PAHSMA) 2021
Cover design by Diana Chamma

The Penitentiary Precinct Conservation Project was a major conservation project
for the PAHSMA. The structural stabilisation and first tranche of archaeological
research excavations were part-funded with specific grants from the Tasmanian
Government and the Commonwealth Government. The excavations of the ablutions
yard and laundry were funded from PAHSMA budgets and supported by in-kind
allocations from the University of New England as part of a continuing collaboration
in archaeological research. The writing of this book took place while Richard Tuffin
was employed by the University of New England.

ASHA
AUSTRALASIAN SOCIETY FOR
HISTORICAL ARCHAEOLOGY

PORT
ARTHUR
HISTORIC
SITES

une
University of
New England

CONTENTS

LIST OF FIGURES

LIST OF PLATES

LIST OF TABLES

ACKNOWLEDGEMENTS

The authors wish to thank the PAHSMA Board, CEO Stephen Large and the Executive Leadership Team for underwriting the research approach to archaeological work in the Penitentiary Precinct Conservation Project and for approving major funding to conduct the excavation series. In particular we acknowledge Dr Jane Harrington, Director Conservation and Infrastructure for supporting this work as a major PAHSMA project.

None of the work would have been possible without the dedicated archaeologists, PAHSMA staff, colleagues and volunteers who worked on the excavation in the first place:

Excavation team (penitentiary) 2013 volunteers: Adelia Tan, Ané van der Walt, Ben James, Bob Stone, Bronwyn Woff, Charlotte Gardner, Chelsea Morgan, Chris Burbury, Fiona Shanahan, James Cole, Jeffrey Pearson, Lauren Davison, Leah Ralph, Megan Rowland, Najat Skeate, Pamela Chauvel, Steven Hall and Teagan Lane.

Excavation team (ablutions area): Laura Bates, Lauren Davison, Jeanne Harris, Rhian Jones, Henry Lion, Ronan McEleney, Fiona Shanahan and Zvonka Stanin.

Excavation team (laundry area): Laura Bates, Emma Church, Lauren Davison, Josh Gaunt, Adam Pietrzak, Michelle Richards and Sam Thomas.

PAHSMA staff (past and present): Nicky Corbett, Matt Dillon, John Featherstone, Jodie Green, John Hack, Jane Harrington, Susan Hood, Naomi Jeffs, Jo Lyngcoln, Marty Passingham, Gareath Plummer,

Ted Plummer, Michael Smith, Jody Steele, Caitlin Vertigan, Annita Waghorn and Peter Williams.

Photogrammetry expert: Peter Rigozzi.

The members of Conservation Volunteers Australia, under the supervision of John Hueston.

UNE for providing personnel and in-kind support, particularly Professor Martin Gibbs, Associate Professor David Roberts and Professor Hamish Maxwell-Stewart.

Radiology Tasmania for their critical assistance with developing and undertaking the X-ray program.

Hansen Yuncken for logistical and programming support in the archaeological monitoring phases of the 2014 structural stabilisation work.

The Tasmanian Heritage Council and the Tasman Council for statutory approvals for the excavation series.

Aboriginal Heritage Tasmania for advice on excavation planning issues.

INTRODUCTION

The penitentiary is the most well-known structure at one of Australia's most visited historic heritage sites – the former male penal station of Port Arthur, Tasmania (1830–77). The imposing brick edifice has been captured in millions of photographs and depicted in hundreds of illustrations. Its angular façade, broken at intervals by the regimented lines of iron-barred windows, sits in stark contrast to the soft green of the manicured grass that surrounds it. Like much of the park-like nature of the modern historic site of Port Arthur, it can be difficult to reconcile such a scene with what we know about its past. Today, the penitentiary represents the challenge of giving access to difficult and complex pasts through site conservation, research and interpretation.

The obvious story of the penitentiary is told through the historical record and the upstanding architecture. Its high walls were built from clay dug, shaped and fired by prisoners, its frames and floors from timber felled and hewn by convict gangs. Beginning its life in the 1840s, as a flour mill and granary designed to convert convict-grown wheat into ration flour, by the 1850s it had become the place where these convicts were incarcerated. This book takes these stories and adds other layers, both metaphorical and literal, delving beneath the grass to tell the story of Port Arthur's most imposing structure via archaeological practice. Through those things left behind – the sandstone footing of a wall, the accumulated dust of years, or the lost object – we gain insight into previously unwritten histories, from the intensely personal to the bigger social, economic and political contexts.

This book is about archaeological excavations which took place in and around the penitentiary between 2013 and 2016. During 2013–15 the Port Arthur Historic Site Management Authority (PAHSMA) carried out a series of investigations linked to stabilisation works within the structure, as well as the reinstatement of interpretive elements associated with the former muster ground. In 2016 a large-scale investigation of the former ablutions and laundry spaces adjacent to the penitentiary took place. Together, this suite of excavations facilitated critical conservation work on an important historic structure. It also presented us with an opportunity to engage with the lesser-known aspects of Port Arthur's fascinating past, providing a window into the spaces where convicts worked and spent their limited free time.

The archaeological excavations – and therefore this book – also delved back beyond the history of the penitentiary. From the moment the penal station was first established in 1830, the area became a hub of industrial and penal activity, the site of work yards, wharves and workshops. The construction of the flour mill and granary between 1842 and 1845 stands as the perfect symbol for the administrators' never-ending quest for economy, its story intertwined with wider goings-on in colonial Tasmania and the faraway corridors of power in London.

These investigations provided an opportunity to understand some of the key aspects of the penal station's past. Through its early history we can learn about how economy was incorporated into penal regimes and how station administrators sought to balance day-to-day management realities against the expectations of colonial and British governments. The site's later history provides insight into how prison populations were managed, as well as how these populations managed to express agency and individuality throughout their incarcerated lives. The configuration of these spaces, as well as the material culture left behind, tells us much about the administrators' attitudes toward the management of the unfree men in their charge.

This book examines these aspects through an integrated application of the methods and approaches of history and archaeology. It is a work of historical archaeology, melding records created by the administrators and – more rarely – the unfree, with the very physicality of the places and spaces that they created. It is not designed to provide an exhaustive accounting of the excavation or the artefacts that were found. There are reports for those who wish to lose themselves in this type of minutiae. Instead, we want to talk about histories – both big and small, of a space and the lives that were carried out within it. Within this space we find the genesis of the modern prison and prisoner. Only through multidisciplinary investigations such as the one outlined in this book can we even start to understand such beginnings.

About this book

This book began life as archaeology reports, written by and for PAHSMA. Although the preparation of such reports is an essential part of any excavation, they can be incredibly dry, full of tedious descriptions and tables of artefacts. While they are an essential part of any investigative program, these reports do not lend themselves to engaging reading.

This book aims to distill the results of our excavations into palatable form, divested of most of the strictures of archaeological reporting. In Chapter 1 we open with a short history of Port Arthur, establishing how and why this isolated station came to fulfill such an important role in the management of transported convicts in Australia. We also outline the known history of the area in which the excavation was situated, establishing why this small patch of waterfront is so important for understanding how the penal station was formed and how it developed over half a century.

In Chapters 2 and 3, we provide a narrative that sets the changes to the natural and built landscape of the penitentiary precinct against an expansive context, demonstrating how this contained landscape reacted to influences ranging from the local to the global. To do this, we draw upon the results of the historical and the archaeological investigations, weaving a developmental narrative with the lives and labours of Port Arthur's unfree and free.

In Chapter 4 we present the results of the archaeological investigations in a format that favours immediate comprehension. Context lists, matrices and endless descriptions of stratigraphy have been relegated, replaced by photographs, illustrations and maps. It is designed to provide the archaeological background to Chapters 2 and 3. The whole section has been divided according to the five main phases of occupation that we identified as a result of the investigation: an early industrial waterfront phase, the two main phases of penitentiary occupation, an intermediate phase of activity, and post-abandonment. This phasing is discussed in more detail at the introduction to Chapter 2.

For those interested in the raw archaeological information, an online data repository containing the original excavation reports has been established.

The repository is located at: https://open.sydneyuniversitypress.com.au/recovering-convict-lives.html

A collection of photogrammetry can be found at: https://une.pedestal3d.com/r/68pm-yOWaL?sorting=1

A detailed overview of how Port Arthur evolved during the convict period can also be found at: www.convictlandscapes.com.au/portarthur

About the site

Port Arthur is located on the Tasman Peninsula, south-east Tasmania. With the peninsula accessible only by sea or via a narrow isthmus, it is easy to see why its security and isolation made it an attractive location for a penal settlement. Clustered around Mason Cove, the boundaries and layout of today's historic site remain much as they were during the convict period. The bulk of the settlement is located on the southern side of the cove, spread along the eminence known as Settlement Hill. Officers' quarters, the church and cleared ground stretch to the cove's west, while the station's former dockyards and the modern visitor centre occupy the northern ground.

The penitentiary stands on the southern side of Mason Cove, occupying ground at the base of Settlement Hill that was formerly waterfront until reclamation of the bay commenced in 1854 (Figures 0.1 and 0.2). To the rear of the penitentiary (south west) runs the elevated formation of Champ Street, then – as now – the settlement's main thoroughfare.

Much of the structure that we see today was actually built between 1842 and 1845, when a large brick flour mill and granary were erected on the former site of a waterside lumber yard and workshops (Figure 0.3). The largest portion of the structure housed a large 35-foot overshot waterwheel, the mill machinery and a timber treadwheel. The latter was a punishment device for convicts, the motive power generated by 48 men stepping on the treads of a 12-foot wheel. The power of man and water were harnessed to the grinding machinery. The smaller portion of the building housed a granary and offices.

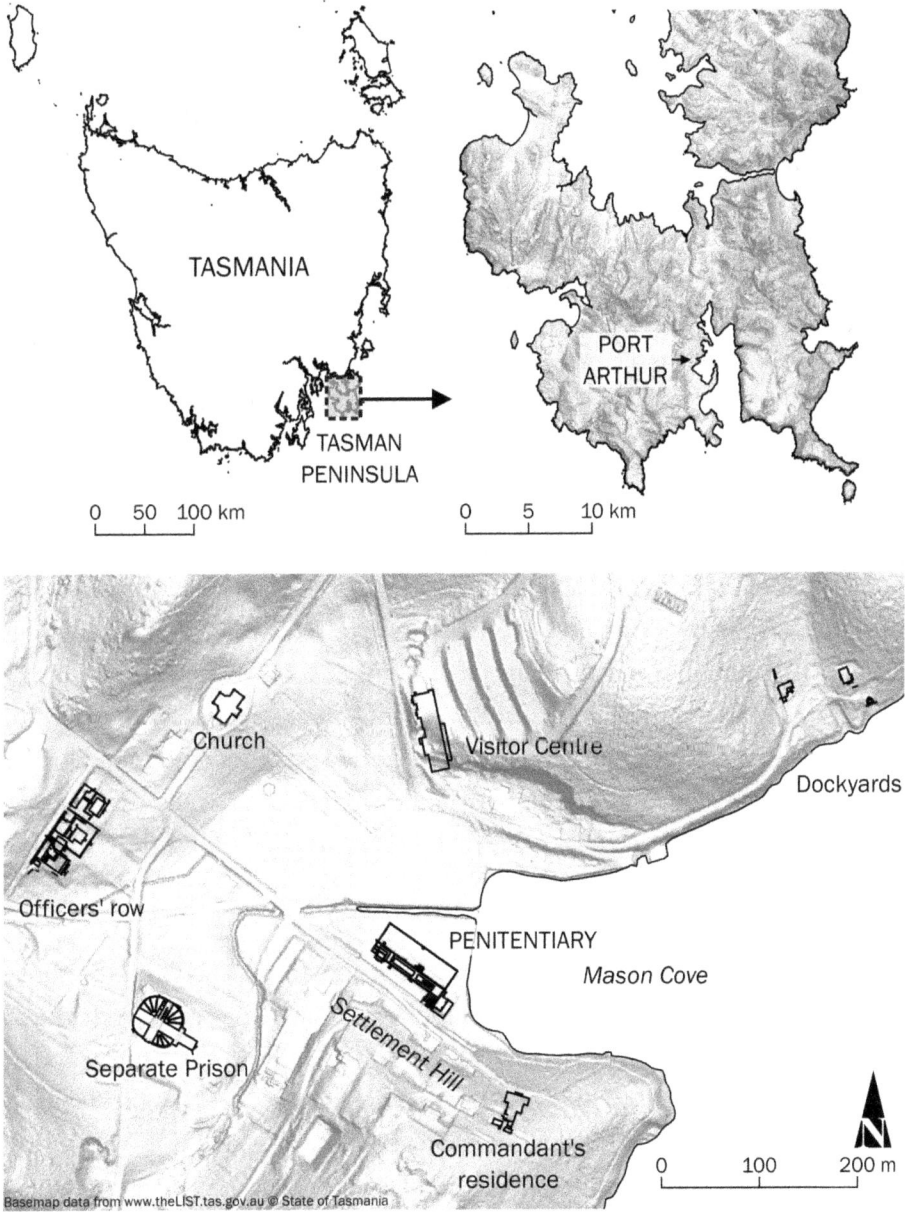

Figure 0.1. The location of Port Arthur and its penitentiary.

Figure 0.2. The penitentiary is situated at the base of Settlement Hill (left), on the former edge of Mason Cove. The cove was partly reclaimed during the 1850s. (Hype TV for PAHSMA, 2017)

Alterations to the structure between 1854 and 1857 turned it into a secure penitentiary building capable of incarcerating 480 prisoners (Figure 0.4). The mill and granary were gutted, leaving behind a retrofitted shell containing cells, a mess hall, dormitory, chapel and library. A new bakehouse was built to the west and a building for watchmen added to the east. At the front of the building a muster ground was laid out on newly reclaimed ground, while to the rear were added exercise yards, ablutions buildings and a laundry.

The structure that remains today reflects both these phases of the building's occupation: an 1840s façade and the remnants of an 1850s interior. Much of the latter, including the structure's roof, was lost in an 1897 fire during the post-convict period. Fire and salvage claimed the penitentiary's ancillary structures, with the muster ground, exercise, ablutions and laundry spaces levelled and grassed over. This is how they remained for much of the 20th century. Today, thanks to the archaeological investigations, the area has been landscaped and interpreted to reflect its use between 1856 and 1877 (Figure 0.5).

Throughout this book, reference will be made to five main areas where excavation occurred: the penitentiary, encompassing the area of the former mill and granary; the bakehouse, referring to the footprint of that building; the muster ground; and the ablutions and laundry areas (Figures 0.6 and 0.7). Of these, the penitentiary, bakehouse and laundry were enclosed, multi-storey and multi-roomed buildings. The muster ground and ablutions were largely open, the latter fitted with exercise yards, shelters and sheds.

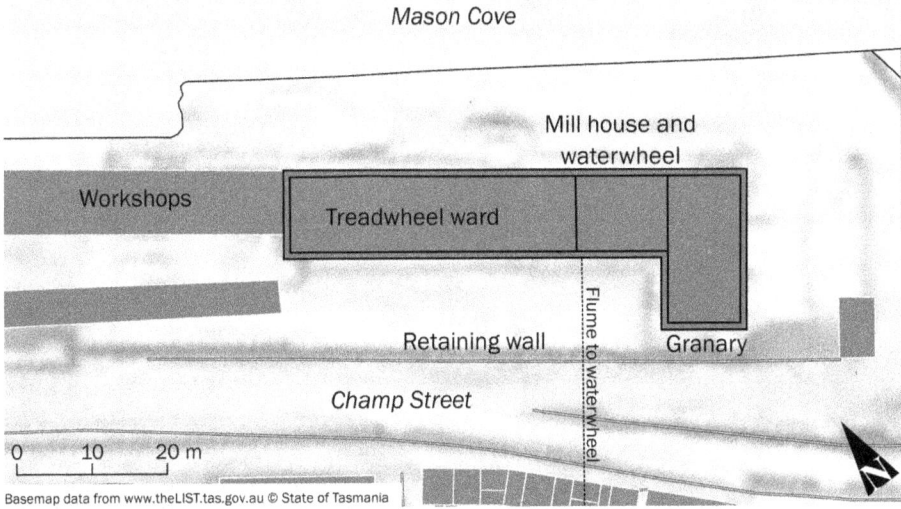

Figure 0.3. Detail plan showing the layout of the mill and granary in 1846.

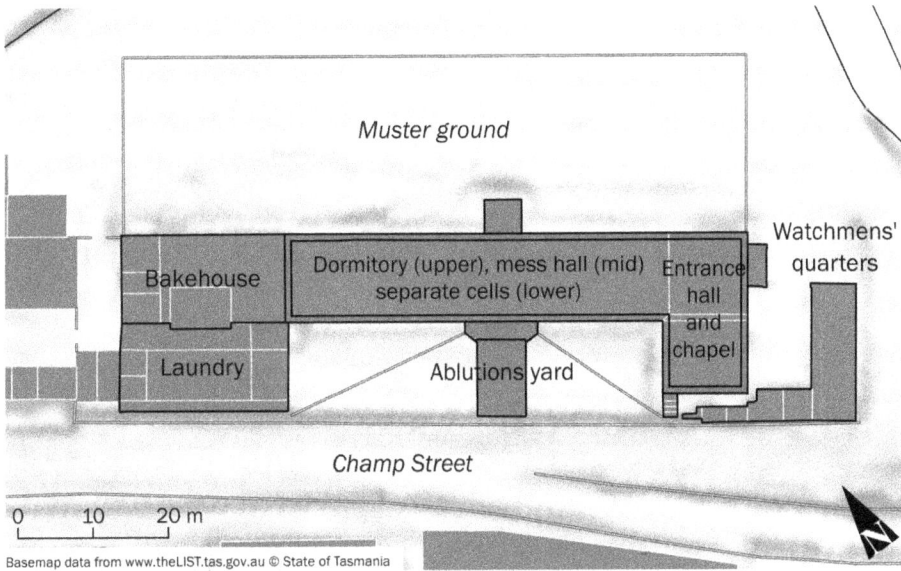

Figure 0.4. Detail plan showing the layout of the penitentiary in 1857.

Figure 0.5. View looking east from the location of the bakehouse over the penitentiary. The muster ground is on the left, with the ablutions area on the right. Champ Street runs above the ablutions area. (Hype TV for PAHSMA, 2017)

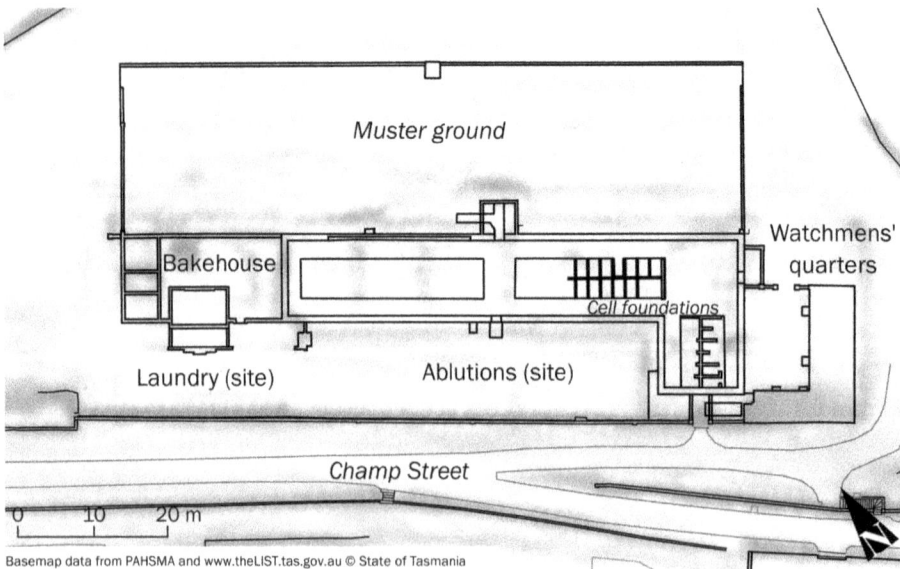

Basemap data from PAHSMA and www.theLIST.tas.gov.au © State of Tasmania

Figure 0.6. Plan showing the penitentiary today.

8

Figure 0.7. Aerial view of the penitentiary. (Hype TV for PAHSMA, 2017)

Project background

The archaeological excavations upon which this book is based were carried out during 2013–16 (Figure 0.8). They were undertaken as part of the larger penitentiary precinct conservation project which began in 2011. The project has been guided by the *Conservation Management Plan 2011: Penitentiary Precinct, Port Arthur Historic Site, Tasmania* and involved the large-scale conservation and structural work within the main penitentiary building, as well as improvements to existing drainage infrastructure.[1]

Integral to the work was a program of archaeological excavations and monitoring. These were tied to a series of significant research and interpretive goals, outlined in *Research Design for Archaeological Excavations within*

---

1   Andronas Conservation Architecture, 2011, 'Conservation Management Plan: Penitentiary Precinct, Port Arthur Historic Site, Tasmania', Melbourne.

Figure 0.8. Photo taken from the muster ground during conservation works in 2015. (PAHSMA 2015)

the Penitentiary Precinct, Port Arthur Historic Site. The high research value stemmed from the excavations' potential to provide information on the use and evolution of Port Arthur's waterfront space, as well as the lifeways of the convicts and supervisors associated with the penitentiary.

The first program of investigation was a series of 22 research excavations completed in 2013 in advance of conservation work. This was followed in 2014 and 2015 by a program of archaeological monitoring by PAHSMA staff and Pragmatic Cultural Heritage Services as the conservation work progressed.

The excavations in 2016 comprised the open-area excavation of the ablutions and laundry areas (Figure 0.9). The former was excavated by a team of seven archaeologists between January and May 2016. During November and December 2016 the laundry was excavated by a team of five archaeologists. These large investigations resulted from the need to carry out further conservation works within the precinct, at the same time as providing an opportunity to research and interpret some of the lesser-known stories and areas of the site.

Authorship

As with all good works, the making of this book has been a collaborative effort. After directing the 2016 excavations, Richard Tuffin completed the reports, mapping and illustrations and, together with the results from the 2013 work, then turned them all into this book. During this time he worked for PAHSMA, then as a Postdoctoral Research Fellow for the University of New England.

David Roe, Archaeology Manager at PAHSMA, was the driving force behind the investigation, arguing for the importance of incorporating a well-planned archaeological research project into the penitentiary stabilisation works program. He oversaw the completion of the 2013 archaeological works, as well as the later 2016 program.

Sylvana Szydzik, Conservation Project Officer at PAHSMA, was in charge of the post-excavation handling and cataloguing of artefacts during the investigation of the laundry area. Since that time, she has been instrumental in the implementation of the artefact x-ray program at PAHSMA.

Ashley Matic directed the 2013 research excavations and returned to Port Arthur in 2014 (as Pragmatic Cultural Heritage Services) to conduct the primary monitoring of the stabilisation project's in-ground works.

E. Jeanne Harris was a consultant on the excavation of the ablutions area, in charge of post-excavation artefact handling and cataloguing of all the assemblages. Jeanne produced the reporting from which the analysis of the artefacts was derived.

Figure 0.9. During the 2016 excavations of the ablutions area. (PAHSMA 2016)

Chapter 1

A SHORT HISTORY OF PORT ARTHUR

Prior to the advent of British settlement in Van Diemen's Land (as Tasmania was known until 1856), the region that would later be the site of the Port Arthur station was occupied by the Pydairrerme Aboriginal group. Evidence of their occupation is found across the Tasman Peninsula, particularly in the form of the shell middens which still dot the peninsula's coastal zones. Today, few such middens survive around the immediate area of the convict station, the shell having been harvested for the purposes of lime production during the convict period.

The first permanent British settlement on the Tasman Peninsula was located on its western reaches, a 300-acre parcel of land granted to William Gellibrand. Stock was run on the property and a timber slab and shingle hut constructed. The property was resumed by the government soon after Port Arthur's establishment, Gellibrand receiving a compensatory grant of land elsewhere in the colony.[1]

The reasons for Port Arthur's initial settlement are mixed. Early surveys of the peninsula in 1828 (Figure 1.1) had identified the plentiful natural resources of the region, in particular the impressive stands of trees growing along parts of the coast and in the hinterland:

---

1   George Arthur, Lieutenant Governor, to Sir George Murray, Secretary of State, 3 March 1831, CO280/28 no. 16, reel 247, Tasmanian Archives (TA).

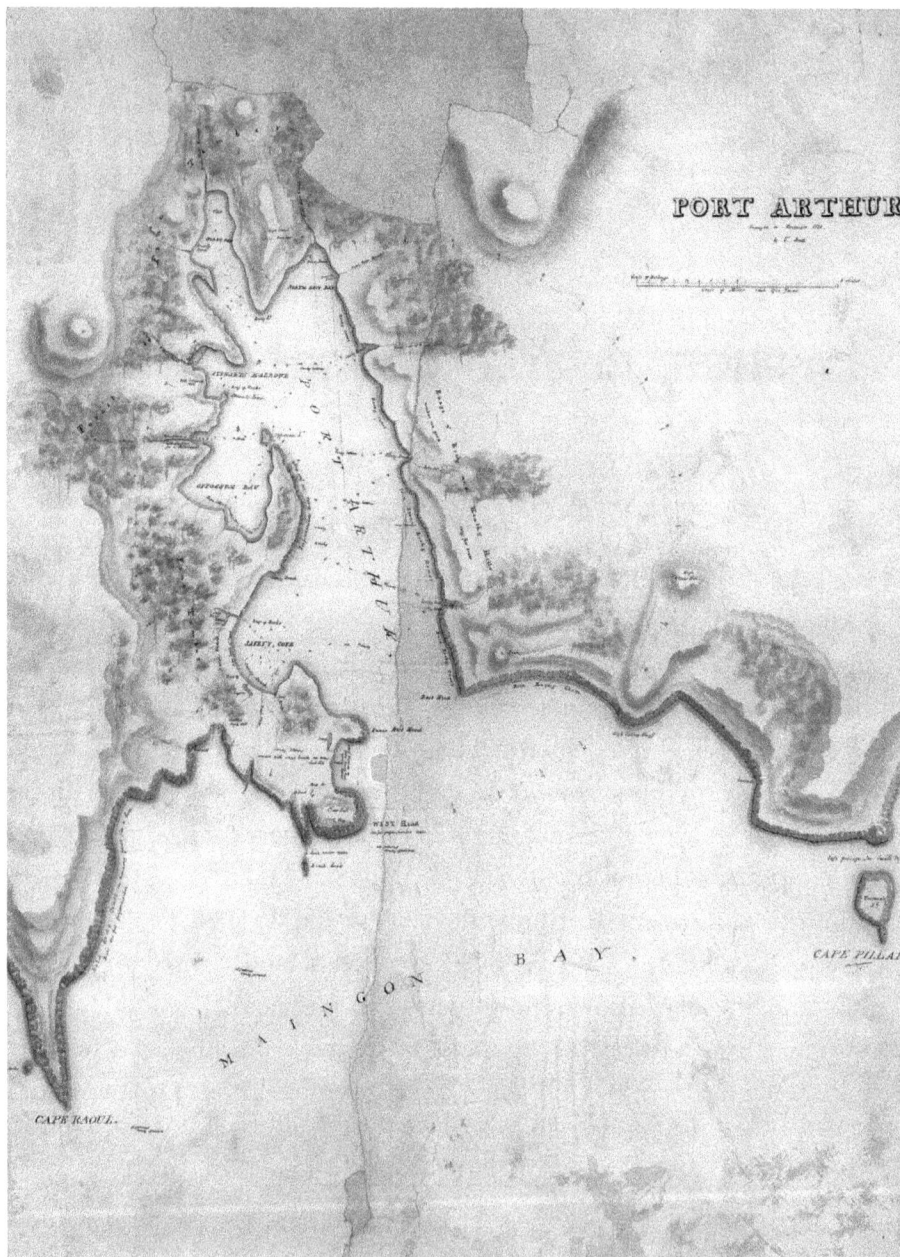

Figure 1.1. An 1828 survey completed by surveyor Thomas Scott, showing the sheltered harbor of Port Arthur. (T. Scott, 'Port Arthur', November 1828, AF397/1/1, Tasmanian Archives)

Stewarts Harbour [Port Arthur's harbour] about 7 leagues from the entrance of the Derwent affords good shelter for Ships of any burthen, and fresh water easily procured with good anchorage near the place where the Timber may be taken on board. The Timber which is in great quantities are Gum, Stringy Bark, Myrtle, Lightwood and Sassafras, all of which appears to be of good quality and may employ any number of men for several years – it may at present be had near the water side and about ½ a mile from Shore.[2]

The presence of such abundant timber reserves was particularly attractive to the government, which at that time was actively searching for a replacement for the Birch's Bay convict timber-getting station (1824–30). Located south of Hobart, the operation at Birch's Bay was troubled by accusations of inefficiency and, perhaps more worryingly, an increasing scarcity of timber (Figure 1.2).[3]

Surveys of the Tasman Peninsula noted its advantageous situation, located half a day's sail from Hobart. At the time, the government was wrestling with the very real difficulty of maintaining a penal settlement on the west coast of the island. Splendidly isolated and therefore considered ideal as a place of punishment, Macquarie Harbour penal station (1822–33) was, however, incredibly difficult to keep in supply, with an inhospitable climate that also stymied attempts at self-sufficiency.[4] The Tasman Peninsula, far easier to communicate with and with a climate that positively encouraged all things agricultural, offered a tempting alternative.

A key role in the station's formation was played by the then Lieutenant Governor of Van Diemen's Land, George Arthur. Arthur had been the principal architect of the system of convict management that enveloped the colony from the mid-1820s, cementing and systematising Van Diemen's

---

2   J. Welsh and R.A. Roberts, to John Burnett, Colonial Secretary, 6 February 1828, CSO1/217/5215, TA.

3   P. Macfie, 'Government Sawing Establishments in Van Diemen's Land, 1817–1832', in John Dargavel, Denise Gaughwin, and Brenda Libbis (eds), *Australia's Ever-Changing Forests V: Proceedings of the Fifth National Conference on Australian Forest History*, Canberra, 2002, pp. 105–31.

4   H. Maxwell-Stewart, *Closing Hell's Gates: The Death of a Convict Station*, New South Wales, 2008, pp. 9–13.

Figure 1.2. Map showing the location of places mentioned in the historical overview.

Table 1.1. Lieutenant Governor George Arthur's hierarchical system of prisoner management.

1st Class	To consist of such Men, whether Mechanics or Labourers, as from especial good conduct will be permitted to sleep out of Barracks, and to work for themselves the whole of each Saturday
2nd Class	Those for whom Barrack accommodation will be provided, & who, subject to the continuance of good behaviour, will be allowed to work for themselves the whole of each Saturday
3rd Class	Men employed on the Public Words who will be released from work at noon every Saturday, subject however to the condition of good conduct
4th Class	Refractory, a disorderly character, to work in Irons, either in the Towns, or on the Roads, under the sentence of a Magistrate
5th Class	Men of the most degraded and incorrigible character who will be worked in Irons and under the sentence of a Magistrate & kept entirely separate from other prisoners
6th Class	Men removed to Maria Island subject to the Classification of the Commandant there
7th Class	Men removed to Macquarie Harbour subject to the classification of the Commandant there

Land's place as a British penal colony.[5] Arthur devised a hierarchical system of prisoner management that covered the colony (Table 1.1).[6]

Arthur envisaged that the Tasman Peninsula would become a key part of this system, replacing the need for the secondary penal centres of Macquarie Harbour and Maria Island (1825–32) which currently formed the foundation of his system.[7] Arthur's ambition encompassed the whole of the peninsula, estimating that 8,000–10,000 convicts could be accommodated on it, the prisoners utilising the natural resources to erect the infrastructure of their own prison, in the process clearing and 'taming' land considered waste. With

---

5   S. Petrow, 'Policing in a Penal Colony: Governor Arthur's Police System in Van Diemen's Land, 1826–1836', *Law and History Review*, Vol. 18, No. 2, 2000, pp. 351–95, p. 356.
6   'Government Order', Colonial Secretary's Office, 9 August 1826, CSO 1/10/155, TA.
7   George Arthur, Lieutenant Governor, to Viscount Goderich, Secretary of State, 15 February 1833, CO280/39 no. 8, reel 254, TA.

the number of arrivals to the colony gradually increasing, he estimated that up to 7,000 new arrivals every year could be kept on the peninsula prior to their distribution amid the colony, the great project doing away with the need for expensive penitentiaries in Britain entirely.[8]

It was with this grand scheme in the back of his mind that Arthur assented to the creation of the new Port Arthur station. The *Derwent* was dispatched with a complement of convicts and rank-and-file soldiers of the 63rd Regiment under the leadership of Assistant-Surgeon John Russell.[9] The ship made for the eastern side of the Tasman Peninsula, where the early surveys had noted the presence of the deep, sheltered harbour. The *Derwent* dropped anchor on 20 September 1830 in a small cove on the harbour's western side, where rocky shores gave way to a sandy beach at the cove's head. Stores and a prefabricated building were hauled ashore by the convicts and the work began on claiming a settlement from the thickly timbered bush.

The composition of Port Arthur's early intake illustrates the intentions of this fledgling settlement. In one of the first musters undertaken, in March 1831, of the 90 prisoners then at the station, over 46 per cent (41) were in timber-related trades.[10] Many of the men had been transferred from the now-defunct Birch's Bay station. A smaller group had served time at Macquarie Harbour, shipped to Port Arthur as part of a staged release prior to being assigned to settlers in the rest of the colony.

The men were put to work clearing the blue gums (*Eucalyptus globulus*), stringybarks (*Eucalyptus obliqua*) and swamp gums (*Eucalyptus ovata*) that

---

8   Robert Smirke to Lieutenant-Colonel Davies, 19 May 1832, *Report from the Select Committee on Secondary Punishments*, British Parliamentary Papers, London, 1831–32 (547), p. 134.

9   The number of convicts in the first contingent is unclear. Historian Doug Munro provides a figure of 33. However, documents indicate that the *Derwent* carried 18 men from Macquarie Harbour and a further nine were directed from chain gangs around Hobart – making for a total of 27. Supplies for 50 convicts and 15 soldiers were carried on the *Derwent*. Memorandum, unknown author, 7 September 1830, CSO 1/483/10748, TA; John Burnett, Colonial Secretary, to Affleck Moodie, Commissariat Officer, 8 September 1830, CSO 1/483/10748, TA; Memorandum, John Burnett, Colonial Secretary, 15 September 1830, CSO 1/484/10749, TA; D. Munro, 'From Macquarie Harbour to Port Arthur: The Founding of a Penal Settlement', *Tasmanian Historical Research Association*, Vol. 36, No. 3, 1989, pp. 113–24, p. 113.

10   'Return of 90 Prisoners employed at the Public Works at Port Arthur for the preceding two months', John Russell, Commandant, CSO1/511/11180, TA.

grew down to the water's edge, focusing on the hill framing the cove's southern edge and the banks of the small stream at the cove's western margin. A cluster of timber slab and shingle huts went up near this stream, accommodating the convicts, to the east of which were the stores and workshops. Barracks for the military, residences for the station commandant and offices, as well as administration offices, were scattered on the hill, the eminence becoming known as Settlement Hill (Figures 1.3 and 1.4).

Within three years of settlement, the convict population of Port Arthur had reached 475, with the consolidation of the encompassing penal peninsula well underway.[11] In addition to timber, sandstone was located and worked, charcoal produced, lime slaked from gathered shell and clay pits dug to supply the raw stuff of brick and tile.[12] Roads and trackways were pushed north and west of the settlement, linking it to the military guard post of Eagle Hawk Neck, which effectively sealed the peninsula by land.

Although the peninsula never became a penal hub on the scale first envisaged by Arthur, it quickly became established as the colony's most important centre of secondary punishment, a position confirmed by the closure of the Maria Island penal station in 1832, followed a year later by Macquarie Harbour.[13] Port Arthur's penal security was assured in 1835 when an act was passed by the Legislative Council imposing a three-mile exclusion zone around the Tasman Peninsula, with those who broke the cordon facing property impoundment and a steep fine.[14] The key was further turned in the lock when Slopen Island, off the west coast of the peninsula, was withdrawn from private leasehold.[15]

---

11 William Gore Elliston, *Statistical Returns of Van Diemen's Land, from 1824 to 1839*, (Hobart Town: William Gore Elliston, 1839), Enclosure no. 37.

12 R. Tuffin and M. Gibbs, 'Early Port Arthur: Convict Colonization and the Formation of a Penal Station in Van Diemen's Land 1830–35', *International Journal of Historical Archaeology*, Vol. 23, 2019, pp. 568–95, pp. 581–82.

13 Munro, 'From Macquarie Harbour to Port Arthur: The Founding of a Penal Settlement', p. 119.

14 'An Act to consolidate and amend certain of the laws relating to the Courts of General Quarter Sessions and to the more effectual punishment and control of Transported and Other Offenders', 1835, no. 2, 6 Wm. IV, published in *The Hobart Town Gazette*, 20 August 1835.

15 *Hobart Town Courier*, 25 September 1835; Charles O'Hara Booth, Commandant, to John Montagu, Colonial Secretary, 21 September 1835, CSO 1/829/17594, T.A.H.O. [untranscribed transcripts of Ian Brand, PAHSMA].

Figure 1.3. Illustration of Port Arthur in 1833. (Unknown artist, 'Port Arthur, Van Diemen's Land, ca. 1833', AG5929, Tasmanian Museum and Art Gallery)

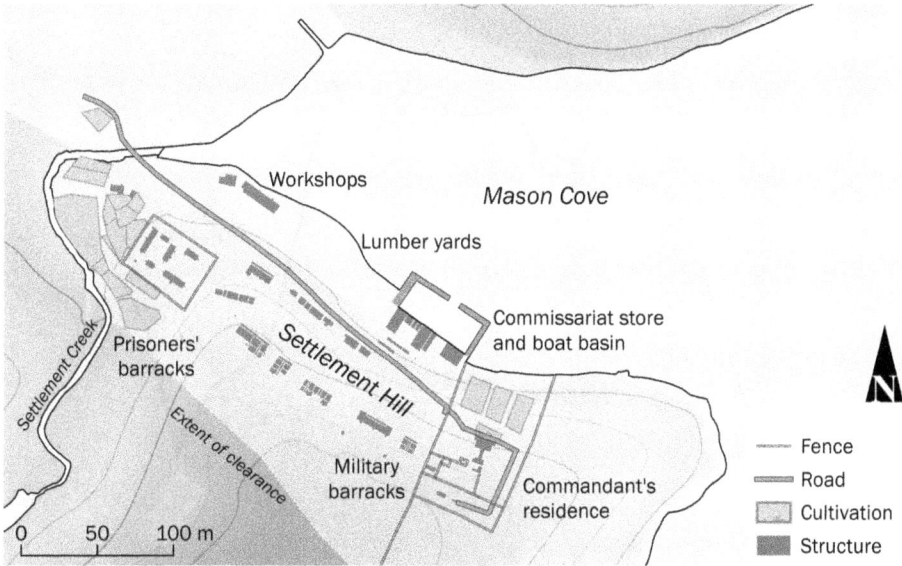

Figure 1.4. By 1833 the settlement had substantially grown from its original cluster of huts.

With the consolidation of the penal peninsula, Arthur had a detailed map prepared and forwarded to his British superiors.[16] Its inked outlines and shaded relief conveyed to them a wild and untamed landmass perfectly suited to the control, coercion and profitable employment of Britain's convicts. Arthur sold his concept well.

Under Captain Commandant Charles O'Hara Booth (1833–44), Port Arthur became administratively responsible for two new stations: a coal mine (1833–48) on the peninsula's western arm (known as Coal Mines), and Point Puer (1834–49), a dedicated station for juvenile male convicts situated across the bay from Port Arthur.

16 George Frankland, 'Notice on Tasman's Peninsula with reference to the Map, constructed from the Surveys of George Woodward and James Hughes', 29th January 1834, CO280/46 no. 13 reel 257, TA; George Arthur, Lieutenant Governor, to Viscount Goderich, Secretary of State, 15 February 1833, CO280/39 no. 8, reel 254, TA.

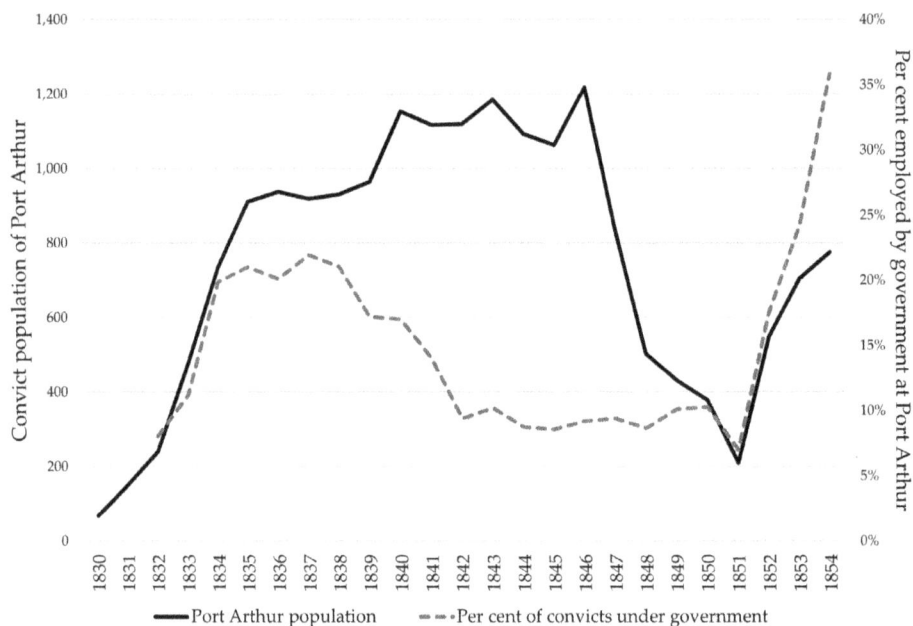

Figure 1.5. Port Arthur's population during 1830–35. The total proportion of men under sentence retained by the government is also illustrated. (British Parliamentary Papers, CSO records, Tasmanian Archives)

As the 1830s progressed, Port Arthur and Coal Mines cemented their place as the colony's penal foundation.[17] From 1834–40, around 20 per cent of male convicts in Van Diemen's Land in government service (as opposed to those who were assigned to free settlers or with a ticket-of-leave) spent time at Port Arthur. For those who were never sent to the station, the experience of those who were would have been well known, either through reports in the colonial press, or through direct exposure to men who had served time there (Figure 1.5).

By the end of the decade the settlement contained over 1,100 men undergoing sentence, overseen by military and civil officers, who were in turn often accompanied by their families. The settlement itself had sprawled beyond its initial boundaries on the south side of Mason Cove, occupying cleared land to the west and north of the cove (Figure 1.6). Sandstone, brick

---

17   I. Brand, *The Port Arthur Coal Mines: 1833–1877*, Launceston, 1993; Tuffin and Gibbs, 'Early Port Arthur', p. 587; H. Maxwell-Stewart, 'The Rise and Fall of John Longworth: Work and Punishment in Early Port Arthur', *Tasmanian Historical Studies*, Vol. 6, No. 2, 1999, pp. 96–114, pp. 107–08.

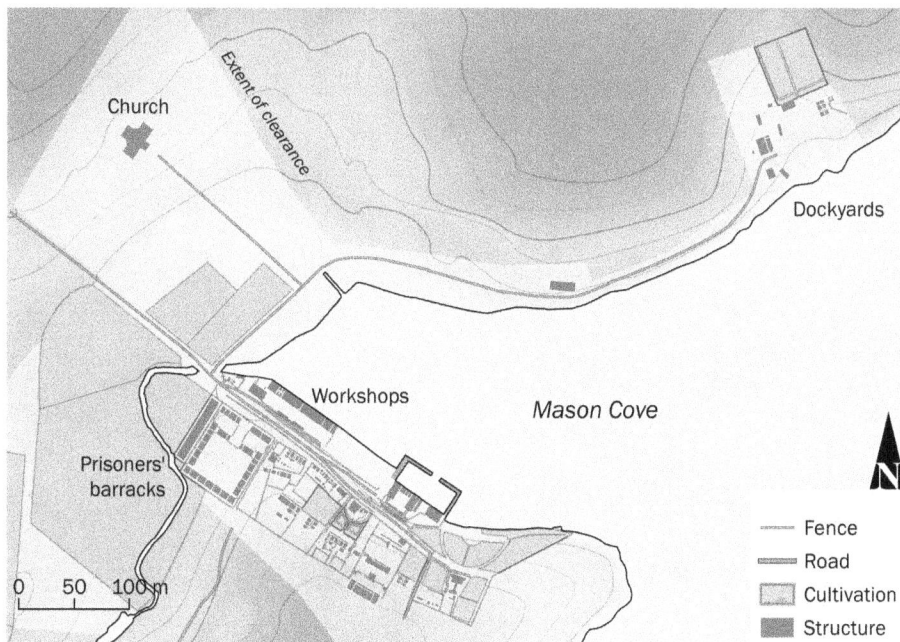

Figure 1.6. By 1840 Port Arthur had sprawled to encompass Mason Cove.

and timber buildings covered Settlement Hill, with a palisaded prisoners' barracks replacing the original hut cluster. An impressive sandstone church was built in 1836, looking down upon the settlement from an elevated position to the west (Figure 1.7).

At some remove from the settlement, a dockyard (1834–48) was established. During its time it produced 15 ships of over 200 tonnes for the colonial and private service, as well as hundreds of smaller boats and buoys.[18] The yard serviced the Colonial Marine, with shipping constantly employed on the half-day's journey to Hobart, transporting prisoners, staff, supplies and products made at the station.

The onset of the 1840s triggered a massive upheaval in how convicts were administered in Van Diemen's Land. Growing dissatisfaction with the perceived variable experience of transported convicts under the assignment system saw both British and colonial governments agree to its complete

18   M. Nash, 'Convict Shipbuilding in Tasmania', *Tasmanian Historical Research Association*, Vol. 50, No. 2, 2003, pp. 83–106, pp. 88, 105–06.

Figure 1.7. This 1843 illustration shows Port Arthur from the northern side of Mason Cove. The convicts in the foreground are preparing ground for cultivation. (Unknown author, 'Port Arthur, Tasmania, 1843', SV6B/Pr Arth/5, Mitchell Library, State Library New South Wales)

overhaul.[19] Where formerly the majority of convicts on arrival were assigned to free settlers as unfree labourers, the 'probation' system saw newly transported male prisoners placed in purpose-built stations (the system was not put in place for female transportees until 1844).[20] At these stations the prisoners were to serve a term of probationary imprisonment prior to release as wage-workers in the private service. Implemented from 1839, the first probation stations did not appear until 1841. By 1844 over 40 establishments operated across the colony, the number and their capacity barely keeping

---

19   J. Ritchie, 'Towards Ending an Unclean Thing: The Molesworth Committee and the Abolition of Transportation to New South Wales, 1837–40', *Historical Studies*, Vol. 17, No. 67, 1976, pp. 144–64.

20   R. Tuffin and M. Gibbs, '"Uninformed and Impractical"? The Convict Probation System and Its Impact Upon the Landscape of 1840s Van Diemen's Land', *History Australia*, Vol. 17, No. 1, 2020, pp. 87–114, pp. 91–93; I. Brand, *The Convict Probation System: Van Diemen's Land 1839–1854*, Hobart, 1990.

pace with an unparalleled and unexpected influx of transportees arriving in Van Diemen's Land.[21]

The Tasman Peninsula played a key role in probation's course. While Port Arthur was ring-fenced as an ultra-penal establishment, six new stations were created in 1841 and 1842, in addition to the existing Point Puer and Coal Mines (Figure 1.8).[22] Although nominally independent, these new stations were administratively linked to Port Arthur, the experience of that station's officers used to smooth their formative years. The penal settlement also acted as a logistical hub, providing construction materials and manufacturing support.

The probation period at Port Arthur saw a number of large-scale capital works that drew heavily upon the station's resources and labour skill base. The largest of these was the construction of the flour mill and granary (1842–45) and the associated mill race, dam, underground aqueduct and flume (a channel for conveying water) required to get water to the wheel. Works were also carried out across the station to meet the accommodation needs of the increased civil and military bureaucracy, with residences constructed and barracks extended. To meet the needs of all these works, sources of sandstone, dolerite, clay and timber were exploited with increasing intensity, opening up the station's hinterland like never before.[23]

The end of the 1840s brought with it a change in circumstances. During the later probation period Port Arthur had increasingly been made an ultra-penal settlement. This meant that it received the worst-behaved convicts from other stations, resulting in a decrease of its convict population. With less labour to go around, works at the settlement were restricted to tasks requisite only for station maintenance. Despite this, work did commence on

---

21 A situation largely exacerbated by the cessation of transportation to New South Wales in 1840. See Tuffin and Gibbs, 'Uninformed and Impractical'? The Convict Probation System and Its Impact Upon the Landscape of 1840s Van Diemen's Land', p. 95; N. Townsend, 'A 'Mere Lottery': The Convict System in New South Wales through the Eyes of the Molesworth Committee', *Push from the Bush*, Vol. 21, 1985, pp. 58–86.

22 J. Thompson, *Probation in Paradise: The Story of Convict Probationers on Tasman's and Forestier's Peninsulas, Van Diemen's Land, 1841–1857*, J. Thompson, Hobart, 2007.

23 R. Tuffin and M. Gibbs, 'The Archaeology of the Convict Probation System: The Labor Landscapes of Port Arthur and the Cascades Probation Station, 1839–55', *International Journal of Historical Archaeology*, Vol. 24, No. 3, 2020, pp. 589–617, pp. 18–22.

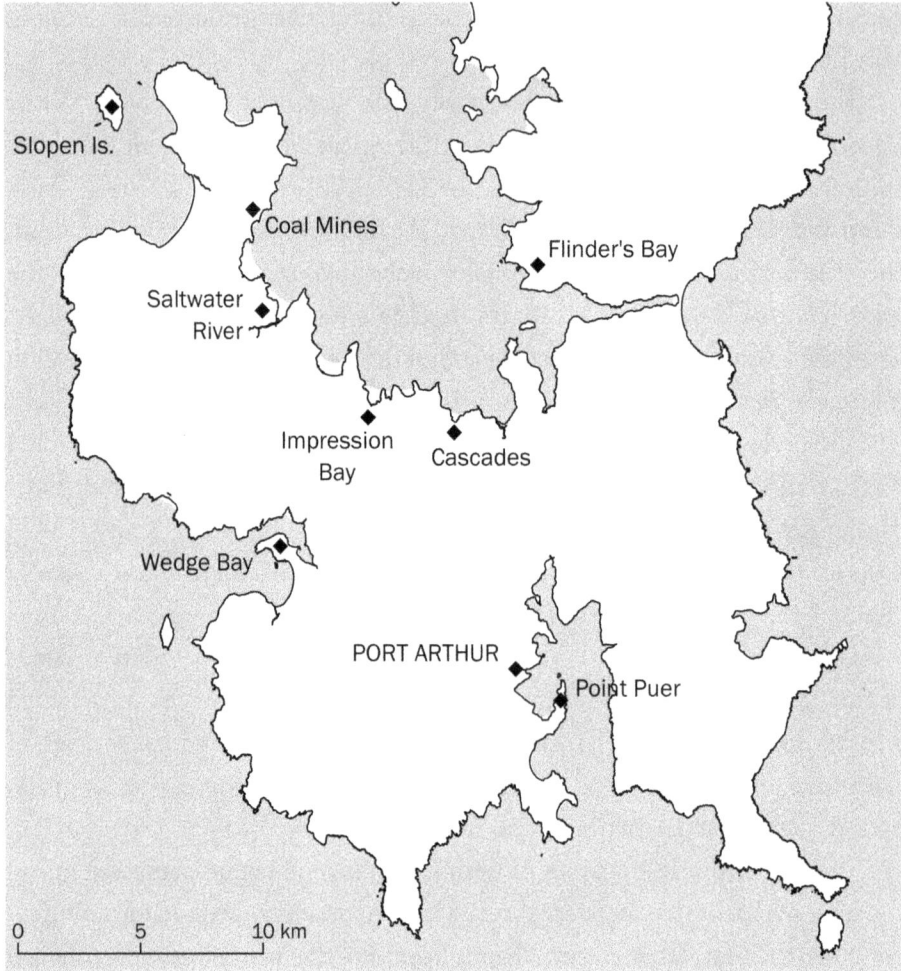

Figure 1.8. Map of the Tasman Peninsula showing the stations operational during the probation period.

one major capital work. Constructed between 1848–52, the Separate Prison (also known as the Model Prison), was a cruciform-shaped prison built to facilitate the implementation of the separate system of confinement. Holding convicts in silent confinement for 23 hours a day, the prison marked Port Arthur's turn away from corporal methods of punishment (like the lash) and toward a punitive focus on the prisoner's mind.

During the early 1850s Port Arthur entered a sustained period of growth (Figure 1.9). This was a result of the closure of many of the probation stations throughout the colony, as Britain sought to lessen its penological

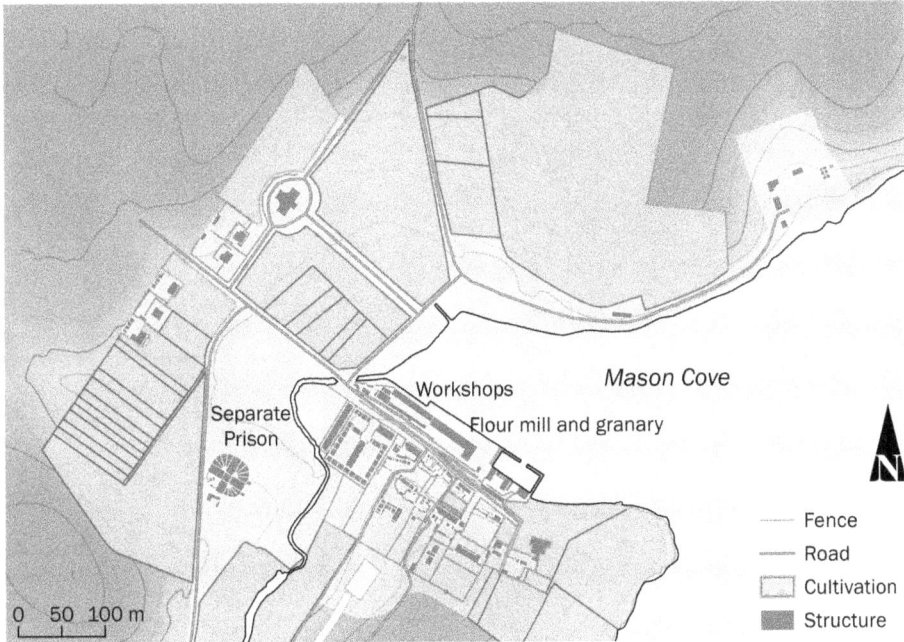

Figure 1.9. The extent of the settlement in 1850.

responsibility in the faraway colony.[24] Prisoners, administrators and material were centralised at a few establishments, with Port Arthur a major receptacle of this rationalisation program (Figure 1.10).

The growing population brought with it problems of accommodation and self-sufficiency. Proposals for improved prisoner accommodation had circulated since 1846, but the station's population downturn had meant that such expansion was little justified. When the convict population once again began to increase after 1851, investigations into improving accommodation were renewed. As a result, the decision was made to convert the former flour mill and granary into a self-contained prison complex.

Beginning in 1854, the conversion process took nearly four years and resulted in the entire structure being completely remodelled. Ancillary structures were also constructed, including the addition of a bakehouse, cookhouse and ablutions area, as well as the rebuilding of the adjacent industrial workshops. A contemporaneous project also saw the tidal sands

24   R. Tuffin, 'The Evolution of Convict Labour Management in Van Diemen's Land: Placing the 'Penal Peninsula' in a Colonial Context', *Tasmanian Historical Research Association*, Vol. 54, No. 2, 2007, pp. 69–83.

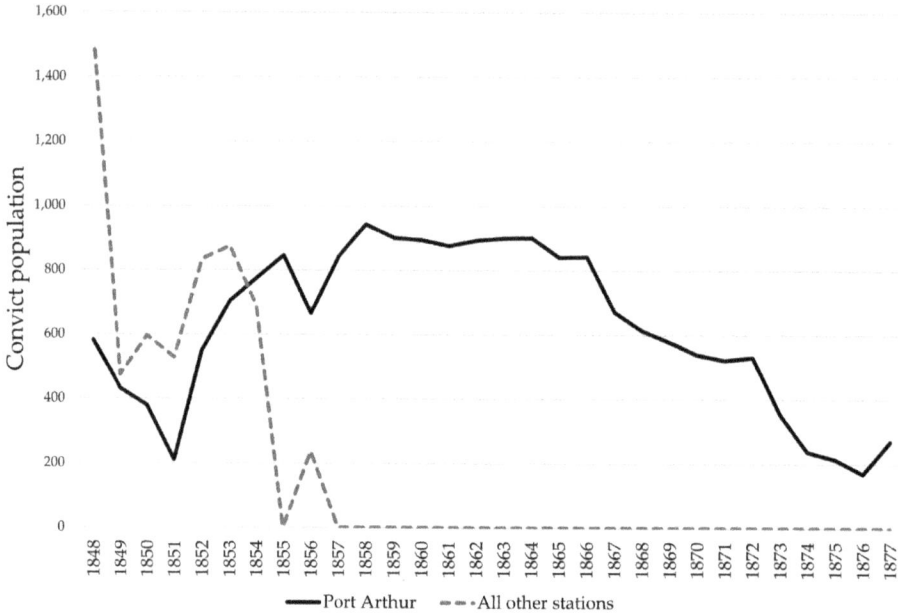

Figure 1.10. Port Arthur experienced a growth in convict population, just at the time other stations on the Tasman Peninsula were beginning to close. (Sources: British Parliamentary Papers; House of Assembly, Tasmania)

at the head of the bay infilled in a massive feat of reclamation, enabling the provision of a parade ground, a storage area for the workshops and the space for a range of covered sawpits (Plate 1.1).

The 1850s and early 1860s were a period of economic vigour at the station. Though overtly industrial operations like the coal mines and dockyards had closed, there was an increased focus upon the self-sufficiency of the penal establishment. A farm was opened near the settlement, running a dairy and piggery. Upwards of 30 acres were placed under crop, with wheat, potatoes, hops, cabbage, potatoes, leeks, carrots, beans and leeks grown to subsidise the settlement's ration requirements. A salt works was even started, producing over 80,000 lbs (36 tonnes) during its nine-year operation.[25] Timber and sandstone were harvested on a large scale, aided by the addition of iron-railed tramways that enabled raw materials to be moved to the settlement with an unparalleled level of efficiency.

---

25 Tabulated from returns of manufacture contained in British Parliamentary Papers, 1860–1871.

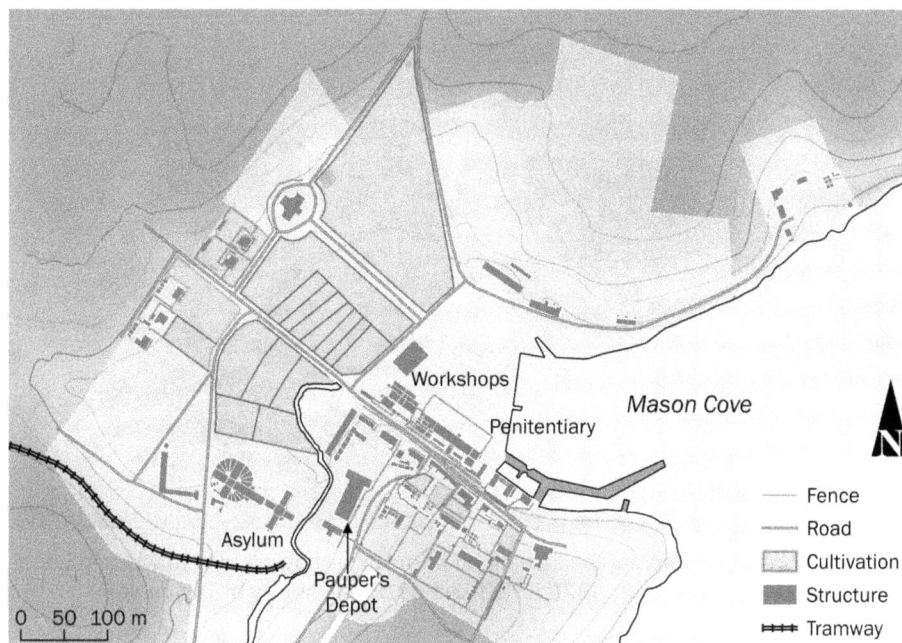

Figure 1.11. Port Arthur in 1865.

An enormous quantity of products was generated in the settlement workshops. Here blacksmiths, nailers, tinplaters, tailors, shoemakers, wheelwrights and carpenters worked to produce material for the station and for export. A steam boiler provided power to a sawmill and bone mill, the latter used to grind bone meal for fertiliser.

In the 1860s, the construction of two buildings at the settlement heralded the final stage of Port Arthur's convict occupation (Figures 1.11 and 1.12). In 1862 work commenced on the paupers' dormitories, followed in 1864 by the asylum (built in 1864–68). Constructed to enable better care of a population that was increasingly aged and infirm, these buildings symbolised Port Arthur's shift towards the provision of welfare for institutionalised men. Unwilling or unable to build lives outside prison walls, these men circulated between the establishments at Port Arthur and the New Norfolk asylum.

In 1871 the administration of Port Arthur was transferred from the Convict Department to the colony.[26] The station's population was a mixture

---

26   S. Petrow, 'Claims of the Colony: Tasmania's Dispute with Britain over the Port Arthur Penal Establishment 1856–1877', *Tasmanian Historical Research Association*, Vol. 44, No. 4, 1997, pp. 221–40, p. 222.

Figure 1.12. A photograph of the settlement from 1871, showing the crowded nature of Settlement Hill. ('Port Arthur', 1871, LPIC102-1-69, State Library of Tasmania)

of men convicted in the colony and Britain. Port Arthur's final years saw a slow decrease in its population, as the remaining prisoners were removed to New Norfolk and Hobart. Fewer prisoners required fewer guards and administrative officers; those who remained acted as caretakers for the last convicts and the buildings that had once incarcerated them (Plate 1.2). Finally, in 1876, the order to abandon the settlement was given, the last prisoner stepping aboard the departing steamer the following year.

Surveys of all the Tasman Peninsula's convict settlements were carried out during 1876–78, dividing into lots the land which had been cleared and reclaimed by the labour of convicts over the previous 47 years (Figure 1.13). Port Arthur was parcelled up and sold to private interests, each treating their purchased lots differently. Some viewed the buildings as quarries, knocking them down and selling the timber and masonry. Others sought to take advantage of a burgeoning tourist industry, as people flocked to the former penal settlement to see for themselves a place they had only read sensational accounts of in print.[27] Former administration buildings and officer's quarters, including the commandant's residence, were converted into hotels and cafes.

---

27   D. Young, *Making Crime Pay: The Evolution of Convict Tourism in Tasmania*, Hobart, 1996.

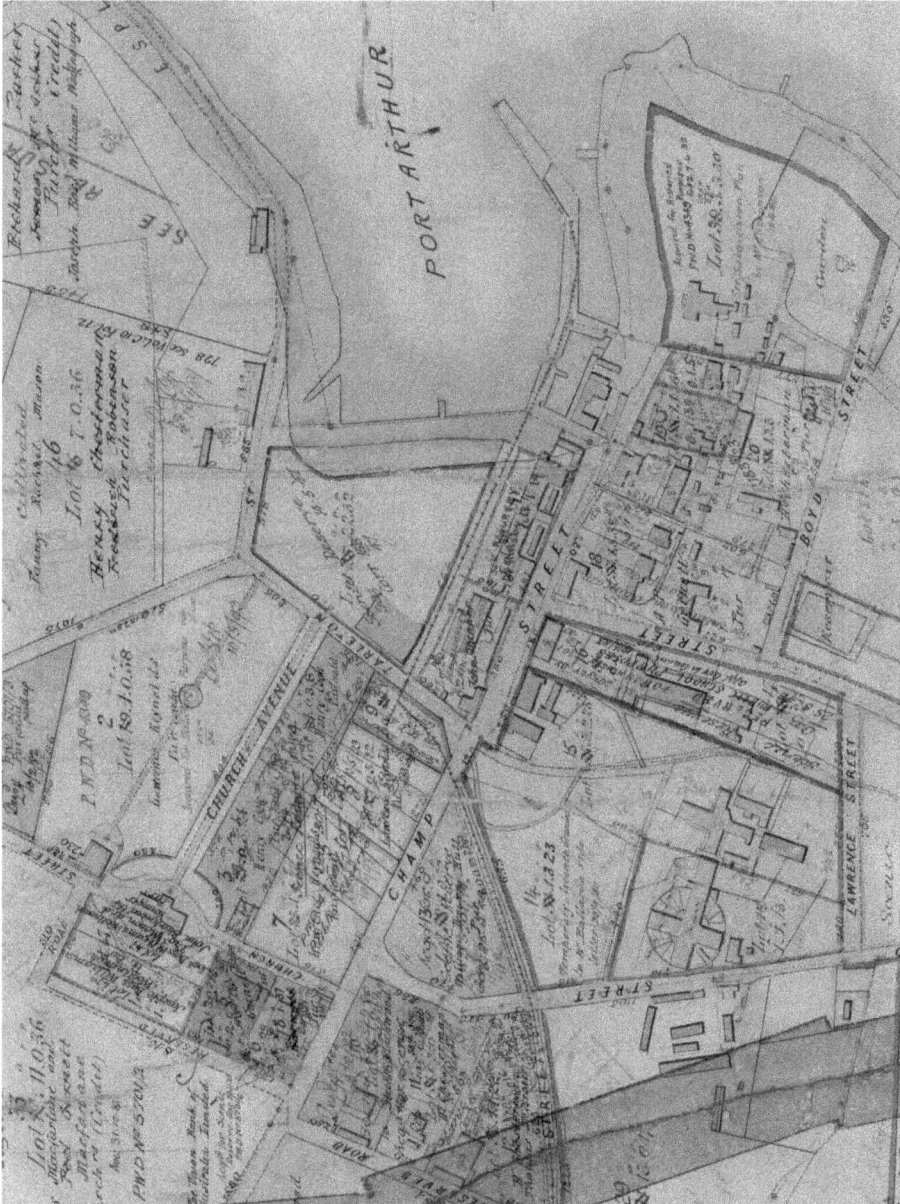

Figure 1.13. Survey plan of the settlement completed by Archibald Blackwood in 1877. (Archibald Blackwood, 'Diagrammetrical survey', 1877, AF397/1/6, Tasmanian Archives)

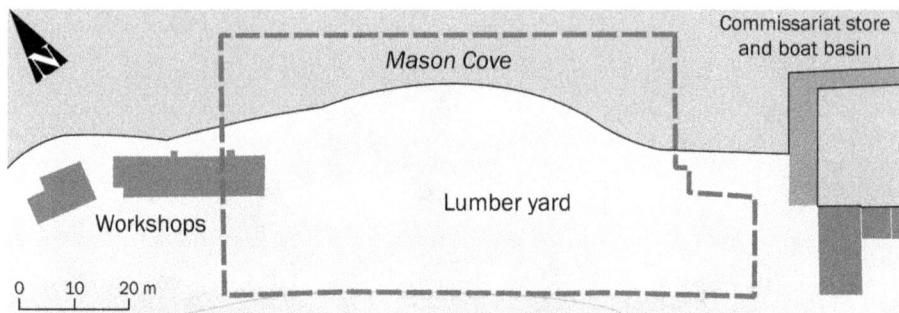

Figure 1.14. Plan of the waterfront in 1833, showing the extent of the later penitentiary precinct (dotted outline).

Devastating bushfires in 1895 and 1897 claimed a number of buildings, including the largest buildings like the hospital, separate prison and penitentiary. Despite this, the Port Arthur township, now renamed Carnarvon, continued to flourish. Its value as a space of scenic beauty and its potential as a tourist site was recognised when it was gazetted by the Scenery Preservation Board in 1916. A gradual purchase of buildings and land returned it to public property, and from 1971 the site was managed by the National Parks and Wildlife Service. The formation of the Port Arthur Conservation Development Project in 1979 introduced a new level of conservation, research and interpretation, albeit at the expense of the township. The last resident of the township, Pat Jones, died in 1985. Since 1987, the site has been managed by the Port Arthur Historic Site Management Authority.

Development of the penitentiary precinct

During the convict period, the area occupying the southern side of Mason Cove – extending from the mouth of Settlement (later Radcliffe) Creek to the garden fronting the commandant's residence – changed in reflection of the various pulses of station development. As Port Arthur evolved from timber-getting camp to penal settlement, industrial prison and, finally, welfare hub, the waterfront changed with it.

From the earliest days, the southern shore was the site of the settlement workshops, the focus of successive attempts to make the settlement an economic and self-sufficient prison. The construction of the flour mill

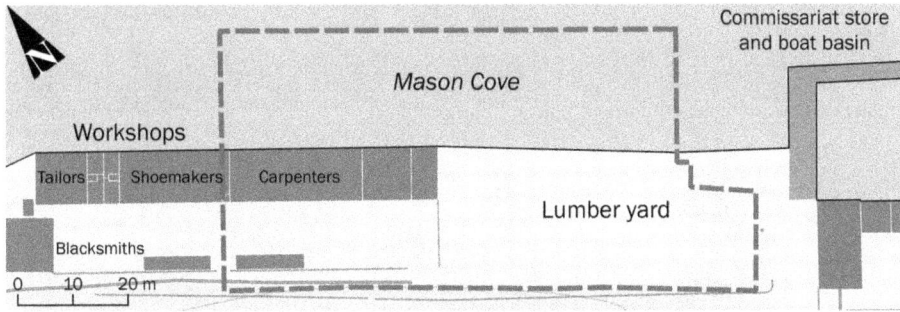

Figure 1.15. Plan of the waterfront area in 1836. Champ Street runs along the bottom of the plan.

and granary between 1842 and 1845 was the ultimate expression of this drive toward sufficiency, in the process creating one of contemporary Port Arthur's most visually striking edifices. The subsequent remodelling of this structure during 1854–57, and the accompanying changes to the foreshore, demonstrated a move toward an industrial prison.

The following overview uses the historical phasing derived from the results of the archaeological investigation (see Chapter 4).

Industrial waterfront phase, 1830–54

During the station's initial phase, the southern portion of Mason Cove witnessed a concerted building program as the infrastructure of industry and goods transport was constructed (Figure 1.14 and Plate 1.3). A range of workshops was constructed in 1831, housing Port Arthur's blacksmiths and shoemakers. To the east of this a wharf and lumber yard were established.

As the settlement rapidly grew during the mid-1830s, the original range of workshops was remodelled and extended. By 1836 the workshops comprised a weatherboard structure housing carpenters, coopers, woodturners, tailors and shoemakers (Figures 1.15 and 1.16). A separate masonry structure housed the nailers and blacksmiths. Extended south-east along the waterfront, the workshop's northern footing was incorporated into the sea defences beginning to formalise the original shoreline. A retaining wall demarcated the line of Champ Street, with a ramp leading down to the back of the workshops. A number of weatherboard structures were also added to the rear of the workshops, comprising a constables' quarters and lumber store.

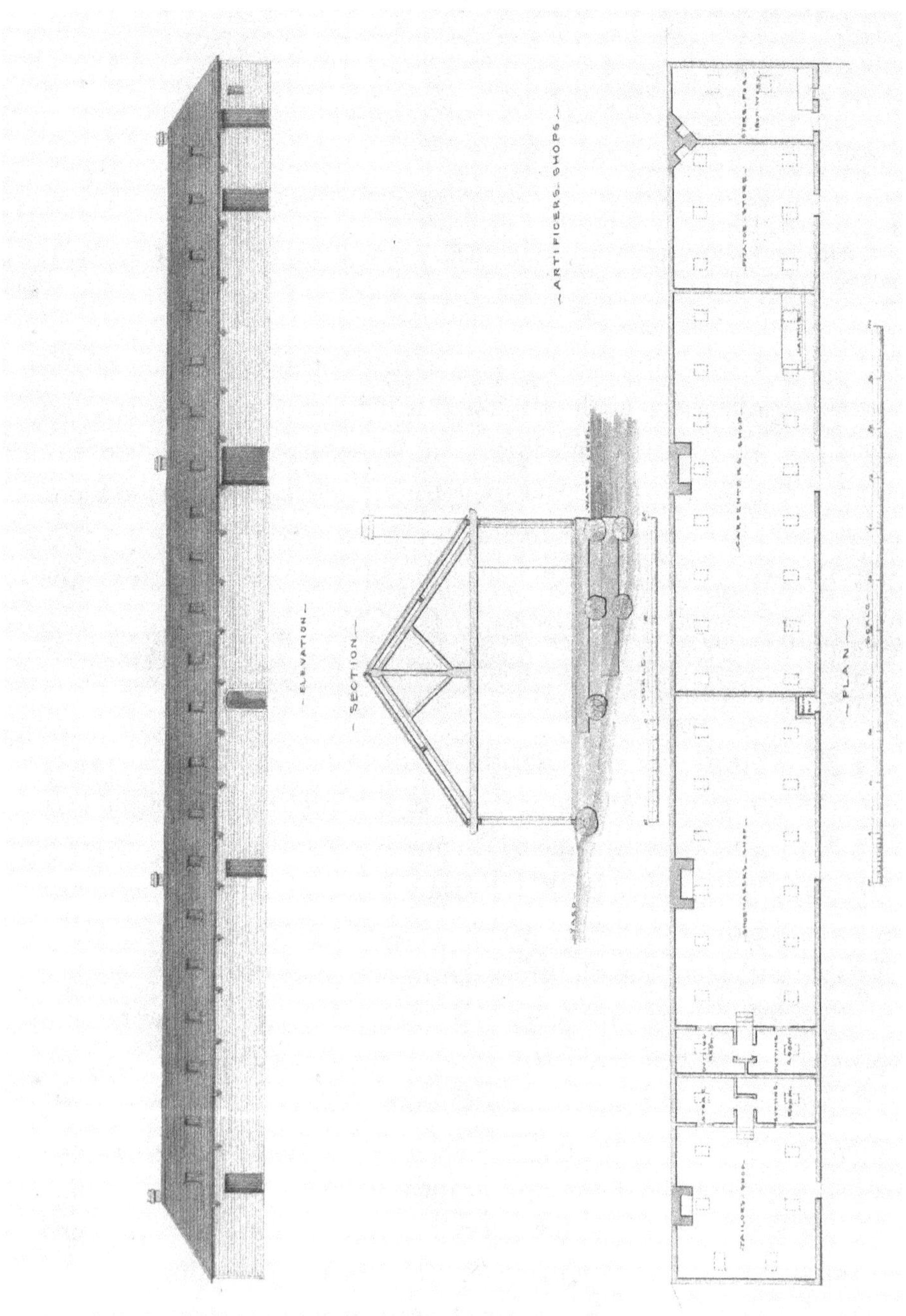

Figure 1.16. Henry Laing's illustration of the waterfront workshops. Note the cross-section showing the original shore and the log-and-earth reclamation overlying. (Henry Laing, ca. 1836, 'Artificer's shops', CON 87/1/35. Tasmanian Archives).

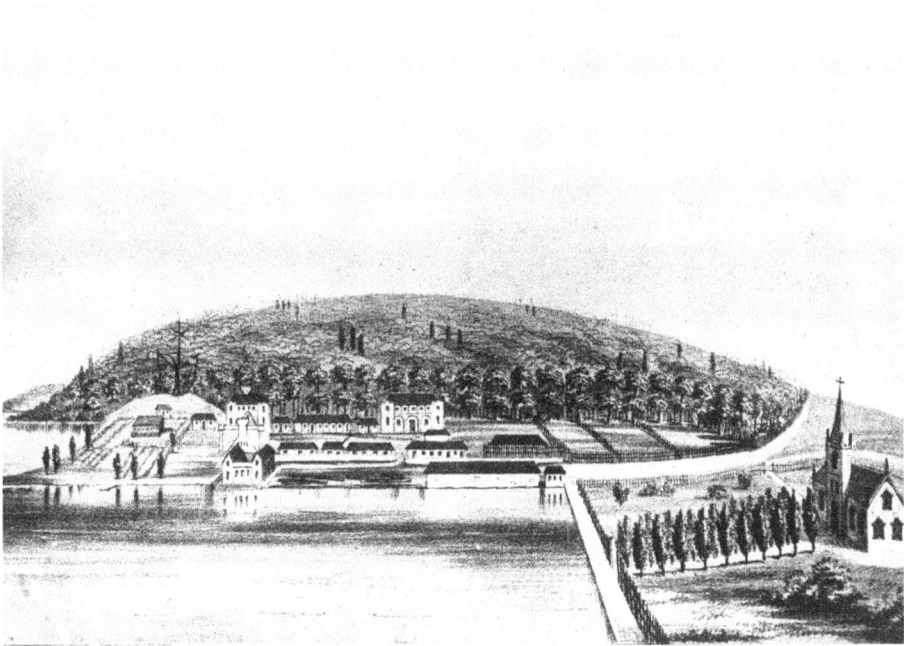

Figure 1.17. Illustration showing the settlement in 1842. The waterfront workshops are clearly visible, as are piles of logs in the adjacent timber-working area. (Captain Hext, ca. 1842, 'The penal settlement of Port Arthur, Van Diemen's Land, Tasmanian Archives)

The 1842 commencement of the flour mill and granary resulted in the demolition of the eastern end of the workshops, the new structure built upon the site of the former lumber yards (Figures 1.17 and 1.18). The building was divided into three main sections: the granary, the waterwheel and mill house, and the treadwheel ward (Figure 1.19). The granary was essentially a separate building from the mill and treadwheel ward, although it shared a single roof with them. The whole was built on an 'L-shaped' plan, with the granary accommodated in the shortest wing (Plate 1.4). The treadwheel was located in the longest ward. Both sections contained multiple storeys.

An engineer from Hobart, Alexander Clark, was appointed to oversee both mill construction and the attendant hydraulic engineering systems. Clark's services were required as there were no Royal Engineers (who provided construction oversight for the Convict Department) with the requisite experience. Arriving on site in January 1843, Clark found work had already begun on excavating the water race required to bring water to the

Figure 1.18. Illustration from 1851–52 showing the completed flour mill and granary. The second black vertical stripe on the building marks the situation of the 35ft (10.7 m) water wheel. The external cistern is depicted below. (Unknown author, 'Port Arthur, from across the cove', ca. 1851–52, Q1686, Tasmanian Museum and Art Gallery).

wheel.[28] Although he found the site chosen for the mill was 'quite suitable' he noted that substantial work was required to keep the waters of Mason Cove at bay.[29]

Foundations were laid in February, with those of the mill house completed the following month.[30] Unsuitable ground to the east meant the granary, which had originally been planned to run parallel with the shoreline, instead had to be built at a perpendicular angle to it – making the building 'L-shaped'.[31] Work continued on the mill building throughout the

---

28 Alexander Clark to J.C. Victor, Commanding Royal Engineer, 28 January 1843. Transcripts of Ian Brand, *Buildings and Structures A-F*, v. 2, PAHSMA, p. 270.

29 Alexander Clark to J.C. Victor, Commanding Royal Engineer, 28 January 1843. Transcripts of Ian Brand, *Buildings and Structures A-F*, v. 2, PAHSMA, p. 270.

30 Alexander Clark to J.C. Victor, Commanding Royal Engineer, 25 March 1843. Transcripts of Ian Brand, *Buildings and Structures A-F*, v. 2, PAHSMA, p. 275.

31 Alexander Clark to J.C. Victor, Commanding Royal Engineer, 25 March 1843. Transcripts of Ian Brand, *Buildings and Structures A-F*, v. 2, PAHSMA, p. 275.

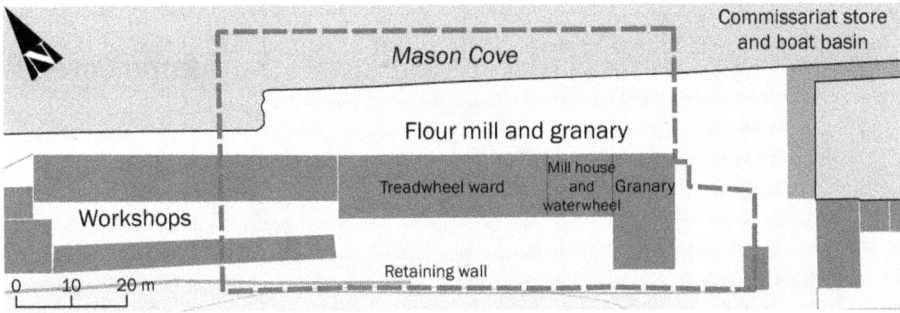

Figure 1.19. Plan of the waterfront area in 1846.

year, with the 35-foot (10.70 m) waterwheel in place by August.[32] Both store and mill house were roofed by April the following year.[33]

At the beginning of 1844 imported millstones arrived and were installed, with work also commencing on the foundations of the attached treadwheel building.[34] By the end of the year, the treadwheel sections and associated machinery had been installed, with the wheel making its first powered revolution (with 26 prisoners) in March 1845.[35] The treadwheel initially comprised six separate sections of 12 feet (3.65 m), spaced out on a central shaft, but was increased to eight by the end of the project.[36] The building was roofed soon after.

During the construction period, work had simultaneously proceeded on the complex system of dam, mill race, reservoir, underground aqueduct, underground piping and overhead flume required to bring the water to the mill (Figure 1.20). The design of the water system encountered difficulties

---

32 Alexander Clark to J.C. Victor, Commanding Royal Engineer, 26 August 1843. Transcripts of Ian Brand, *Buildings and Structures A-F*, v. 2, PAHSMA, p. 281.
33 Alexander Clark to J.C. Victor, Commanding Royal Engineer, 16 March 1843. Transcripts of Ian Brand, *Buildings and Structures A-F*, v. 2, PAHSMA, p. 292.
34 Alexander Clark to J.C. Victor, Commanding Royal Engineer, 16 March 1843. Transcripts of Ian Brand, *Buildings and Structures A-F*, v. 2, PAHSMA, p. 292; Alexander Clark to J.C. Victor, Commanding Royal Engineer, 25 March 1843. Transcripts of Ian Brand, *Buildings and Structures A-F*, v. 2, PAHSMA, p. 288;
35 Alexander Clark to J.C. Victor, Commanding Royal Engineer, 13 February 1845. Transcripts of Ian Brand, *Buildings and Structures A-F*, v. 2, PAHSMA, p. 344.
36 Alexander Clark to J.C. Victor, Commanding Royal Engineer, 28 April 1845. Transcripts of Ian Brand, *Letterbook of Alexander Clark*, v. 20, PAHSMA, p. 130; K. Preston, 'Prison Treadmills in Van Diemen's Land: Design, Construction and Operation, 1828 to 1856', *Tasmanian Historical Research Association*, Vol. 60, No. 2, 2013, pp. 81–99, pp. 92–95.

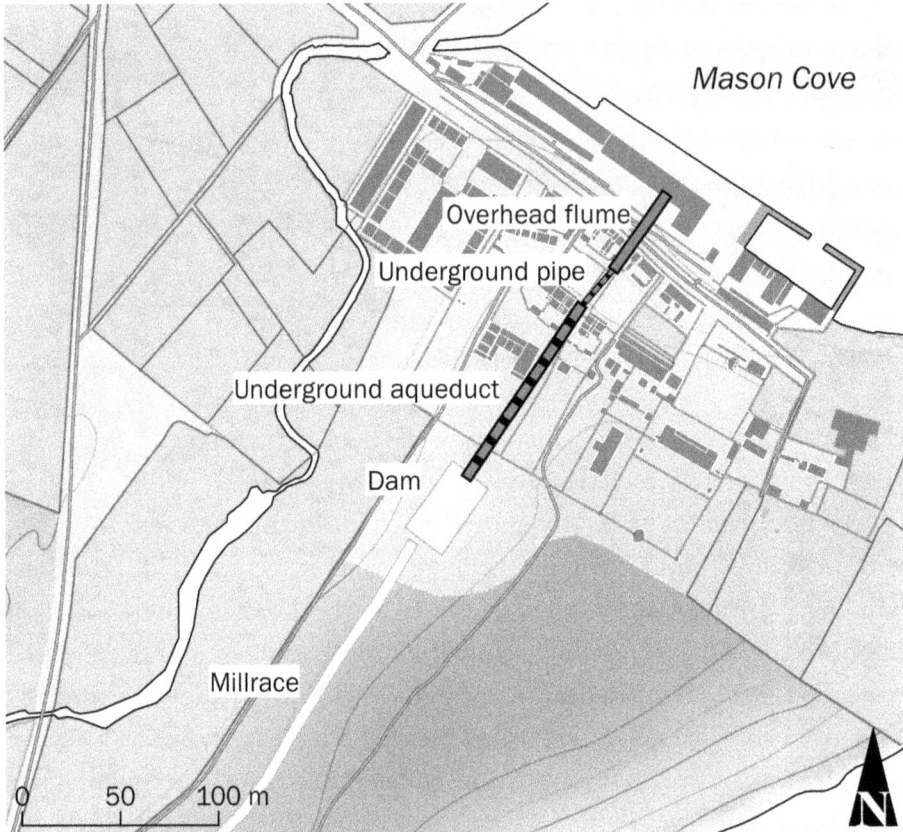

Figure 1.20. The water was supplied to the mill via a composite system that was eventually found wanting.

due to the distance that the water was required to travel from the dam on the upper stretches of Settlement Creek (1.50 km) and the presence of existing buildings on Settlement Hill. The last element of the system built was the flume running to the back of the mill over Champ Street. This was completed in June 1845, with water run through it for the first time soon after.[37]

Between 1842 and 1845 the area behind the mill was used for the storage of materials and as working space. The Champ Street sandstone retaining wall was constructed at the same time as the treadwheel building and was two-thirds complete by March 1845.[38] The wall incorporated a pier to

---

37   Alexander Clark to J.C. Victor, Commanding Royal Engineer, 7 April 1845. Transcripts of Ian Brand, *Buildings and Structures A-F*, v. 2, PAHSMA, p. 352.

38   Alexander Clark to J.C. Victor, Commanding Royal Engineer, 13 February 1845. Transcripts of Ian Brand, *Buildings and Structures A-F*, v. 2, PAHSMA, p. 344.

support the overhead flume. The side fronting Mason Cove comprised a strip of land reclaimed as part of the mill and granary's construction. It was likely also used as a storage and working area, and as the site of the terminal cistern of the waterwheel pit.

Penitentiary Phase I: 1854 – ca. 1862

The mill was almost immediately a failure, which we discuss in detail later in the book. By 1848 proposals for the building's conversion to house prisoners had been made.[39] By the 1850s the whole structure was being used as a store (Figure 1.21). Remodelling commenced in 1854 and was completed in 1857. This work was accompanied by the reclamation of part of Mason Cove, creating space for the penitentiary's muster ground.

This renovation saw the internals of the old structure gutted to make way for infrastructure to house 484 convicts. The size of the building enabled some form of classification, with a twin-tiered row of back-to-back separate cells accommodating 136 of the settlement's most recalcitrant inmates 'deemed desirable to exclude from the general dormitory' (Figure 1.23).[40] Two floors above was a dormitory sleeping a further 348 better-behaved convicts.[41] The building was also outfitted with a mess hall, situated between the cells and the dormitory. A chapel and library were also added (Figures 1.22 and 1.24).

To the west of the building, a bakehouse and cookhouse were added, further overprinting some of the earlier workshops. This structure was commenced around 1855, though it was not listed as completed until 1858.[42] A two-storey structure, it contained a main cooking area, in which were situated two large bread ovens and basins, and a scullery and storerooms

---

39   G.H. Courteney, Superintendent, to J.S. Hampton, Comptroller General, 2 August 1848, MM62/1/24, A1122, no.10759, TA.
40   James Boyd, Commandant, to William Nairn, Acting Comptroller General, 10 August 1857, *Convict Discipline and Transportation*, British Parliamentary Papers, London, 1859 (August), p. 181.
41   James Boyd, Commandant, to William Nairn, Acting Comptroller General, 10 August 1857, *Convict Discipline and Transportation*, British Parliamentary Papers, London, 1859 (August), p. 181.
42   James Boyd, Commandant, to William Nairn, Acting Comptroller General, 7 August 1858, *Convict Discipline and Transportation*, British Parliamentary Papers, London, 1859 (August), p. 203.

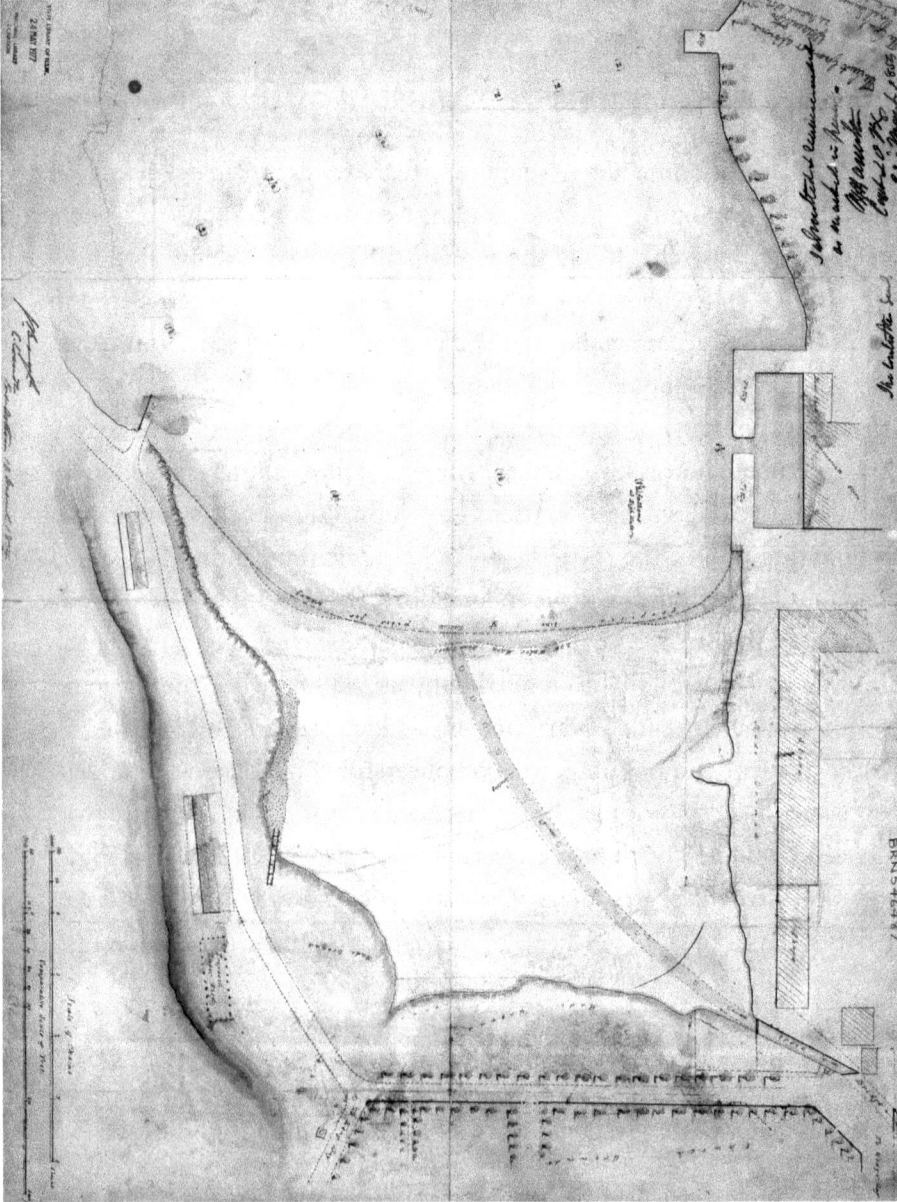

Figure 1.21. Rough plan of Mason Cove showing the proposed reclamation. By this time the flour mill and granary is labelled a 'store'. (Unknown author, Plan of Port Arthur waterfront, 1852, maps/0894, Mitchell Library, State Library of New South Wales)

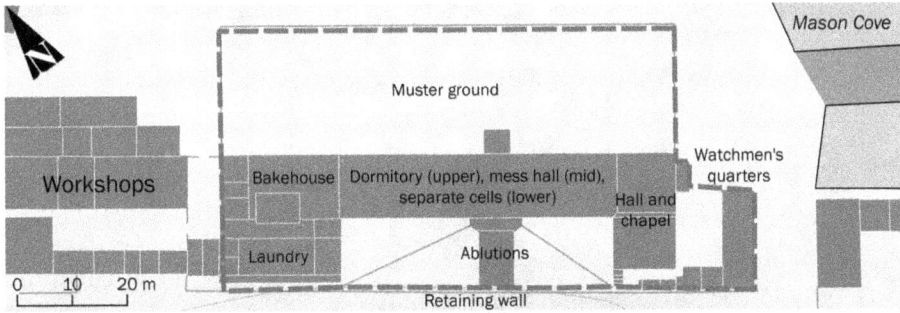

Figure 1.22. Plan of the area in 1857.

located at its western end. The upper floor was occupied by a clothing store. A hoisting machine – a form of dumb waiter – connected the bakehouse to the mess hall.

With the conversion of the mill well underway in 1855, the erection of a range of buildings comprising 'laundry, receiving room, hot air drying room, clothing and other stores' was mentioned in returns as still yet to occur.[43] Evidently this work was completed before 1857, as in this year reference was made to exercise yards, privies and lavatories, kitchen and bakery, clothing store, laundry and drying room.[44] The laundry building was situated to the south of the bakehouse and cookhouse, the ablutions area to the east behind the bulk of the penitentiary.

A plan from ca. 1856 depicts the ablutions and laundry areas during this first phase (Plate 1.5). According to the plan, the ablutions area comprised two yards flanking a central building (Plate 1.6). Entry to the ablutions was made through a door at the rear of the penitentiary, or via the laundry into the western yard. Prisoners exiting from the penitentiary passed through a portal, from which they had a choice of seven separate entrances. Three of these led into the large central ablutions block and the remaining four into the yards flanking it.

---

43   James Boyd, Commandant, to J.S. Hampton, Comptroller General, 4 January 1855, *Convict Discipline and Transportation*, British Parliamentary Papers, London, 1854–5 (1916) (1988), p. 25.

44   James Boyd, Commandant, to William Nairn, Acting Comptroller General, 10 August 1857, *Convict Discipline and Transportation*, British Parliamentary Papers, London, 1859 (August), p. 181.

Figure 1.23. Interior view of the penitentiary separate cells in the former treadwheel ward, taken post-1877. (Unknown author, 'Cell gallery – Penitentiary, Port Arthur', n.d., NS1013/1/1657, Tasmanian Archives)

Figure 1.24. View showing the penitentiary, likely during conversion works as neither the clocktower nor bakehouse are shown. Note the construction materials stacked outside the building and the sawing frame (complete with convict) to its east. (Unknown author, untitled illustration of Port Arthur, ca. 1854–56, Allport Library and Museum of Fine Arts, State Library of Tasmania)

The yards were depicted as being divided diagonally, with each division of the yard fitted with shelter sheds and fireplaces. In the eastern yard there were two back-to-back fireplaces located centrally in the dividing wall, as well as a fireplace on the outer eastern wall of the central building. All the fireplaces were covered by shelters. Covered seating was situated along the base of the Champ Street retaining wall and the penitentiary's eastern wing.[45]

The western yard was shown as being a mirror-image of the eastern, with a diagonal wall defining two spaces with covered seating and fireplaces. In the south-western corner of the yard, an entrance led into a long narrow passageway between the rear of the laundry and the Champ Street retaining wall. In this narrow space was a bank of 27 lavatory troughs for washing.

The central building was depicted as an ablutions shed, in which were situated privies, urinals and washing troughs. There were three openings into the northern end of the structure. Approaching from the penitentiary, the

---

45 James Boyd, Commandant, to William Nairn, Acting Comptroller General, 10 August 1857, *Convict Discipline and Transportation*, British Parliamentary Papers, London, 1859 (August), p. 181.

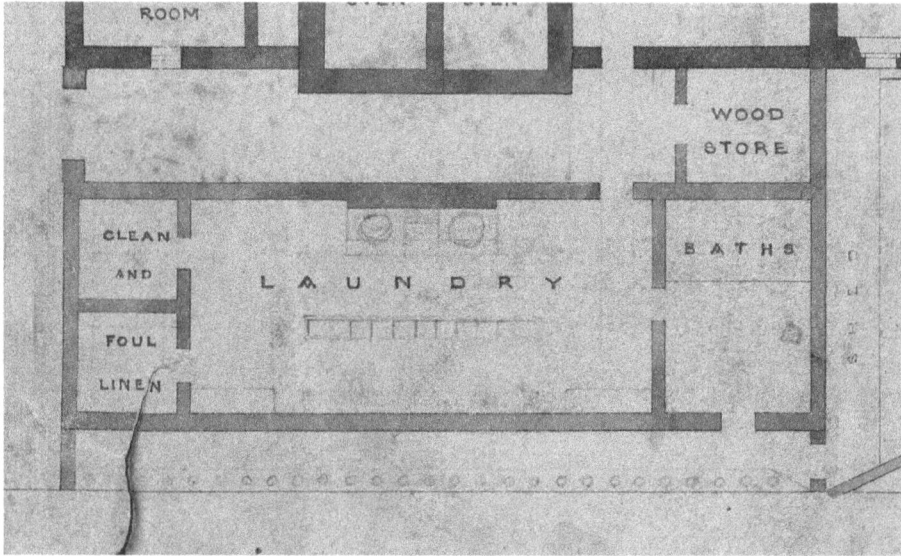

Figure 1.25. Detail of ca. 1856 plan, showing laundry area. (Plan of Port Arthur penitentiary, ca. 1856, PXD 52, Mitchell Library, State Library of New South Wales)

right-hand entrance provided access to the western side, where fifteen privies lined the wall. Along the rear wall of the structure were eight partitioned urinal enclosures. The eastern side of the structure was occupied by four freestanding washing troughs, with a doorway leading back out to the portal. An enclosed space marked as 'Inspection' ran down the structure's centre, only accessible from the portal.

The privies and urinals appear to have not required subsurface drainage; the waste was collected for use on the settlement farm:

> All matter from the latrines and urinals are removed to the Farm and the vessels cleansed daily; underground sewerage is purposefully avoided, all drains have a good fall and discharge themselves freely.[46]

The plan indicates that at this time the laundry area comprised seven separate spaces delineated by masonry walls (Figure 1.25). Only four of these spaces were roofed: the clean and foul linen stores, laundry and bathhouse.[47] An unroofed passageway was situated between the rear of the bakehouse and

---

46 'Interrogatories ... Penal Settlement, Pauper and Lunatics' Depot, Port Arthur, Tasman's Peninsula, 15 November 1865, CO 280/369, reel no. 1966–67, p. 87.

47 Lander, 'Port Arthur Penal Station, Tasmania', 5 August 1858, HM 133, PAHSMA Collection.

the laundry, providing access from the bakehouse and laundry area to the workshops to the west. A wood store was located at the eastern end of the passage. Similarly, an unroofed space was situated between the southern rear of the laundry and the Champ Street retaining wall. This space was accessed via the bathhouse, with an entrance also through to the ablutions yard.

Within the bathhouse, the baths were situated in the northern half of the space. From the bathhouse, another doorway led into the laundry proper. In this space two large coppers sat against the northern wall, either side of the centrally located chimney. Two square objects, possibly drying tables, were situated in the south-eastern and south-western corners of the room, between which a drying rack may have been depicted. A linear feature shown in the centre of the space likely depicted washing tubs. Two small stores for dirty and clean linen were located in the western extent of the building, accessed from the laundry.

Penitentiary Phase II: ca. 1862 – settlement close

In the ca. 1856 plan a number of features were earmarked for demolition. The dividing walls of both yards are marked 'to be removed' and an annotation at the top of the plan states that all the fireplaces in the yards are to be removed.

In 1862, documents refer to the 'conversion of a certain building into a day room for the effective convicts in the back-yard of the penitentiary.'[48] This 'certain building' was the yard's central structure. A subsequent report in 1864 stated 'The lavatories etc., in the back yard of the penitentiary have been reconstructed, and a day room provided for the prisoners.'[49]

This documentary evidence is supported by a plan completed ca. 1863, which purportedly shows the newly reconstructed lavatories and urinals (Figure 1.26 and Plate 1.7). It also indicates that the conversion works did not extend to the main penitentiary or the bakehouse. The change is further borne out by a later 1870s plan, which, though simpler, does show

---

48 James Boyd, Commandant, to William Nairn, Comptroller General, 28 July 1862, *Convict Discipline and Transportation*, British Parliamentary Papers, London, 1863, p. 69.
49 James Boyd, Commandant, to William Nairn, Comptroller General, 10 August 1864, *Annual Reports on the Convict Establishments at Western Australia and Tasmania*, British Parliamentary Papers, London, 1865 (June), p. 51.

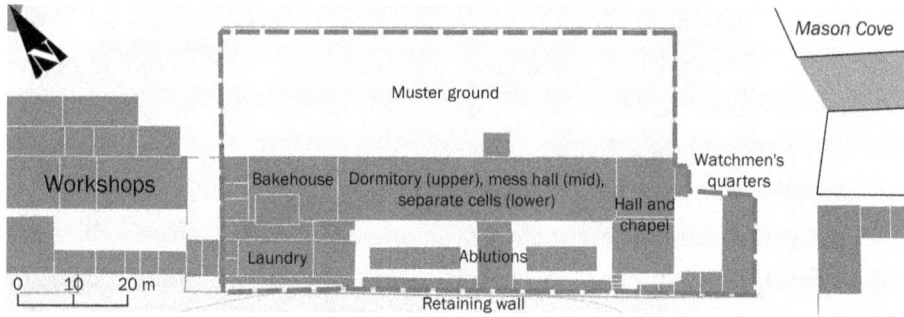

Figure 1.26. Plan showing the area in 1865.

the day room, water closets and lavatory as being in the same position as the earlier plan.[50]

The ca. 1863 plan indicates that the portal between the penitentiary and central structure had been reconfigured and the number of entrances reduced to three: one into the central building, the remaining two into the flanking yards (Figure 1.27). The central building, which had originally housed the washing basins and urinals, was completely refitted, its purpose changing from ablutions block to day room. Benches were situated around the interior wall and a fireplace located at the southern end of the building.

In the eastern yard, the diagonal partition and fireplaces were all removed. In their stead a shed was added in the centre of the yard. No obvious entrances to the shed are shown, indicating an open-sided structure. At the rear (south) of the yard, where there had once been timber shelters, was placed a stretch of 19 'water closets' and six urinals. These were enclosed by a shingled-roofed, lattice-screened shelter, placed in the same location as the original Phase I shelters. Both the closets and urinals were individually partitioned, the plan indicating that a five-holed drain was situated within each urinal partition. As during the first phase, waste matter was collected for use at the settlement's farm.

As with its earlier incarnation, the western yard became a mirror-image of the eastern, with the fireplaces and diagonal yard wall removed and a centrally located shed built. The shed was of a similar design to that in the west yard. The wall separating the laundry from the yard was pushed east to accommodate a hot-water boiler and its attendant chimney. A bank of 34 lavatory basins under

---

50   Unnamed plan, 1870, HM 1870/1, PAHSMA Collection.

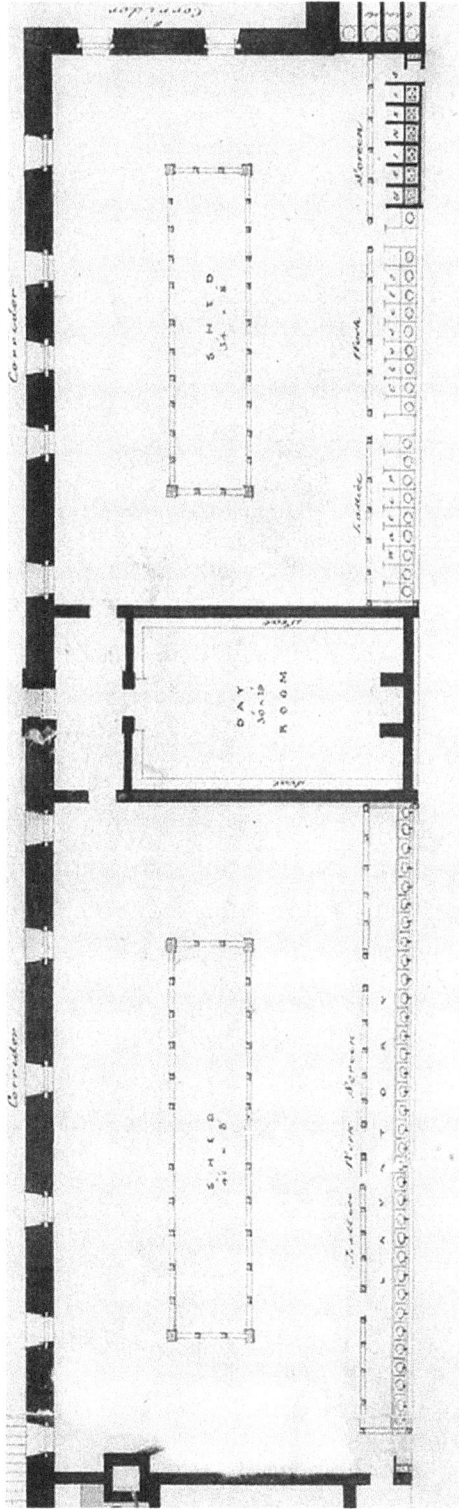

Figure 1.27. Detail of ca. 1863 plan showing the ablutions area. (Unknown author, untitled plan of penitentiary Port Arthur, ca. 1863, PWD 266/1/1779, Tasmanian Archives)

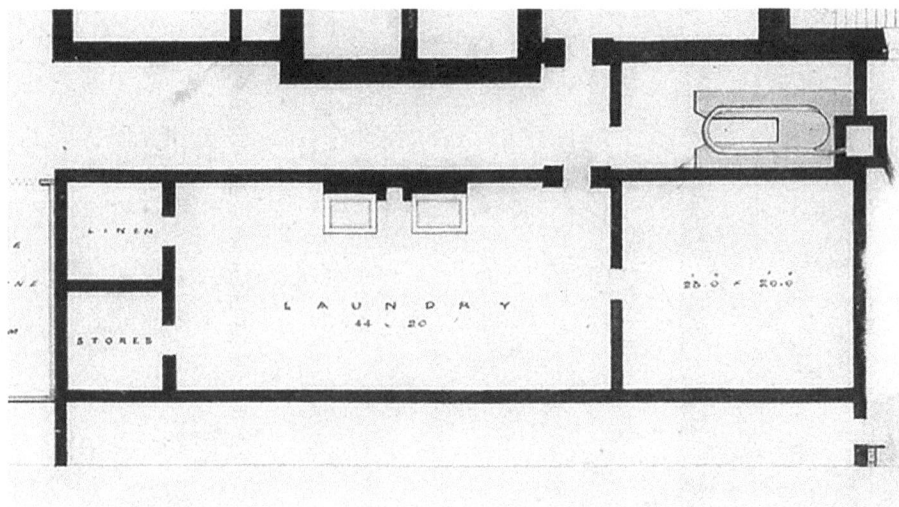

Figure 1.28. Detail of ca. 1863 plan showing the laundry area. (Unknown author, untitled plan of penitentiary Port Arthur, ca. 1863, PWD 266/1/1779, Tasmanian Archives)

a lattice-fronted shelter lined the yard's southern wall. As in the eastern yard, the shelter was situated in the same location as the Phase I shelter. The plan suggests that the lavatory basins were not separately partitioned.

The plan indicates that the remodelling works resulted in the extension of the laundry into the western ablutions yard (Figure 1.28). This largely affected the building's eastern extent, leaving its western mostly untouched. The long space at the laundry's rear remained, and the entrance to the western yard of the ablutions yard was retained. The entrance into the laundry was blocked at this time, suggesting that the space could only be accessed from the ablutions yard. A later 1870s plan labels this elongated space as a 'Bath Room'. Earlier records mention the construction of a 'new bath room' in 1864, which had been completed in 1865 and 'supplied with hot and cold water.'[51]

---

51 James Boyd, Commandant, to William Nairn, Comptroller General, 10 August 1864, *Annual Reports on the Convict Establishments at Western Australia and Tasmania*, British Parliamentary Papers, London, 1865 (June), p. 51; James Boyd, Commandant, to William Nairn, Comptroller General, 14 August 1865, *Annual Reports on the Convict Establishments at Western Australia and Tasmania*, British Parliamentary Papers, London, 1866 (May), p. 29.

Figure 1.29. Photograph of the penitentiary during the convict period, likely early 1870s. (J.W. Beattie, 'Port Arthur, past & present', n.d., DSM/986.8/B, p. 29, Mitchell Library, State Library of New South Wales)

A reference in 1871 recorded the presence of ten separate baths.[52]

In the building's west, the linen stores were retained in the same configuration, with the laundry space also remaining in its original layout. In the east, the old wood store was extended and converted into a house for a boiler and its attendant chimney. Providing hot water, the boiler also allowed the prisoners' provisions to be cooked by steam.[53] The historical use of the space east of the laundry was not recorded. Accessible only from the laundry building, it is unlikely to have been retained as a bathhouse.

A settlement plan from 1870 indicates that the boiler and bath spaces had been roofed toward the end of the settlement's life. This may have been associated with the works on the bathhouse noted above.

---

52 James Boyd, Commandant, to Governor's Secretary for Penal Establishment, 8 April 1871, 'Report of the Select Committee, with Minutes of the Proceedings, and Evidence', No. 127, *Journals of the House of Assembly*, Hobart, 1871 (Vol. 22), p. 17.

53 James Boyd, Commandant, to William Nairn, Comptroller General, 10 August 1864, *Annual Reports on the Convict Establishments at Western Australia and Tasmania*, British Parliamentary Papers, London, 1865 (June), p. 51.

The post-convict period

By the mid-1870s the penitentiary was suffering from neglect, a fact borne out by the comments of a visitor in 1876, who noted that 'the wood-work and especially the flooring [of the day room and lavatory] was going to rack and ruin.' The degradation was complete by 1889 (12 years after closure), when a correspondent for the *Tasmanian Mail* recorded how the 'weatherboard erections' adjacent to the penitentiary had completely collapsed and were overgrown with weeds. Despite this, an 1889 survey plan shows that the laundry and day room were evidently still standing in some form or another (Figure 1.30).

The penitentiary was not sold in the 1889 land sales, the asking price of £800 obviously being considered too high (Figure 1.31).[54] The matter was taken out of everybody's hands when, on 31 December, the penitentiary was gutted by fires. While the masonry shell of the penitentiary and bakehouse remained upstanding in some form, the timber ablutions block and what remained of the laundry stood no chance of survival.

Over the following decades the parlous state of the structure proved of ongoing concern to the Carnarvon town council (formed when Port Arthur became a township) and the Tasmanian government, the latter having assumed control of it by 1913.[55] The penitentiary survived plans for its demolition, instead undergoing extensive 'tidying' through the removal of unsafe elements and the clearing of debris. In the 1930s William Radcliffe, storekeeper and landowner at Port Arthur, built a large wooden shed just west of the laundry ruin – where the workshops had once stood – to house his museum pieces.[56] These included curiosities dug up from around Radcliffe's property, including the penitentiary space. With Radcliffe's death in 1943, management passed to his widow, who, with the Scenery Preservation Board's backing, moved the museum off the historic site.[57] The old museum was levelled in 1959 and the site left to grass over.[58]

---

54 *The Mercury*, 13 March 1889.
55 Note, September 1913, LSD/324/975x. Transcripts of Ian Brand, *Buildings and Structures A-F*, v. 23, PAHSMA, p. 324.
56 Young, *Making Crime Pay*, p. 121.
57 Young, *Making Crime Pay*, p. 135.
58 Young, *Making Crime Pay*, p. 135.

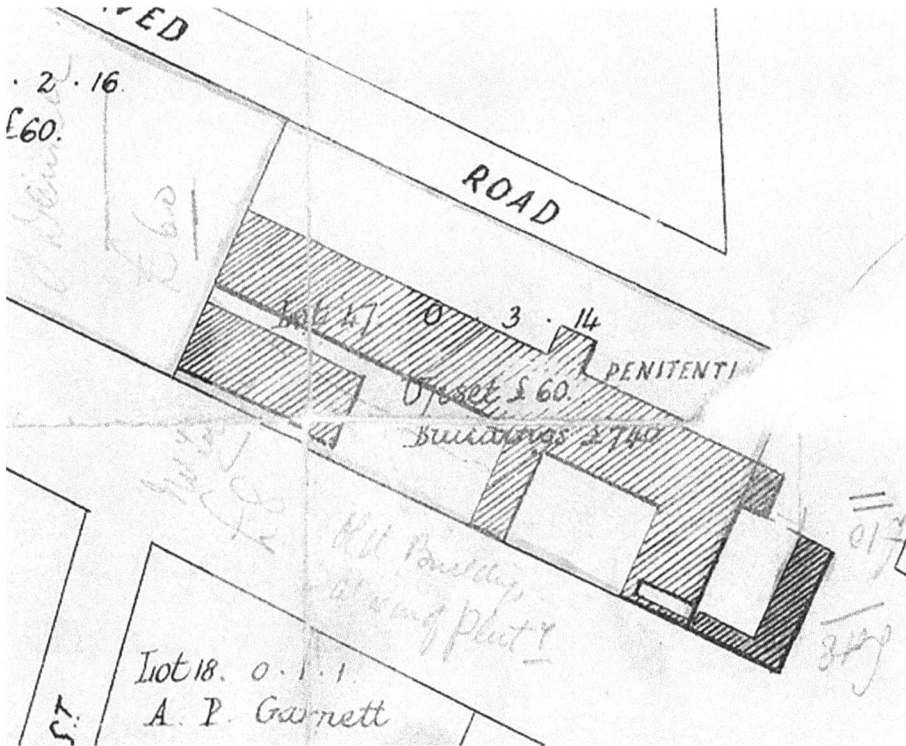

Figure 1.30. Detail of 1889 survey, showing the remnant structures in the laundry and ablutions area. (Unknown author, 12 March 1889, 'Lots for sale on the ground at Port Arthur', PWD 266/1/1777, Tasmanian Archives)

From that point on, the main issue was the safety of tourists clambering around the slowly degrading penitentiary and bakehouse. No construction took place in the former laundry and ablutions block area, the space being left open until the late 1960s when, during 1967–71, a concerted works program was undertaken to stabilise the penitentiary ruin. This saw the space being used for the parking of heavy machinery and storage of building materials. The area remained fenced off and closed to the public until June 1998, when access from the penitentiary and workshops range was reinstated. The lawn covering was improved and a single interpretative sign installed.

Figure 1.31. View of the ablutions area in the 1890s, prior to the 1897 fire. (Unknown author, 1890s, untitled photograph of Port Arthur penitentiary, Tasmanian Archives)

Chapter 2

THE STORY OF THE PENITENTIARY PRECINCT

The penitentiary that we see today largely represents one particular aspect of Port Arthur. Its brick and sandstone walls predominantly speak of the period 1854–77, when it became the incarcerative epicentre of the penal station. Over time, earlier incarnations of the building and the site have become obscured. The archaeological investigations of 2013–16 were able to strip back and define these obscuring layers, reshaping and refining the historical, architectural and archaeological understandings that we already had.

The excavations cast new light on all aspects of Port Arthur's convict period history, from the formation of a timber-getting camp, to the decline of an industrial prison – even to the processes that accompanied the purposeful forgetting of the convict landscapes. Archaeological and historical research found that the post-1830 occupation of the site can be divided into a series of phases: the use of the waterfront between 1830 and 1854, the conversion and occupation of the penitentiary between 1854 and 1877, and the period after the penitentiary was abandoned.

1830–1854	Industrial waterfront phase	
1854–1877	Penitentiary conversion and occupation	
	1854 – ca. 1862	*Penitentiary – Phase I*
	ca. 1862	*Penitentiary – Intermediate Phase*
	ca. 1862–1877	*Penitentiary – Phase II*
>1877	Post-abandonment	

The following chapter brings together a story that spans the entirety of Port Arthur's 47-year convict-period history: from the station's beginnings through its evolution into an industrial prison. It is a story of how space was formed and re-formed and adapted to penal requirements.

Settlement of a penal station

The decades of intense activity after 1830 have obscured or destroyed much of Port Arthur's pre-British settlement landscape. Within the settlement's bounds no trees survive from before 1830. The shape of its encircling hills has been altered by levelling and building. Even the outline of the bay has been masked by years of reclamation. We get glimpses of the place before the arrival of the British, captured in the maps, illustrations and descriptions committed to paper during the station's formative years. Yet the interest of their authors was more often turned toward the landscape's economic value: trees reduced to planks and beams, shell beds to building mortar, clay to bricks, stone to masonry, the sheltered harbour to a place of safe anchorage.

During the archaeological excavations we uncovered sections of dolerite bedrock, providing us with a small window into this lost landscape. This was a landscape that pre-dated the penal station by 6,500 years, the point at which the sea level stabilised near its present-day levels.[1] Its origins, of course, go back much, much further, the earliest visible stone on the Tasman Peninsula dating to the Devonian (416–360 million years ago).[2] During the Triassic and Permian (200–300 million years ago), the sedimentary mudstones and sandstones that comprise a large part of the peninsula were laid down as part of a great period of glaciation. Where beds of these later became exposed close to the surface, they became sources of building stone and gravel to be worked by the convict labourers.

Dolerite stone was formed 200 million years ago, caused by a major intrusion of magma from below the earth's crust. This iron-hard igneous

---

1   C. Sharples, *A Coastal Erosion Hazard Assessment for the Port Arthur and Coal Mines Historic Sites, Tasman Peninsula, Tasmania*, report prepared for Port Arthur Historic Site Management Authority, Tasmania, 2017, p. 49.

2   Bill Cotching, n.d., *Geology of Tasmania*, unpublished report, https://www.billcotching.com/Geology%20of%20Tasmania.pdf.

stone breaks through the surface across the peninsula and defines much of the landmass's edges where it meets the sea. Around the greater Port Arthur harbour it emerges as a gently sloping shelf of stone, often covered by cobbled dolerite eroded by the water out of its parent stone (Plate 2.1). Much of this shoreline has been lost from Mason Cove, plundered of its stone and covered by waterfront improvements. We do know from contemporary accounts that the doleritic shore extended around the sides of the cove, its head marked by a sandy beach exposed at low tide. This beach was later buried under reclamation fill in the 1850s.[3]

The archaeological excavations found great flat sections of dolerite, gently sloping toward the line of the original shoreline. Some outcrops of dolerite were split, jagged pieces jutting from the overlaying clays which had settled over millennia. The difficulty faced by the convicts of working the stone was evident. When they began to cut into the earth for their walls and building platforms, the closely outcropping dolerite was simply exposed and not modified. Instead they used the stone as a firm footing for structures, like the imposing bulk of the Champ Street retaining wall in the 1840s, or for the foundations of the 1850s laundry building.

The difficulties of working the dolerite and consolidating Port Arthur's early shoreline meant that the station's first arrivals instead focused on the tasks of clearance, timber-getting and the construction of the first buildings. While the bedrock may have proved difficult to work, the convict builders did take advantage of the rounded dolerite boulders and cobbles which covered the shoreline and were suspended within the clays. As the ground of Settlement Hill was cleared and buildings and roads constructed, these loose stones were stockpiled and incorporated into the footings, walls and building pads of the new structures (Figure 2.1). The use of this fieldstone dolerite was gradually superseded when clay was found to make bricks and sandstone quarries opened. Today, some of the sites where these stones were used are still visible on Settlement Hill.

Up until 1833 Mason Cove was largely left much as it had been found. Only small amounts of reclamation took place along its southern side, with a

---

3   T. Owen and J. Steele, *Port Arthur 2002, Sawpit and Tannery Complex Excavation Report*, report produced for the Port Arthur Historic Site Management Authority, 2002, p. 19.

Figure 2.1. Dolerite fieldstone retaining wall on Settlement Hill. This stone would have been collected during clearance activity between 1830 and 1833. (PAHSMA 2020)

timber wharf and jetty constructed to allow the direct loading and unloading of boats. The three earliest depictions we have of the settlement all date to 1833, after three years of occupation (Figures 1.3, 1.14 and Plate 2.2). They show buildings of accommodation and security for military and civil staff situated on the higher ground of Settlement Hill, buildings to accommodate and punish the convicts located at the lower, far eastern end of settlement, and the stores and workshops built on the foreshore. This was a template that Port Arthur would adhere to for the entirety of the convict period.

The mid-1830s was a time of consolidation and formalisation at the settlement, triggered by Port Arthur's increasing importance as a place of penal incarceration and labour. The focal area of the waterfront reflected the changes going on at the settlement. Work began on straightening the shoreline, with gridded logs, rock and rubble used to create a seawall fronting the bay.

The natural sloped profile of the terrain was modified, the clays overlying the shelving dolerite levelled. This excavated material was then used to consolidate the shoreline. Few artefacts or building materials were found within these redeposited layers. This was not surprising, considering that little demolition/salvaging of structures would have been taking place in the early 1830s. This meant that masonry by-products which would have otherwise made their way into such reclamation fill were not available. Instead, the loose dolerite boulders used for walls and footings were also used to bulk out the reclamation material.

The process of levelling and infilling the waterfront meant that the distinction between the areas north and south of Champ Street became sharper. The ground south of the workshops was cut back to accommodate the buildings, leading to the need for a retaining wall along the waterside edge of the road, as well as the provision of a ramp to allow access to the lower waterfront area.

The consolidation of the terrain was accompanied by work to formalise the infrastructure. By 1834 a large boat basin had been added in front of the Commissariat store, built from a grid of logs (Plates 2.3 and 2.4). Around this time the earliest workshops, situated near the mouth of the creek, were replaced by a larger range of buildings. The original building was a prefabricated storehouse brought on the first transport. Rapidly erected, it provided a relatively secure place to store six months' worth of provisions.[4] It also provided a home for Port Arthur's growing subset of convicts engaged in manufacturing tasks.

The need for these workshops was linked to decisions made early in the settlement's life. Initially, Lieutenant Governor Arthur had resisted diversification of labour away from a central focus on timber-getting.[5] There had always been a small number of convicts engaged in tasks which facilitated the station's self-sufficiency, with a carpenter, bricklayer and a gardener sent to the settlement in October 1830.[6] Despite Arthur's reservations, as the station's prisoner population increased, opportunities to expand the manufacturing focus of the station arose.[7]

---

4   Memorandum, George Arthur, Lieutenant Governor, 7 September 1830, CSO 1/483/10748, TA.

5   Captain Mahon, Port Arthur Commandant, to John Burnett, Colonial Secretary, 23 September 1831, note by George Arthur, Lieutenant Governor, 21 October 1831, CSO 1/484/10749, TA.

6   John Russell, Assistant Surgeon 63rd Regiment, to John Burnett, Colonial Secretary, 2 October 1830, CSO 1/477/10639, TA.

7   Captain Mahon, Port Arthur Commandant, to John Burnett, Colonial Secretary, 6 March 1832, CSO 1/483/10748, TA.

In mid-1831 manufacturing for export was instituted, initially with broom making as a way of employing men incapable of more intense forms of labour.[8] In July of the following year an order was given to form a shoemaking gang at the station, where the men would 'work at their trades in the service of the Government'.[9] Thirty-two shoemakers and tailors in the gangs of Hobart and Bridgewater were ordered to be sent to the station, leading to a four-fold increase in the population of the shoemaking gang by December.[10]

Initially the shoes and boots were maintained and manufactured with leather shipped to the settlement (Plate 2.5).[11] This leather was sourced through the Commissariat, which received it through tender from British or colonial sources.[12] The footwear was used locally at the settlement by convicts and free residents alike, the convict labourers undertaking repairs. Men's, women's and children's footwear was exported from the settlement by the thousand to other parts of the colony. This greatly diminished the burden on the Commissariat, which had formerly sourced footwear for convict uniforms from England.[13]

The growth of the manufacturing trades soon outstripped Port Arthur's capacity to house the labour force. Despite taking over the prefabricated store on the waterfront after the new Commissariat store was built in 1833, that space soon became inadequate.[14] This led to the approval in May 1834 of a new range of workshops, including a 'far more extensive' shop for the shoemakers.[15]

---

8   John Russell, Assistant Surgeon 63rd Regiment, to John Burnett, Colonial Secretary, 19 July 1831, CSO 1/483/10748, TA.

9   Memorandum, John Burnett, Colonial Secretary, 17 July 1832, CSO 1/477/10639, TA.

10   Josiah Spode, Principal Superintendent, to John Burnett, Colonial Secretary, 10 August 1832, CSO 1/477/10639, TA.

11   Mr Reilly, Ordnance Office, to John Burnett, Colonial Secretary, 15 October 1832, CSO 1/477/10639, TA.

12   Charles O'Hara Booth, Captain Commandant, to John Burnett, Colonial Secretary, 12 August 1833, CSO 1/477/10639, TA.

13   George Arthur, Lieutenant Governor, to Under Secretary Hay, 21 May 1827, *Historical Records of Australia*, Series III, Volume IV, Tasmania, April–December 1827, The Library Committee of the Commonwealth Parliament, 1923, p. 56.

14   George Arthur, Lieutenant Governor, to John Burnett, Colonial Secretary, 27 December 1832, CSO 1/632/14299, TA [transcripts of Ian Brand, PAHSMA]; J Gibbons, Commandant, to John Burnett, Colonial Secretary, 23 September 1832, CSO 1/613/13997, TA.

15   Memorandum, George Arthur, Lieutenant Governor, 5 May 1834, CSO 1/716/15655, TA.

Figure 2.2. Detail of the 1833 illustration, showing the waterfront area. The workshops are to the right. Convicts are visible working at a sawpit in the lumber yard. (Unknown artist, 'Port Arthur, Van Diemen's Land, ca. 1833', AG5929, Tasmanian Museum and Art Gallery)

The new buildings were constructed from weatherboard, with their waterside foundations incorporated into the sea defences along the shore.[16] Space was provided in the shops for tailors, shoemakers and carpenters. A masonry-built blacksmith's workshop was set further back from the shore, partly cut into the slope and housing forges for nail-making and larger work.

The formalisation of Port Arthur's shoreline also occurred in the area east of the workshops, where the old timber wharf had been located. The straightening of the shoreline, as well as the addition of the workshops and the Commissariat store either side, created a rectangular working area below Champ Street. It was given over to a set of sawpits and a lumber yard, creating a zone of labour that extended right along the waterfront (Figure 2.2). Walls and fences defined the area, which had been levelled to expose sections of the dolerite bedrock, in a fashion similar to the workshops area.

It was on this resultant flatter ground that the station's industrial enterprise was focused. Logs, metal, leather and stone flowed in from Port Arthur's hinterland and the holds of visiting vessels. The products of sawpit, smithy, wheelwright, shoemaker, tailor and mason flowed out from the workshops and yard. Walls, palisades and structures served to define an important area

---

16   Henry Laing, ca. 1836, 'Artificers shops', CON 87/1/35, TA.

of control and coercion, an area that was limited in the number and type of prisoners who could access it. By the time the new range of workshops had been constructed in 1835, more than 80 convicts were employed in the area, this workforce accounting for over 14 per cent of the settlement's 700-strong population (Figure 2.3).[17]

Despite the physical attempts to define this area as a zone of strictly controlled labour, the temptations offered to prisoners by the availability of tools that could facilitate escape, or materials that could be bartered, meant that the waterfront workshops area was the scene of numerous offences. William Prussia had arrived at Port Arthur in 1832. Listed as a shoemaker on his transportation to Van Diemen's Land, he had been employed in his trade at the station.[18] In the following year he was arraigned before the Commandant on a charge of being accessory to the night-time burglary of the workshops. For this charge he received 75 lashes.[19]

The shops that Prussia and his accomplices broke into were the old prefabricated stores from the first period of settlement. When these were replaced as part of the greater waterfront consolidation, the new premises appear to have been more secure, with no further burglaries recorded. However, convicts continued to take advantage of their access to tools and materials. In 1836 Thomas Rares was suspected of giving a bradawl to a fellow prisoner, who used it to aid their escape.[20] The following year Joseph Wilkes and Edward Preston were arraigned for taking advantage of their positions of trust and producing private work in the blacksmiths' and shoemakers' shops.[21]

By exposing the early dolerite and clay layers in the excavations, it got us thinking about the early site formation processes at Port Arthur: what the landscape was like before convicts arrived in September 1830 and how this landscape was modified to suit the station's early industrial requirements.

17   'The report of a visit to the Penal Settlement on Tasman's Peninsula, in the 11th month 1834, by James Backhouse and George W Walker', 6 November 1834, 'Distribution of Labour, Tasman's Peninsula 20th November 1834', CSO1/807/17244, TA.
18   Description list, William Prussia, #137, *Maria*, CON23/1/3, TA.
19   Conduct record, William Prussia, #137, *Maria*, CON31/1/34, TA.
20   Conduct record, Thomas Rares, #443, *Earl St Vincent*, CON31/1/34, TA.
21   Conduct record, William Preston, #1159, *Aurora*, CON31/1/35; conduct record, Joseph Wilkes, #1389, *Gilmore*, CON31/1/46, TA.

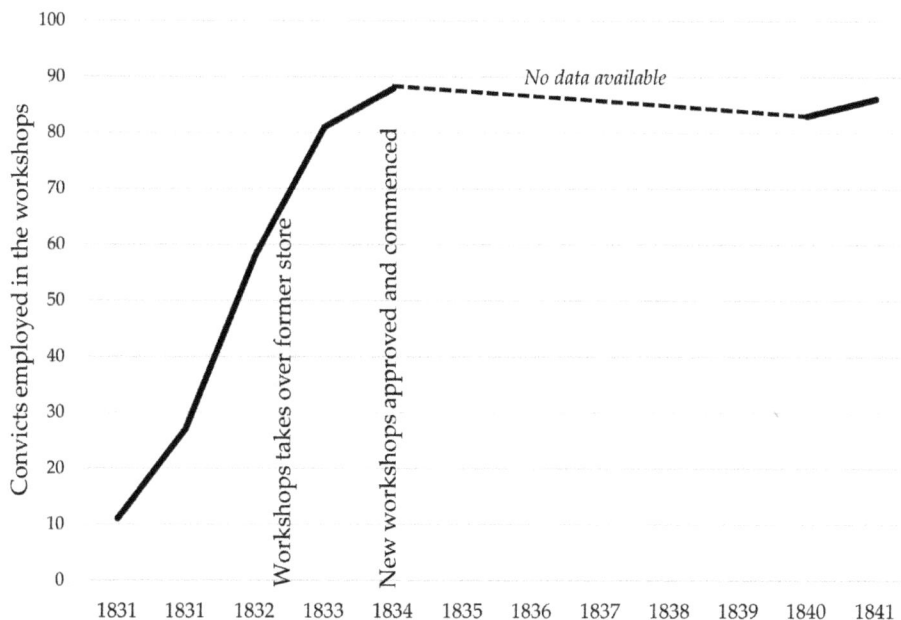

Figure 2.3. Graph illustrating the rapid rise of the number of convicts employed in the waterfront workshops between 1831 and 1834.

It was clear from the shallow nature of the bedrock that significant landscaping had taken place: the removal of the loam and clay overburden as part of terracing and levelling activity. This created a waterfront terrace, its seafront edge stabilised by a log seawall, its landward margin overlooked by the Champ Street thoroughfare.

This waterfront consolidation and the construction of the new and expanded workshops marked Port Arthur's shift from a place that concentrated primarily on the activity of timber-getting to an industrially focused, permanent station where the prisoner population was engaged in disparate occupations both inside and outside the settlement's core bounds. As the station became the colony's sole location for secondary punishment after 1833, more and more of its unfree population were devoted to labour designed to facilitate self-sufficiency in construction, clothing and agriculture. The informally organised timber camp was now becoming a multi-faceted organisation with more complex infrastructure and organisational requirements.

Impetus was given to this sufficiency drive from 1841 when Port Arthur was reclassified as a probation punishment station. The colony-wide

Figure 2.4. Impression Bay probation station. (Unknown author, 1845–55, 'Impression Bay station, Premaydena', Tasmanian Archives)

emergence of probation as a system brought with it a major push by the Convict Department at its new and existing stations to make operations as economically efficient as possible. This included both overt profit-making enterprises – such as the opening of a coal mine – as well as actions to lessen the daily cost burdens of clothing, rationing and superintending prisoners. As a result, stations were required to clear and cultivate vast acreages to provide food, as well as work the timber, clay and stone resources that might sit nearby (Figure 2.4).

At Port Arthur, where a decade of settlement had seen much of this economic activity already occur, the authorities turned their attention to a grand and complex undertaking that would theoretically turn the station into a powerhouse of economy and self-sufficiency. Begun in 1842, the flour mill and granary would consume material and available labour over a three-year period. In the end, indeed almost as soon as the building was completed, it became evident that this grand undertaking was a failure on a monumental level.

Convict management: profit and punishment?

It is one of the more incongruous pairings: the penitentiary that began life as a flour mill. Its thick brick walls once contained the undeniable trappings of industry: a giant 35 ft (10.50 m) wooden waterwheel, grinding gear with three pairs of millstones, a capacious granary and Commissariat offices. In an obvious concurrence of economy and penology, the mill also contained a treadwheel. Twelve feet in diameter, it was formed from eight cylinders, each of which could take up to six convicts at a time – allowing 48 men to work on the wheel at one time. With the mill and granary repurposed in the 1850s to house the infrastructure of confinement, the layered history of this building and its surrounds illustrates the seemingly dichotomous foundation of a place like Port Arthur: a place where the need to confine and coerce an unfree population sat – sometimes uncomfortably – side-by-side with the need to extract an economic return, all against a backdrop of a continually changing penal philosophy that required almost constant rearrangements of buildings and the landscapes in which they were set. The history and archaeology of today's penitentiary precinct perfectly encapsulates the tension that lay at the heart of the management of convict labour: the tension between 'profit and punishment'.

The economics of a ration

A complex series of conditions came together to trigger the construction of the flour mill and granary. Its foundations were laid in 1838 by events that occurred well away from the Tasman Peninsula, when the wheat fields of New South Wales were struck by a disease that devastated the harvest.[22] The farmers of Van Diemen's Land profited from the disaster, which in turn led to the planting of increased acreage across the colony. Such an increase in the wheat yield required a commensurate increase in the colony's milling capacity, encouraging the establishment of mills throughout Van Diemen's Land.

---

22   R. Tuffin, 'A Monument to Folly? The Port Arthur Flourmill and Granary', *Tasmanian Historical Studies*, Vol. 9, 2004, pp. 124–28, pp. 127–28.

For the Convict Department, the wheat export boom of the late 1830s was to cause difficulties in supplying rations to the thousands of convicts working for the government. This situation was exacerbated from the introduction of probation in 1839, after which all newly arrived convicts were placed into government-run stations. As a result, the number of convicts maintained by the government jumped from over 5,600 in 1839 to nearly 8,000 in 1841 and close to 12,000 the following year.[23]

All these prisoners required a daily ration, of which flour was an integral component. During 1841 the daily approved intake per prisoner was 1.5 lbs (700 g) of flour, alongside an allowance of vegetables, meat and salt (Figure 2.5).[24] The flour was predominantly used to make the bread consumed with every meal – equating to a loaf per day. At that rate of ration, the Commissariat was required to source 5.5 tons of flour per day for a prisoner population of 8,000. On the Tasman Peninsula, the Commissariat officer, Thomas Lempriere, estimated in 1839 that daily flour consumption at Port Arthur, the coal mines and Point Puer alone was 1.25 tons.[25]

During the 1830s, wheat had been supplied to the Commissariat through a system of tender, providing a valuable source of income to the colony's farmers and merchants.[26] The wheat bound for the Tasman Peninsula was ground in Hobart, thereby incurring the costs of production, refinement and transportation before it could be included in the convicts' diet.[27] With the peninsula stations comprising a sizeable percentage of rationing requirements, this placed a considerable drain on the Commissariat.

At the end of 1838 a board had been convened to investigate the possibility of employing the Port Arthur convicts in the large-scale cultivation of

23   R. Tuffin, 'The Convict Population of Van Diemen's Land: Landscapes Project Database 1', April 2020, Excel database, University of New England, https://hdl.handle.net/1959.11/28597, DOI: 10.25952/5ea24c915db7b.
24   'Regulations of the Probation System', 1 July 1841, Enclosure No. 4 in: John Franklin, Lieutenant Governor, to Lord Russell, Secretary of State, 9 July 1841, *Convict Discipline and Transportation*, British Parliamentary Papers, London, 1843 (158), pp. 38–41.
25   'Return of Provisions etc remaining in Her Majesty's Magazines on Tasman's Peninsula with the estimated duration at the present rate from 1 April 1839 inclusively', Thomas Lempriere, Port Arthur, 11 April 1839, CSO49/1/7, TA.
26   'Statement of Prices of Flour at which the Tenders Were Accepted from 1st April 1839 to 31st March 1840', 22 April 1839, CSO49/1/7, TA.
27   Memorandum by H.G. Darling, Deputy Assistant Commissary General, 21 May 1838, CSO5/129/3067, TA.

Figure 2.5. Rationing measures from the collection of the Tasmanian Museum and Art Gallery. (S617, S906, S2008.28, S2008.27)

wheat.[28] The aim of their enquiry was to deduce if the Tasman Peninsula could become a rationing hub for the rest of the convict establishments in the colony. The board found against the idea, stating that such an enterprise would jeopardise Port Arthur's security and the peninsula's penal nature.[29]

Despite these misgivings, in 1839 P. Roberts, an officer of the Commissariat, raised the idea of not just growing the grain at Port Arthur, but also grinding it.[30] His justification was that it would bypass Hobart in the supply chain, as the wheat would come directly to the peninsula from the Midlands grain-growing regions. A saving would ensue, as well as an improvement in quality, with the Commissariat directly overseeing

28 John Montagu, Colonial Secretary, Government Order, 18 October 1838, CSO5/129/3067, TA.

29 Josiah Spode, Principal Superintendent, Charles O'Hara Booth, Captain Commandant, to John Montagu, Colonial Secretary, 12 January 1839, CSO5/129/3067, TA

30 Peter Roberts, Deputy Assistant Commissary General, to John Montagu, Colonial Secretary, 22 July 1839, CSO5/204/5011, TA.

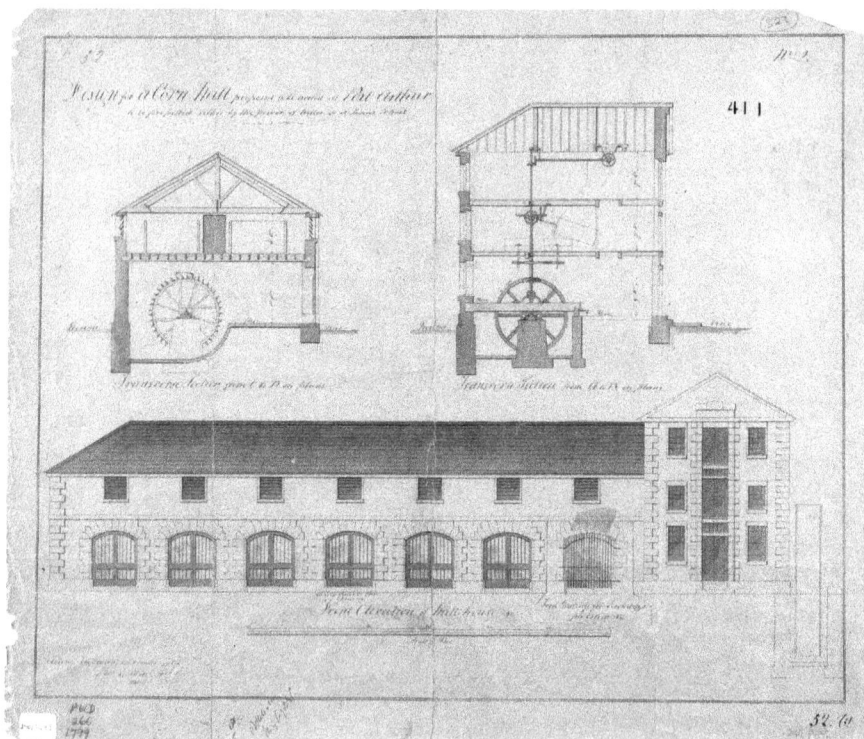

Figure 2.6. Elevation and sections drawn by William Cart, Acting Foreman of Works, for a mill to be 'propelled either by the power of water or a Tread Wheel'. (William Cart, 1839, 'Design for the Corn Mill proposed to be erected at Port Arthur', PWD266/1/1799, Tasmanian Archives)

the grinding process. Commandant Booth concurred, and the lieutenant-governor referred the matter to the Commanding Royal Engineer.[31] William Cart, Port Arthur's Foreman of Works, was tasked in August 1839 with investigating the project's feasibility.[32]

Two months later, Cart forwarded a number of plans and elevations for a water mill and granary (Figures 2.6 and 2.7).[33] He suggested the station's

---

31 Charles O'Hara Booth, Captain Commandant, to John Montagu, Colonial Secretary, 3 August 1839, note by John Montagu, Colonial Secretary, 13 May 1839, CSO5/204/5011, TA.
32 R. Kelsall, Commanding Royal Engineer, to William Cart, Acting Foreman of Works, 16 August 1839, CSO5/204/5011, TA.
33 William Cart, Acting Foreman of Works, to R. Kelsall, Commanding Royal Engineer, 21 October 1839, CSO5/204/5011, TA. Plans: 'Design for a Corn Mill Proposed to Be Erected at Port Arthur', 1839, PWD266/1/1798–99, 1801, 1803, TA.

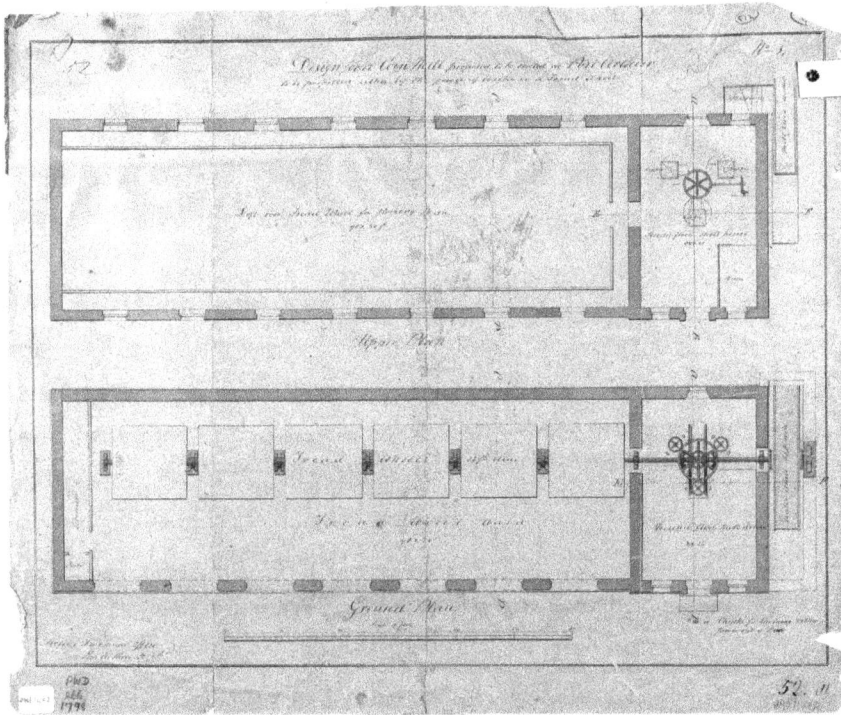

Figure 2.7. Plans drawn by Cart showing the treadwheel sections and grinding gear. (William Cart, 1839, 'Design for the Corn Mill proposed to be erected at Port Arthur', PWD266/1/1798, Tasmanian Archives)

waterfront as the ideal location, as it would enable a good flow of water to the wheel from the settlement's stream. In an unasked-for addition, he also added a design for a treadwheel. This was supported by Booth, who believed it would afford 'a description of labor at times much required on the Settlement'.[34]

Although the inclusion of a treadwheel was not favoured by the Commanding Royal Engineer, Roger Kelsall, such additions had begun to find favour in the prisons of the British Isles (Figure 2.8).[35] When they were constructed in the colonies, their power was often harnessed to grind flour, with

---

34 Charles O'Hara Booth, Captain Commandant, to Matthew Forster, Acting Colonial Secretary, 29 May 1840, CSO5/204/5011, TA.

35 R. Kelsall, Commanding Royal Engineer, to William Cart, Acting Foreman of Works, 28 October 1839, CSO5/204/5011, TA; D. H. Shayt, 'Stairway to Redemption: America's Encounter with the British Prison Treadmill', *Technology and Culture*, Vol. 30, No. 4, 1989, pp. 908–38.

treadwheels installed in prisoners' barracks at both Hobart and Launceston.[36] Such instruments ensured that the convicts remained productive – even as they were being punished.

Kelsall forwarded Cart's original plans, with the proviso that the treadwheel would not proceed, to Lieutenant Governor Franklin in November 1839.[37] Permission was provided within the fortnight.[38] However, although new plans and elevations for a water-powered mill and granary were produced in ca. 1840, works did not commence for another three years.[39] The project received assent numerous times, in November 1839, July 1841, April 1842 and December 1842.[40] Although the record is silent on the reasons for the extensive delay, it is likely that the exigencies caused by the introduction of probation led to the mill project being quietly shelved almost as soon as it first received sanction. When giving his permission, Franklin included the caveat that works could only proceed if there was 'no material reduction in the Convict Establishment of the Colony … in contemplation'.[41] The need for such reductions immediately appeared on the horizon with the advent of probation, which necessitated the unparalleled expansion of the network

36 M. Gibbs, 'The Enigma of William Jackman, 'the Australian Captive': Fictional Account or the True Story of a 19th Century Castaway in Western Australia', *The Great Circle*, Vol. 24, No. 2, 2002, pp. 3–21, p. 7; J. Birmingham, I. Jack, and D. Jeans, *Industrial Archaeology in Australia: Rural Industry*, Victoria, 1983, pp. 28–31.

37 R. Kelsall, Commanding Royal Engineer, to Matthew Forster, Acting Colonial Secretary, 13 November 1839, CSO5/204/5011, TA.

38 Matthew Forster, Acting Colonial Secretary, to R. Kelsall, Commanding Royal Engineer, 29 November 1839, CSO5/204/5011, TA.

39 The undated and unsigned plans are likely a series of three held by the Tasmanian Archives. Booth refers to the production of plans in February 1840, which may be the revisions. These were later used by Kelsall in 1841 as part of his cost estimates. 'Design for a Corn Mill Proposed to Be Erected at Port Arthur', n.d. [ca. 1840], PWD 266/1/1800, 1802, 1804, TA; R. Kelsall, Commanding Royal Engineer, to John Montagu, Colonial Secretary, 14 June 1841, CSO5/204/5011, TA; Charles O'Hara Booth, Captain Commandant, to Matthew Forster, Acting Colonial Secretary, 29 May 1840, CSO5/204/5011, TA.

40 John Montagu, Colonial Secretary, to George Maclean, Assistant Commissary General, 8 July 1841, CSO22/57/704, TA; G.J Boyes, Colonial Secretary, to Charles O'Hara Booth, Captain Commandant, 1 April 1842, CSO22/57/704, TA; G.J Boyes, Colonial Secretary, to J.C. Victor, Commanding Royal Engineer, 7 December 1842, CSO22/57/704, TA.

41 Matthew Forster, Acting Colonial Secretary, to R. Kelsall, Commanding Royal Engineer, 29 November 1839, CSO5/204/5011, TA.

of stations across the colony and so entailed an increased drain upon both colonial and British coffers.[42]

The situation on the ground at Port Arthur also did not allow for such large-scale works. In mid-1840 work had commenced on the long-delayed and much-needed military barracks at Port Arthur.[43] This large construction project, as well as works on new barracks at Point Puer, meant that Booth considered it 'utterly impossible' to begin work on the mill at the same time. Later, in 1842, work on the new brick-built hospital also interfered with its commencement.[44] However, by 1842 the situation in the colony had once again changed, causing the Port Arthur mill to become a priority.

At the end of 1839 the Commissariat had predicted a season of unusually high wheat prices, driven upward by increasing immigration to the Australian and New Zealand colonies.[45] They were at the mercy of the market, having to issue tenders for wheat over a year before they would actually receive it in store. This led to an uncertainty of supply, cost and quality that sat badly with the department's officers. By 1841 it looked as if the predictions were coming true. In May, George Maclean, Assistant Commissary General, advised Franklin that advertisements had been placed for the flour required to meet Port Arthur's ration requisition, their usual contractor having slowed production due to insufficient water.[46] Maclean enquired as to why the work on the Port Arthur mill had not begun. With the first of the probation stations appearing on the Tasman Peninsula in March 1841, the Port Arthur mill was 'now more than ever wanted.'[47]

Through 1842 the Commissariat became increasingly irritated at the delays. Instructions were once again issued to commence the work in March, although the works on the Port Arthur hospital necessitated further delay.

---

42 Tuffin and Gibbs, '"Uninformed and Impractical"? The Convict Probation System and Its Impact Upon the Landscape of 1840s Van Diemen's Land', pp. 94, 97–98.

43 Charles O'Hara Booth, Captain Commandant, to W. Mitchell, Assistant Colonial Secretary, 28 October 1840, CSO5/204/5011, TA.

44 R. Kelsall, Commanding Royal Engineer, to G.J. Boyes, Colonial Secretary, 17 March 1842, CSO22/57/704, TA.

45 P. Roberts, Deputy Assistant Commissary General, to John Montagu, Colonial Secretary, 12 December 1839, CSO5/204/5011, TA.

46 George Maclean, Assistant Commissary General, to John Montagu, Colonial Secretary, 21 May 1841, CSO5/204/5011, TA.

47 George Maclean, Assistant Commissary General, to John Montagu, Colonial Secretary, 21 May 1841, CSO5/204/5011, TA.

PRISONERS WORKING AT THE TREAD-WHEEL, AND OTHERS EXERCISING, IN THE 3RD YARD OF THE VAGRANTS'
PRISON, COLDBATH FIELDS.
(From a Photograph by Herbert Watkins, 179, Regent Street.)

Figure 2.8. The treadwheel at work. (H. Mayhew and J. Binny, *The Criminal Prisons of London*, London, 1868)

While the Commissariat, Royal Engineers and Convict Department traded correspondence and excuses, probation continued to have a marked effect on the location and density of the colony's prisoner population. By mid-1842 there were over 9,000 convicts in government stations, of whom over 30 per cent were in eight stations on the Tasman Peninsula. These 3,000 convicts required over two tonnes of flour per day – not including the ration requirements of free officers, military and their families.[48]

The problem of paying for their upkeep was made all the more dire when, in 1842, the colony entered a severe economic depression. Speculation gave way to inflation and unemployment, with passholding convicts looking for employment particularly hard hit.[49] With no other means of support, they

---

48 'Return of the Different Establishments Road and Probationary Stations at which Prisoners are Employed on the 31st of May 1842', CSO22/61/308, TA, p. 73.
49 Brand, Ian. *The Convict Probation System: Van Diemen's Land 1839–1854*. Hobart: Blubber Head Press, 1990, pp. 24–26.

Figure 2.9. Saltwater River probation station. (J.W. Beattie, 'Saltwater River', 1890, PH30/1/4574, Tasmanian Archives)

were forced back into government depots, where they were at least fed – on government flour. This unexpected situation drained the colony's capacity to sustain its convict population, at the same time as highlighting to Britain the mounting cost of maintaining its share of the prisoner population.

In response, administrators began to concentrate on station self-sufficiency. The Commissariat, in particular, regarded Van Diemen's Land as 'the Granary of the Australasian Colonies' and believed that stations should be able to grow enough wheat and vegetables to cover their ration requirements.[50] On the Tasman Peninsula three of the more established probation stations (Impression Bay, Cascades and Saltwater River) had over 110 acres of wheat under crop by the end of 1844.[51] Of these, Saltwater River was the major supplier of wheat to the Commissariat, its 80 acres producing over 60 tonnes of grain (Figure 2.9). Port Arthur and the Coal

---

50   George Maclean, Assistant Commissary General, to C.E. Trevelyan, Treasury, 17 July 1844, CO280, Vol. 170, No. 165, reel 527, TA.

51   E. Eardley Wilmot, Lieutenant Governor, to Lord Stanley, Secretary of State, 31 January 1845, *Convict Discipline*, British Parliamentary Papers, London, 1845 (659), p. 81.

Mines, both considered at this time to be punishment stations, had no wheat under crop.

It was thus economics that led to the construction of Port Arthur's most imposing edifice. As foreseen as early as 1838, a large proportion of the colony's prisoner population had been concentrated by the Convict Department in the Tasman Peninsula, a situation exacerbated by the introduction of probation. The need to ration so many prisoners led to a concentration on self-sufficiency, resulting in peninsula stations accounting for over 40 per cent of wheat grown at colonial convict stations. The construction of a mill at the Port Arthur station would reduce transport and production costs, and would increase the Commissariat's oversight. To the economically minded officers of the Commissariat, every day that the mill was delayed resulted in further costs that could have been avoided.

A flurry of bureaucratic efficiency saw the services of engineer Alexander Clark engaged in December 1842.[52] In the end, the project he was charged with overseeing took over two years to complete: the first foundation stones were laid in February 1843 and the building completed in June 1845.[53] At some point, likely in 1841, Cart's plan for a treadwheel had been reintroduced.[54] Although it went unremarked in the records, the treadwheel was likely reinstated at the insistence of Franklin, who appeared to have agreed with Booth on the efficacy of such a device. There is no evidence that new plans were ever drawn up, and it appears that the plans from 1839 and 1840 were used as a reference.

The archaeological investigations showed that the treadwheel ward and adjacent mill house were built almost exactly to the scale depicted in the 1839 plan (Figure 2.10). Although the exterior detailing of the building differed markedly from the original plan (including the addition by Clark of a floor above the treadwheel), the interior division between treadwheel and mill workings was the same, as was the space allotted

---

52   G.J. Boyes, Colonial Secretary, to R. Kelsall, Commanding Royal Engineer, 6 December 1842, CSO22/57/704, TA.

53   Alexander Clark, Foreman of Works, to Major Victor, Commanding Royal Engineer, 19 June 1845. Transcripts of Ian Brand, *Letterbook of Alexander Clark*, v. 20, PAHSMA, p. 143.

54   Kelsall refers to the treadwheel in June 1841. R. Kelsall, Commanding Royal Engineer, to John Montagu, Colonial Secretary, 14 June 1841, CSO5/204/5011, TA.

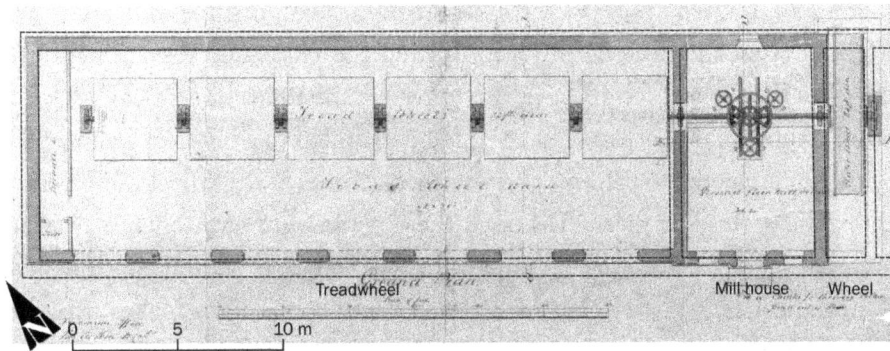

Figure 2.10. Cart's original 1839 plan for the treadwheel and mill house overlaid on the footprint of the mill (treadwheel ward and mill house) derived from the excavation. (William Cart, 1839, 'Design for the Corn Mill proposed to be erected at Port Arthur', Tasmanian Archives)

to the waterwheel (6 feet, or 1.80 metres). The treadwheel was even initially budgeted according to Cart's original design of six sections, although Victor and Clark increased this to eight during the project.[55] Seven pedestals were built to support the treadwheel's central shaft.[56] The whole arrangement powered two of the millstones; the third was powered by the 35 metres overshot waterwheel.

Clark's alterations from the original plan also resulted in the installation of a larger waterwheel. He also abandoned the plan to sink the treadwheel and waterwheel into the ground, due in part to the mill's siting on rocky ground.

The later conversion works of the mill and granary into the penitentiary removed all archaeological evidence of the mill and treadwheel workings, so Cart's plan provides the only visual clue as to the composition of these workings. The granary, even with Clark's last-minute decision to make it L-shaped, was built in close adherence to the plan of ca. 1840: it was the same width and had the same number of storeys and a nearly identical area (2,990 square feet as opposed to the planned 2,880 square feet).

The likely composition of the mill's internal workings can also be found in a contemporary plan for a treadwheel at the penal station of Norfolk Island

---

55   J.C. Victor, Commanding Royal Engineer, to Alexander Clark, 1 September 1843. Transcripts of Ian Brand, *Buildings and Structures A-F*, v. 2, PAHSMA, p. 282.

56   J.C. Victor, Commanding Royal Engineer, to Alexander Clark, 1 September 1843. Transcripts of Ian Brand, *Buildings and Structures A-F*, v. 2, PAHSMA, p. 282.

(Plate 2.6). Drawn up by Victor in April 1845, there is some indication that Clark advised the design and even drafted the plans and elevations.[57] The plan was for a wheel for 48 men, driving two millstones – identical to that at Port Arthur.[58] It shows an offset treadwheel, linked to a series of gears which could be connected to milling or dressing machinery. The wheel was elevated above the ground by piers. Although these plans were probably not an exact representation of the Port Arthur mill, the fact that they were drawn by Victor and Clark just as that mill was nearing completion makes it highly likely that the plan was a close approximation that borrowed heavily from recent experience.

The mill and granary took two years to build, almost double the time initially estimated by the Royal Engineers. When Clark arrived in early 1843, work had already begun on excavating the mill race, meaning that construction of the building and the intended water supply occurred at the same time. In the end, to get the necessary head of water to power the wheel, a small dam was constructed south of the settlement, in the upper reaches of the settlement's creek (Figure 1.20). From this, a 1.20 km race brought water to a secondary dam constructed on the outskirts of the station. To avoid interfering with the extant buildings on Settlement Hill, Clark constructed a 98 m long, brick-built underground aqueduct, at the end of which water ran into an underground pipe (Figure 2.12). This crossed Champ Street on an open overhead flume, which connected with the rear wall of the mill, where the water spilled onto the overshot wheel (Figure 2.11).

---

57 Clark mentions the preparation of a ground plan of a mill with part of a treadwheel ward, as well as an elevation of 'gearing and stone framing' for Victor in late April 1845. The two were also discussing plans for a windmill at Norfolk Island. See: Alexander Clark, Foreman of Works, to Major Victor, Commanding Royal Engineer, 17 April 1845; Alexander Clark, Foreman of Works, to Major Victor, Commanding Royal Engineer, 28 April 1845; J.C. Victor, Commanding Royal Engineer, to Alexander Clark, 7 June 1845. Transcripts of Ian Brand, *Letterbook of Alexander Clark*, v. 20, PAHSMA, pp. 130, 141.

58 J.C. Victor, Commanding Royal Engineer, to William Nairn, Comptroller General, 29 April 1845, in: Eardley Eardley-Wilmot, Lieutenant Governor, to Lord Stanley, Secretary of State, 25 August 1845, CO 280/184, reel 536, no. 124, TA.

Figure 2.11. Illustration of Port Arthur by John Skinner Prout in 1845. This is one of the only depictions of the mill during its operation. The flume running over Champ Street to the mill is visible in the inset. (J.S. Prout, 1845, 'Port Arthur, Tasmania', Mitchell Library, State Library of New South Wales)

Building with convict labour

The story of the mill's construction was one of delays, difficulties and frustration, as Alexander Clark sought to complete the formidable structural and hydro engineering feat. These challenges would be faced again almost a decade later, when the mill was converted into the penitentiary. Using convict labour for everything from skilled trades to monotonous manual labour, such construction programs were common to many colonial convict stations.

The Australian colonies were built on the back of convict labour. Whether a convict was assigned to a free settler or serving time in a government gang or station, labour was a unifying constant. Whether felling trees in the bush, cutting sandstone in a quarry, piecing together shoes in a workshop, or picking apart rope in the quiet of a separate cell, the convict was nearly always at work. As we have seen, there were huge costs

Figure 2.12. View along the underground brick aqueduct. (PAHSMA 2020)

GENTLEMEN CONVICTS — The Centipede.

Figure 2.13. Convicts labouring at Port Arthur in 1836. (T.J. Lempriere, `Gentlemen Convicts: the Centipede', 1836, Dixson Library, State Library of New South Wales)

involved in managing convicts: rations, clothes, superintendence, building construction and maintenance, and physical and spiritual welfare. In many instances, the convict administrators sought to make the prisoner contribute to their own upkeep, such as by growing their own wheat, or by employing them in resource extraction or manufacturing (Figure 2.13).

At a big and important station like Port Arthur, hundreds of convicts worked at many different trades. During the station's life convicts were employed in over 150 occupations, from clerical services to primary production and farm work.[59] The number of bricklayers, masons and carpenters fluctuated according to the projects being undertaken and the number of skilled prisoners available, but some convicts were always employed in the construction and upkeep of buildings. Toward the end of 1841, when work

---

59   R. Tuffin, 'The convict trades of the Port Arthur Penal Station, 1830–77: Landscapes Project Database 2', Excel database, University of New England, https://hdl.handle.net/1959.11/28598, (April 2020), DOI: 10.25952/5ea24d605b30e.

on the large military barracks was nearing completion, over 70 prisoners, or 8 per cent of the total convict population, worked at these trades.[60]

Measuring the quantity and quality of the labour output was a difficult task for the administrators. They were managing a workforce that, at best, resented their labour being appropriated and, at worst, actively sought opportunities to disrupt works. Alexander Clark, during the construction of the mill, reported that a section of the treadwheel was badly damaged in January 1845 by 'accident or inattention'.[61] In the same letter he also reported that much of his workforce had been implicated in a theft from the Commissariat stores and had been imprisoned.[62]

One of the ways the authorities sought to control labour was through the application of rewards and punishments. Prisoners placed in positions of trust sometimes attracted better rations, such as the addition of tea and sugar to their diet.[63] They could also be provided with better accommodation, such as being placed in a ward with fewer prisoners. Should the prisoner misbehave, these rewards could be stripped away. Other punishments included solitary confinement, extension of the prisoner's sentence, and, before 1848, corporal punishments such as flogging.

Another means of controlling convict labour was the allocation of minimum work quotas (Figure 2.14). Such quotas were applied to most of the jobs carried out by convicts, from breaking dolerite stone to digging and carting clay. The authorities also attempted to regulate and itemise construction labour. Regulations from 1849 stipulated that a fit prisoner working as a bricklayer should be laying up to 600 bricks a day.[64] A mason building a dressed stone wall was expected to construct just over one cubic

---

60 Charles O'Hara Booth, Commandant, 'Yearly Return of Work performed by Mechanics and Laborers [sic] at Port Arthur Tasman's Peninsula from the 1st December to 30th November 1841', CSO50/1/8, TA.

61 Alexander Clark, Foreman of Works, to Major Victor, Commanding Royal Engineer, 9 January 1845, C4/1, Royal Society Archives, University of Tasmania (UT).

62 Alexander Clark, Foreman of Works, to Major Victor, Commanding Royal Engineer, 9 January 1845, C4/1, Royal Society Archives, UT.

63 Maxwell-Stewart, 'The Rise and Fall of John Longworth'.

64 'Van Diemen's Land. Convict Department. Revised Scale of Task Work Adapted to the Capacity of the Several Classes of Convicts and Proportioned for the Carious Seasons of the Year', September 1849, GO/33/68, no. 142, TA.

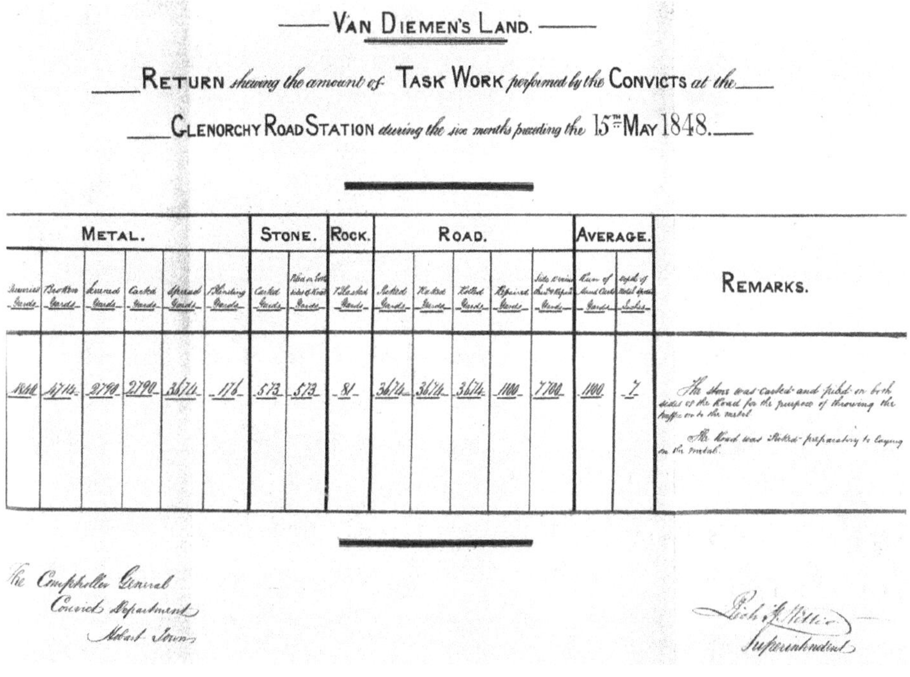

VAN DIEMEN'S LAND.

RETURN shewing the amount of TASK WORK performed by the CONVICTS at the GLENORCHY ROAD STATION during the six months preceding the 15th MAY 1848.

METAL.						STONE.		ROCK.	ROAD.					AVERAGE.		REMARKS.
Quarried Yards	Broken Yards	Screened Yards	Carted Yards	Spread Yards	Blinding Yards	Carted Yards	Piled on both sides of Road Yards	Blasted Yards	Picked Yards	Raked Yards	Rolled Yards	Repaired Yards	Side drains cut & repaired Yards	Run of Hand Carts Yards	Depth of Metal spread Inches	
1844	4714	2790	2790	3674	176	573	573	81	3674	3674	3674	1100	7700	1100	7	The stone was carted and piled on both sides of the Road for the purpose of throwing the traffic on to the metal. The Road was picked preparatory to laying on the metal.

The Comptroller General
Convict Department
Hobart Town

Superintendent

Figure 2.14. Table of work performed at the Glenorchy road gang in 1848. Similar tabulations were kept for Port Arthur's convicts. ('Return shewing [sic] the amount of task work performed', 15 May 1848, GO33/64 no. 123, Tasmanian Archives)

metre per day.[65] Keeping note of these quotas was the job of the overseers, who would have measured the output of work at the end of the day.

The length of the workday was variable. During the summer months, the convicts worked for 10 hours each day.[66] During the depths of winter this was reduced to just over seven hours. Convicts labouring on the settlement, such as those engaged in station construction, would have spent all of these hours working. Those who were required to walk to their places of work, such as in the surrounding bush, included this travel time in their hours of labour.

Working days could be cut short or missed entirely due to heavy rain; labour returns sometimes itemised the amount of time lost to poor

65 'No. 10. Scale of Task Work Adapted to the Capacity of Several Classes of Convicts and Proportioned for the Various Seasons of the Year', *Convict Discipline and Transportation*, British Parliamentary Papers, London, 1849 (1022) (1121), p. 157.

66 'Rules and Regulations for the First Stage of Convict Probation in Van Diemen's Land, 1847', Enclosure No. 6, in: J.S. Hampton, Comptroller General, to William Denison, Lieutenant Governor, 15 November 1847, *Convict Discipline and Transportation*, British Parliamentary Papers, London, 1849 (1022) (1121), pp. 139–51.

weather.[67] Later records indicate that prisoners who had to work in the rain were sometimes given increased rations of tea, sugar and flour.[68] Sometimes, however, it was impossible to find shelter, or the prisoners were working under a particularly vexatious overseer. Martin Cash, who served time at Port Arthur in the late 1830s, recorded working in the bush and getting caught in a heavy shower.[69] The men continued to work, and when Cash returned to the settlement he was forced to spend a cold and damp night in his cell. Such exposure could and did lead to sickness, which placed men in hospital and in turn decreased the amount of labour available.[70]

During every moment of the archaeological excavations, we were surrounded by the products of Port Arthur's convict labour. Like all of Port Arthur's structures and spaces, the buildings and yards of the penitentiary were built by a mixture of skilled and unskilled labour drawn from the station's prisoner population. Every moulded brick, every worked piece of sandstone and every broken piece of dolerite had been quarried, sawn, broken, chiselled and laid according to a system of rewards and punishments, measured and enforced by station overseers.

An example was the dolerite that we found associated with all phases of the site. As explained above, this hard stone is incredibly difficult to quarry. When construction work began on the waterfront, the convicts largely worked around it or used it as a foundation to build upon. During conservation works in 2014, dolerite boulders could only be removed through the use of powered drills and expanding demolition mortars.

When construction of the mill began in 1842, the building was set on a combination of existing and reclaimed land. Our investigations found that the building had been built partly on a raft of newly reclaimed land, and partly on a section of the original shore, on a foundation of dolerite stones mortared together (Figure 2.15). Alexander Clark mentioned the construction of this

---

67   Robert Ballantine, Superintendent Cascades, to Comptroller General, 7 January 1850, CSO 24/126/4130, TA.

68   A.H. Boyd, Civil Commandant Port Arthur, to the Colonial Secretary, 12 April 1873, CSD 7/52/1161, TA.

69   J.L. Burke, *Martin Cash, the Bushranger of Van Diemen's Land*, J. Walch and Sons, Hobart, 1870, in: Brand, Transcripts of Ian Brand, v. 23, PAHSMA, pp. 97–98.

70   F.G. Brock, Colonial Surgeon, to N. Dawson, Principal Medical Officer, 23 November 1848, CO 280/248 reel 576, TA.

Figure 2.15. The footings of the mill were primarily formed from dolerite. This photo shows the foundations for the wall separating the treadwheel ward from the mill house. (PAHSMA 2014)

footing in 1843, recording that the dolerite footings were brought nearly level with the ground surface.[71] This placed the sandstone and brick above the high-water mark, with the dolerite providing an impervious barrier to damaging salts.

Clark wrote of the difficulty of using dolerite: 'There are neither many men here who can work it, nor is there anything but cast steel that can stand it'.[72] Working with picks, bar and hammer, excavating the stone and then reducing it to gravel was intensive and monotonous. However, the presence of tonnes of dolerite from all phases of occupation indicates its versatility.

Breaking dolerite into gravel was a task mostly reserved for convicts undergoing punishment (Figure 2.16). A visitor to Port Arthur in 1842, David Burn, recollected:

---

71   Alexander Clark, Foreman of Works, to Major Victor, Commanding Royal Engineer, 15 February 1842, C4/1, Royal Society Archives, UT.
72   Alexander Clark, Foreman of Works, to Major Victor, Commanding Royal Engineer, 15 February 1842, C4/1, Royal Society Archives, UT.

Figure 2.16. The Port Arthur waterfront and Settlement Hill. In the foreground (right) lies a pile of dolerite boulders and broken gravel. (Image held by the George Eastman Museum, Rochester, New York)

> The most habitual absconders … are not only put in irons, but fastened to a chain, where they are made to break stones under the eye of every passer-by – a punishment the most intolerably galling.[73]

Until 1854 the breaking gang likely worked near the place where the gravel was required. Dolerite found during the archaeological investigations near the site of the 1830s and 1840s workshops was probably broken by a gang stationed at the location. After 1854 the stonebreakers worked from a covered

---

73   D. Burn, *An Excursion to Port Arthur in 1842*, ed. JW Beattie, Hobart, 1850, pp. 35–36.

shed on the north side of the cove. This was situated near a large outcrop of dolerite, from which the stone was sourced.

The conversion of the penitentiary required a vast amount of dolerite, and the shed in the north side of the cove may have been built to facilitate this. Work returns show that convicts were sometimes tasked with breaking up to 16 cubic feet (almost a tonne) of hard stone in a day's work. During the course of the excavation of the ablutions yard, we removed approximately 280 cubic feet of broken dolerite from the west yard surface. Using the taskwork rate as a guide, it would have taken over 17 days for one person, working 10 hours each day, to break this amount of stone. A much greater amount (over 12,000 cubic feet) was required for the dolerite and mortar raft on which the separate cells inside the penitentiary were constructed. Clearly a massive amount of energy was expended by convicts just to prepare the surfacing and foundational gravels.

This energy was being expended in a very labour-intensive manner, designed to take advantage of the need to punish while extracting an economic return. Prisoners assigned to such tasks had few opportunities to interrupt work, other than by going slow – which would attract immediate censure from a watchful overseer. This happened in November 1843 to Patrick Murray, who had his sentence of hard labour extended for not breaking a sufficient quantity of stone.[74]

Convicts working on more complex, collaborative or important tasks had many more opportunities to cause problems – deliberate or otherwise. As already mentioned, Alexander Clark blamed prisoner carelessness for damage sustained during work on the mill's treadwheel. Throughout the life of Port Arthur, convicts were often brought before the magistrate for breaking tools or materials. Recorded offences include damage to saws and other tools, as well as to finished articles such as worked stone, sawn timber and even the foremast of a ship that was being worked on at the settlement dockyard.[75]

---

74   Conduct record, Patrick Murray, #1653, *Emerald Isle*, CON31/1/32, TA.
75   Conduct record, Thomas Wilkinson, #570, *Asia*, CON31/1/45, TA; Conduct record, Morris Hyde, #1591, *Emeror Alexander*, CON31/1/20, TA; Conduct record, John Jubb, #157, *Claudine*, CON31/1/23, TA; Conduct record, James Reynard, #1359, *Augusta Jessie*, CON32/1/5, TA; Conduct record, Edward Pyzer, #1165, *Aurora*, CON31/1/35 TA.

Our excavations gave us an insight into this question of work quality. The offence records capture overt signs of resistance, but our archaeological investigations revealed subtler evidence of prisoners acting against the directions of their overseers. For example, during Phase I in the ablutions area (at the time of the mill's conversion) a series of sumps were installed to service surface drainage circumscribing the yards (Figure 4.33). On the face of it there was nothing wrong with the five brick sumps – two in the east yard and three in the west. They were all built in a similar manner: an open-ended box of bricks, capped by a grated sandstone drain, designed to drain freely from the base.

During our excavations, however, it became clear that the sumps in the east yard performed their purpose tolerably well, while those in the west yard were a complete failure. The sumps in the west yard had been built into thick clay, which did not allow water to drain away. The sumps in the east had been placed in the mixture of redeposited clay and stone that had backfilled the trench footings of the mill. This latter redeposited mix was more porous, allowing the water in the sump to percolate away.

Although this may not immediately suggest sabotage, it does indicate that convicts may have deliberately completed low quality work, or work doomed to failure. They had been tasked with making brick sumps, which they did to the letter. They therefore could not be punished for failing in this task. But they failed to create sumps that worked, with only two in the east yard draining to any degree. By setting the west yard sumps in a non-porous clay, the prisoners left a maintenance issue that would have plagued the administrators for the whole time the ablutions yard was used. There is no evidence that they ever tried to rectify it. It remained an issue until 2016 when the re-landscaping of the ablutions yard finally rectified the drainage issues.

Labour in the laundry

Little is known about the operation of the penitentiary laundry during the life of the penal settlement, and the documentary record does not shed much light. Settlement Regulations for 1868 indicate the role the laundry played in keeping prisoners clean:

> 272. The prisoners are not permitted to wash their persons or clothes on the works, – this must be done at the penitentiary.[76]

Further regulations from the 1860s specified that the prisoners were 'to be provided with clean shirts, twice-a-week in summer, and once weekly in winter months'.[77] Clean socks or stockings were to be issued weekly. These sources appear to indicate that, while shirts and socks were taken care of by the laundrymen, the cleanliness of the rest of the prisoner's uniform itself was a matter for the convict. It is not known how access to the laundry was managed, although it may have coincided with the convicts' Saturday afternoon bath.

Other contemporary sources give some further insight into how the penitentiary laundry might have operated. Henry Mayhew and John Binny's *Criminal Prisons of London* – a survey conducted between 1856 and 1862 – contains a good description of a prison laundry at work:

> On entering the laundry ... we observed two large coppers built into brickwork and supplied with steam by means of pipes ... Adjoining are two new wooden rinsing troughs, with two pipes, to supply them with hot water, and a wringing machine with two crank handles ... There are six washing-boxes, each of them provided with two washing-troughs ... The larger of the troughs is supplied with hot and cold water, and the smaller one with cold water ... They [the prisoners] wash the clothes in the larger one, and use the other for rinsing ... We passed into the ironing-room, which is supplied with six wooden horses, where the clothes are hung up to dry and exposed to the action of steam ... It is also furnished with a large table for folding and ironing the clothes, a mangling machine, and a stove for heating the irons.[78]

Mayhew and Binny's report indicates that this type of setup was common to the prisons of the era. Coppers, heated by either furnace or pipe-fed steam, were used to boil the clothes. The clothes were then wrung before being soaked and scrubbed in washing troughs, after which they were moved into rinsing troughs. The washing and rinsing troughs could be supplied with

---

76 Convict Department, *Rules and Regulations for the Penal Settlement on Tasman's Peninsula*, Tasmania, 1868. Reprint: PAHSMA, Port Arthur, 1991, p. 40.

77 Convict Department, *Rules and Regulations for the Penal Settlement on Tasman's Peninsula*, Tasmania, 1868. Reprint: PAHSMA, Port Arthur, 1991, p. 40.

78 H. Mayhew and J. Binny, *The Criminal Prisons of London*, London, 1868.

piped hot water. The clothes were then again put through a wringer, dried on racks, and finally ironed with heated flat irons.[79]

The size of the laundry operation depended on the number of prisoners to be catered for and whether the prison took in washing from outside to make money. A prison laundry, as recorded by Mayhew and Binny, could have as few as four and as many as 23 prisoners working at any one time. The ratio of those employed in the laundry to the total number of prisoners was found to be roughly similar in each prison surveyed by Mayhew and Binny. On average, the ratio worked out at 1:46, varying from 1:35 to 1:58. In a prison such as Wandsworth, 23 prisoners washed for a total of 830 male and female prisoners.

However, at Port Arthur, it appears that the numbers employed in the laundry were far smaller. H.P. Fry, writing in 1846 – before the construction of the penitentiary laundry – recorded that there were five men washing for the whole station.[80] With a prisoner population of close to 1,200 during this period, if Fry's figures are to be believed, then the men were washing at a ratio of 1:240 – far higher than that recorded by Mayhew and Binny.

In 1862, during the operation of the penitentiary laundry, there were five 'laundrymen' at work.[81] This was at a time when the prisoner population was close to 900. It is likely that these men were split between the various laundry buildings at the station. Separate laundries were constructed for the hospital in 1858 and the paupers' depot in 1863.[82]

From the snippets of information we do have about the penitentiary laundry, we can derive some idea of how it operated. Prior to the introduction of a boiler during Phase II, water would have had to have been boiled separately. It is likely that kettles were suspended above the fireplace situated

---

79 P. Sambrook, *Laundry Bygones*, Shire Publications, United Kingdom, No. 107, 1983.

80 R.H.P. Fry, *A System of Penal Discipline, with a Report on the Treatment of Prisoners in Great Britain and Van Diemen's Land*, London, 1850, p. 172.

81 Return of Labour, 21 June 1862, No. 82, *Journals of the House of Assembly*, Hobart, 1871 (Vol. 10), pp. 28–30.

82 James Boyd, Commandant, to Governor's Secretary for Penal Establishment, 8 April 1871, 'Report of the Select Committee, with Minutes of the Proceedings, and Evidence', No. 127, *Journals of the House of Assembly*, Hobart, 1871 (Vol. 22), p. 17; James Boyd, Commandant, to William Nairn, Acting Comptroller General, 7 August 1858, *Convict Discipline and Transportation*, British Parliamentary Papers, London, 1859 (August), p. 203.

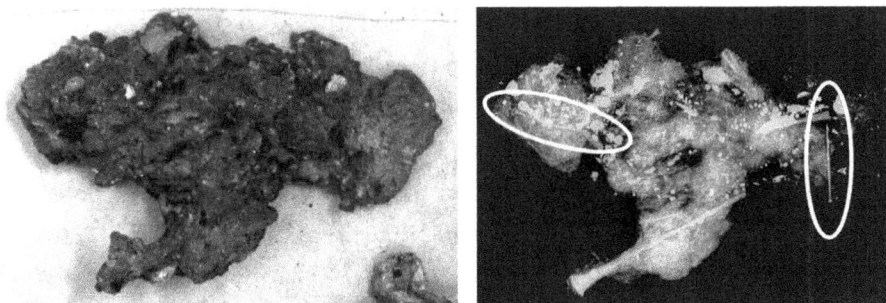

Figure 2.17. One of the radiographed concretions from the laundry, showing sewing pins (circled) and a nail. (PAHSMA 2020)

between the two coppers, supplying a slow but constant supply of hot water. If the ca. 1856 survey plan is reliable, it also appears likely that the laundry was fitted with a number of tables, which would have been used for drying, folding and ironing. In keeping with Mayhew and Binny's survey, it would be expected that the laundry was also outfitted with a wringer and a mangle to aid the drying process. Labour returns list mechanics (skilled convicts) making the requisite tools for the laundry.[83]

The space occupying the eastern extent of the laundry building likely provided an area to carry out ancillary activity. Historical plans suggest it was used as a bathhouse during Phase I, but do not explain what the room was used for after it was expanded during the ca. 1862 conversion. Archaeological evidence, in the form of the high number of buttons recovered, suggests that the space may have been used as a place to repair clothing. This was further supported by the recovery of a small amount of sewing paraphernalia from the deposits within this space (Figure 2.17). Most of the buttons recovered from the area were bone three or four-hole fastenings – the type that was predominantly used on convict uniforms.

Using both historical and archaeological evidence, we were able to examine the penal economy. This hinged upon the drive toward self-sufficiency, as the authorities sought to lessen the burden of transportation on both Britain and the colony. This drive created the environment in which the construction of

---

83   In returns for 1862, 'washing dollies' – long poles with an upturned funnel on one end used during the soaping and soaking stage – are listed among the many items built by the site carpenters. Return of Labour, 21 June 1862, No. 82, *Journals of the House of Assembly*, Hobart, 1871 (Vol. 10), p. 33.

Port Arthur's flour mill and granary seemed like a pragmatic and judicious response to an economic problem. The realities of planning such a work at a penal station, where the labour was being deployed on a myriad of other different tasks, resulted in delays and frustration.

Managing convict labour at Port Arthur presented many challenges that the authorities sought to mitigate through a combination of rewards and punishments. The quantity and quality of the labour was measured by overseers armed with work quotas and backed by the settlement's stringent rules and regulations. However, the historical and archaeological evidence show that the prisoners found numerous ways to subvert the extraction of labour. At times this was through overt means, which often attracted the ire of the authorities. At other times, they evidently used the trust that had been placed in them to undermine the effectiveness of the products they were tasked with making. In this way, Port Arthur's largest and most impressive edifice stands not just as a monument to penal economy and punishment, but also to the labour of those who were forced to create it.

Designing and understanding a penal space

Almost from the beginning, it was clear that the water mill was doomed to failure. The composite water supply system almost immediately proved inadequate, with the already minimal, and seasonally variable, flow of water in the creek further reduced by evaporation and leakage.[84] Instead, the successful operation of the mill relied upon the application of raw labour power through the treadwheel. However, as Port Arthur's population markedly dwindled after 1846, finding the labour to drive the wheel became difficult for the station administrators. In 1848 the deployment of 48 men on the treadwheel would have absorbed 10 per cent of the total prisoner population: men required to carry out labour elsewhere.

Additionally, the economic demands that had driven the construction of the mill in the first place had dissipated throughout the 1840s. Just as Port Arthur's convict population declined, so too did the entire peninsula's: from a peak of nearly 4,000 convicts in seven stations in 1844, to 1,800 in

---

84   Tuffin, 'A Monument to Folly?', pp. 135–37.

five stations by 1848.[85] By the end of 1851, only 700 convicts resided on the peninsula. This decline was mirrored across the colony, as the number of convicts maintained by the government decreased. This, in combination with the colony's slow recovery from the depression, meant that the conditions which had made the construction of the mill such an attractive proposition in the first place had, by the late 1840s, completely dissipated. The scene was set for the building's next phase of life.

To control and coerce

By the time the failures of the mill had become evident, discussion had been going on at Port Arthur for a number of years about improving the capacity of the station to incarcerate its convict population. These proposals were directly tied into wider penological debates about the best way to control and coerce an unfree population. Although an unconventional solution, the conversion of the flour mill and granary structure drew upon a number of key penological theories prevalent in such discussions. Much more than a local response to immediate needs, the conversion's outcome was to reflect global debates about the efficacy of penal regimes.

At the time that Port Arthur was first founded in 1830, Britain penological thinking was in the midst of a revolutionary turn. For almost 50 years, the influence of prison reformers such as John Howard and Jeremy Bentham had introduced a preference for cellular incarceration, moving prison discipline beyond its former focus on corporal punishment. By the 1830s, the prisons of Britain had become fewer, but larger and more systematised.[86] There had been an overhaul of the infrastructure of incarceration, with larger prisons incorporating designs encouraging regimes based on surveillance, classification, economic labour and reform.[87] These ideas had been adopted by influential advocacy groups including the Society for the Improvement of Prison Discipline (from 1816), who went on to produce treatises on prison design. In 1836 a more formal body, the Inspectorate of Prisons, was

---

85 R. Tuffin, 'The Convict Population of the Tasman Peninsula, 1830–77', Excel database, University of New England, May 2020, https://rune.une.edu.au/web/handle/1959.11/28634, DOI: 10.25952/5eaf4d980f63c.

86 R. Evans, *The Fabrication of Virtue: English Prison Architecture, 1750–1840*, Cambridge. New York. Melbourne, 1982, pp. 236–37.

87 Evans, *The Fabrication of Virtue*, pp. 261–309.

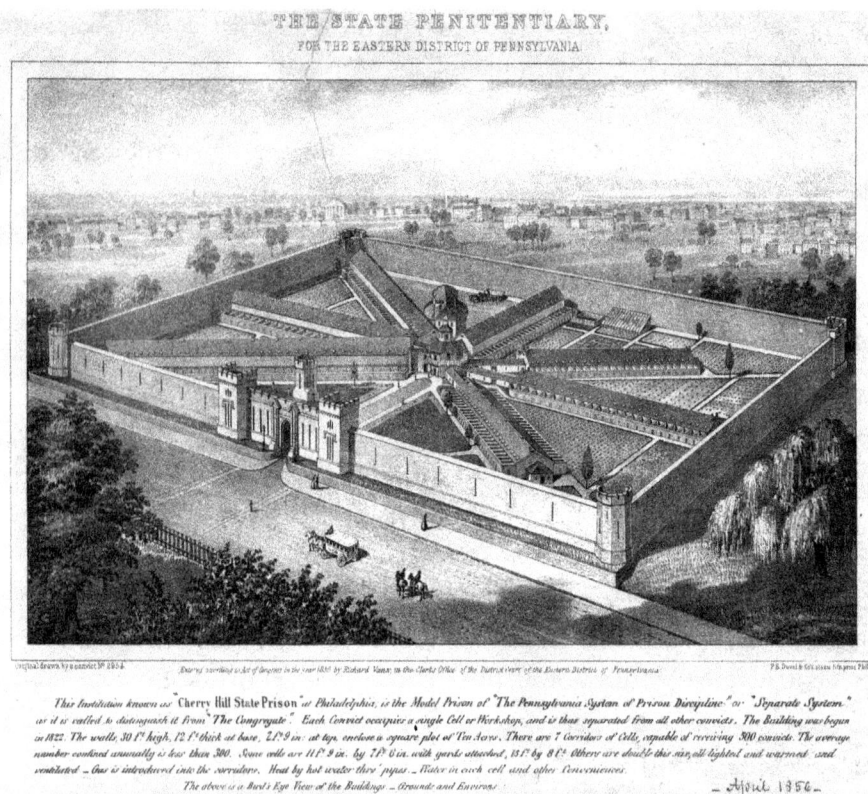

THE STATE PENITENTIARY,
FOR THE EASTERN DISTRICT OF PENNSYLVANIA

This Institution known as "Cherry Hill State Prison" at Philadelphia, is the Model Prison of "The Pennsylvania System of Prison Discipline" or "Separate System," as it is called to distinguish it from "The Congregate". Each Convict occupies a single Cell or Workshop, and is thus separated from all other convicts. The Building was begun in 1822. The walls, 30 f.t high, 12 f.t thick at base, 2 f.t 9 in: at top, enclose a square plot of Ten Acres. There are 7 Corridors of Cells, capable of receiving 500 convicts. The average number confined annually is less than 300. Some cells are 11 f.t 9 in: by 7 f.t 6 in: with yards attached, 18 f.t by 8 f.t Others are double this size, all lighted and warmed and ventilated – Gas is introduced into the corridors, Heat by hot water thro' pipes. Water in each cell and other Conveniences.
The above is a Bird's Eye View of the Buildings – Grounds and Environs – April 1856 –

Figure 2.18. The Eastern State Penitentiary, Philadelphia. (Samuel Cowperthwaite, 1855, Eastern State Penitentiary, Wainwright Philadelphia Lithographs, Library Company of Philadelphia)

formed, with the intention of overseeing the implementation of prison policy throughout the British Isles.[88]

In 1830 an influential publication by Basil Hall brought widescale attention to improved systems of prison discipline then being practised in America.[89] In particular, Hall highlighted two new systems that had been implemented at Auburn Prison in New York, and Eastern State Penitentiary in Philadelphia (Figure 2.18). At the former, prisoners were kept in separate cells during the night and worked alongside each other during the day (known as 'associated labour'), with the labour carried out in enforced silence. This became known as the *silent system*. At Philadelphia, prisoners

---

88   Evans, *The Fabrication of Virtue*, p. 329.
89   B. Hall, *Travels in North America in the Years 1827 and 1828*, 3 Vols., Vol. 1, Edinburgh, 1830.

were kept separated at all times, except when attending religious service and at exercise; this became known as the *separate system*.

Hall's work attracted the interest of William Crawford, later appointed Inspector of Prisons, who produced a report on the American systems for the British Parliament in 1834.[90] Crawford and the Inspectorate advocated the separate system, most notably in an 1837 report that found the separate system to be 'the most rational and efficacious mode which has yet been adopted for the government of prisons'.[91] The system's ascendency was assured by the passage of the New Gaols Act in 1839.[92] The separate system – and the prisons and regimes that it spawned – remained the keystone of penal practice in Britain and numerous other countries for years to come.[93]

Particularly early reflections of these emerging theories can be found at Port Arthur. It is clear that, even as early as 1833, Hall's observations of the American systems were known in the colony. At this time Captain Commandant Booth and the civil engineer John Lee Archer were considering how to expand the station's infrastructure of incarceration, in response to a rapidly increasing population requiring penal sanction. A plan for accommodating up to 700 prisoners was devised, as part of which 237 separate cells were to be constructed according to 'Mr Basil Hall's description of the American plan'.[94] The remainder of the convicts would be accommodated in shared wards (Plate 2.7).

Although the plan was never carried out in full, in 1835 a modified version of it was eventually implemented (Plate 2.9). As part of the new design of the prisoners' barracks, convicts were accommodated in a combination of shared ward and separate cells, reflecting in part the theories finding traction in Britain at the time. Deficiencies existed in the construction of the barracks, particularly in the construction of the separate cells back-to-back and the use of timber. This allowed for communication between the cells and thereby largely negated the benefits of separation intended by the design. Despite

---

90   W. Crawford, *Report of William Crawford, Esq., on the Penitentiaries of the United States, Addressed to His Majesty's Principal Secretary of State for the Home Department*, House of Commons, London, 1834.
91   Inspectors of Prisons for the Home District, 1837, *Extracts from the Second Report of the Inspectors of Prisons for the Home District*, HMSO, London, p. 64.
92   Evans, *The Fabrication of Virtue*, p. 330.
93   Evans, *The Fabrication of Virtue*, pp. 331, 402.
94   Charles O'Hara Booth, Commandant, to John Burnett, Colonial Secretary, 3 June 1833, CSO 1/584/13194, TA.

this, the barracks complex served as the main hub of incarceration until the conversion of the flour mill and granary began in 1854.

There was a large gap between the formulation of new incarceration concepts and their actual implementation. This was markedly so in the colony, where correspondence with Britain, at its quickest, took half a year to complete a round trip. It was somewhat inevitable that the designs that eventuated in the Australian colonies were hybridised versions of the inspectors' strict recommendations. Building design, even the size of the cells, could not be standardised. New separate cells for the Parramatta female factory, New South Wales, were some of the first built (1838–39) according to the separate system, although they had smaller cells and did away with the recommended heating and waste treatment apparatus.[95] Similar modifications were made to new country gaols built at Port Philip, Bathurst, Goulburn and Maitland throughout the 1840s – all supposedly implementing the new design philosophies.[96]

In Van Diemen's Land, the large number of new stations built as part of the probation system in the 1840s were meant to incorporate separate cells for the third (lowest) class of prisoners. However, the dire economic circumstances necessitated a more pragmatic approach to station design that omitted the expense of constructing tens, if not hundreds, of masonry cells at each station. It was not until 1846, as the number of stations across the colony dwindled, that there was a concerted campaign to construct separate cells at those remaining.[97]

At Port Arthur, a growing population of ultra-penal prisoners (men who were serial reoffenders) meant that, by 1846, the decade-old barracks compound was proving inadequate for classification and separation, with the authorities casting around for a solution. In March of that year surveys suggested four separate locations around the station for a new complex.[98] Evidently the expense of creating a new penitentiary from scratch was prohibitive, as the idea was not pursued.

---

95   J.S. Kerr, *Design for Convicts: An Account of Design for Convict Establishments in the Australian Colonies During the Transportation Era*, Sydney, 1984, pp. 105–6.
96   Kerr, *Design for Convicts*, pp. 106–7.
97   Tuffin and Gibbs, 'The Archaeology of the Convict Probation System: The Labor Landscapes of Port Arthur and the Cascades Probation Station, 1839–55'.
98   L.F. Jones, Superintendent, to William Champ, Comptroller General, 15 March 1846, MM62/1/17, A1107, No. 5895, TA.

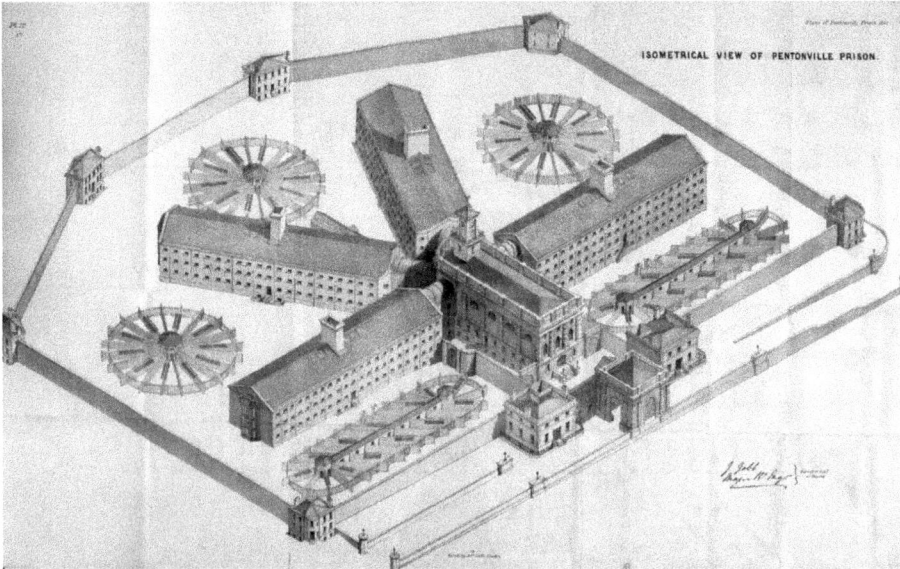

Figure 2.19. Isometric view of Pentonville Prison, as depicted in the 1844 report of Joshua Jebb. (Jebb, 1844, Report of the Surveyor-General of Prisons on the construction, ventilation, and details of Pentonville Prison, London, Houses of Parliament)

By this time, in Britain, the ultimate expression of the separate system had been given form. Designed by Royal Engineer Joshua Jebb, Surveyor-General of Prisons, the construction of Pentonville Prison (built in 1840–42) served as a template for nearly 60 prisons constructed in Britain over the following decade (Figure 2.19).[99]

Six years after the completion of Pentonville, the template was superimposed upon Port Arthur's landscape with the commencement of work on what would become the station's penal centrepiece: the separate prison (Figure 2.20). Begun in 1848, the building was designed to emulate in full Pentonville's system of confinement. Cruciform-shaped, it was designed to hold prisoners in silent isolation for 23 hours a day, with one hour a day for exercise. Prisoners were required to work in their cells, covering their faces with hoods when at exercise and chapel. At chapel, separation was further enforced through the use of individual cubicles (Figure 2.21). However, even

---

99 Inspectors of Prisons for the Home District, 1837, *Extracts from the Second Report of the Inspectors of Prisons for the Home District*, HMSO, London; A. Brodie, J. Croom, and J.O. Davies, *Behind Bars: The Hidden Architecture of England's Prisons*, Swindon, 1999, p. 15.

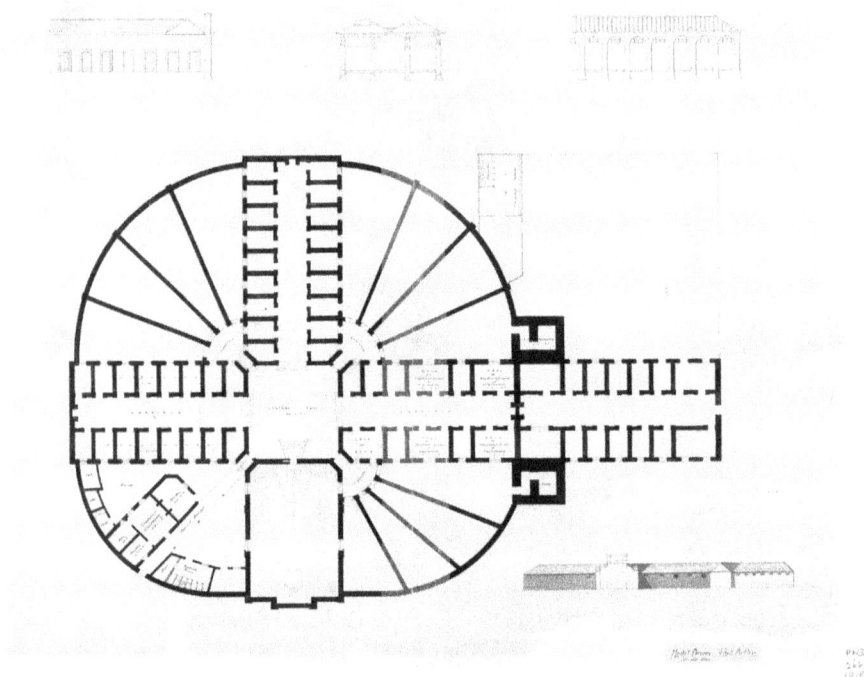

Figure 2.20. A later redrawing of a ca. 1850 plan of the Separate Prison. (Unknown author, 'Port Arthur, Model Prison', PWD266/1/1818, Tasmanian Archives)

this model building failed to adhere completely to the ideals outlined by the inspectors, the cells being smaller, unheated and unplumbed.

The separate prison primarily served to introduce new prisoner intakes to the rigours of the Port Arthur penal station. Newly arrived prisoners were supposed to undergo up to 18 months' confinement, prior to release into the station's general population. The prison was also the destination for recidivist convicts. It acted as a prison within a prison, intended to quell the more rebellious instincts of the prisoners. In this it partly mirrored British establishments such as Pentonville, which themselves served as incarcerative precursors for prisoners being sent out to the Australian colonies.

In late 1850, the report of Lieutenant-Colonel Jebb on the discipline and construction of the new Portland Prison (opened 1848) in Britain reached Van Diemen's Land (Figure 2.22).[100] Designed to hold prisoners who had

---

100 W.T. Denison, Governor, to Earl Grey, Secretary of State, 12 September 1850, *Convict Discipline and Transportation*, British Parliamentary Papers, London, 1851 (1361) (1418), p. 56.

Figure 2.21. View from the pulpit, Lincoln Prison chapel (UK). The chapel of the separate prison was almost identical to this in design. (Richard Tuffin, 2018)

been sentenced to penal servitude undergoing labour on public works, it combined the separate system of confinement with associated labour during the day. These prisons were designed to provide a step between the stringent regimes of a place like Pentonville and probationary release into the colonies. The main prison at Portland was a timber and corrugated iron building, containing 700 separate cells and two association rooms with capacity for 100 men sleeping in hammocks.

With its combination of associated and separate accommodation, Portland Prison serves as an important antecedent for the conversion of Port Arthur's penitentiary five years later. Port Arthur already had its separate prison, where the principles of classification and separation awaited the newly arrived or the recalcitrant. The conversion of the mill would offer improved incarceration accommodation for the remainder of the population, providing a strictly regimented space where they could be confined, coerced and classified.

In this way, the combination of a separate prison and the new penitentiary was designed to serve as an enclosed penal system within the penal station. The convict progressed from a period of separate treatment in one, to associated labour in the other; the speed of this progression depended upon his outward displays of reform. This replicated in miniature the penal system of the British Isles, in particular that employed in Ireland. Introduced in 1854, the Irish Penitentiary System was seen by many as an improvement

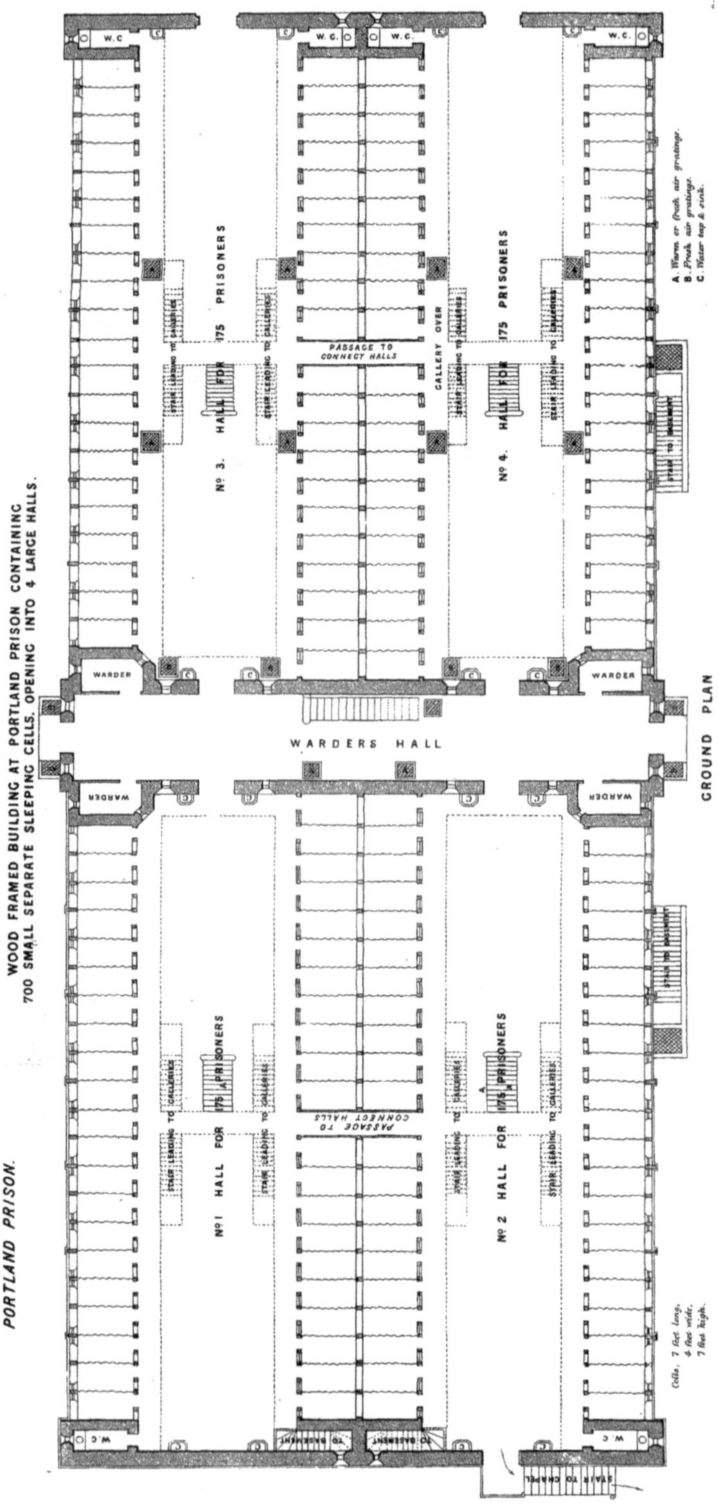

Figure 2.22. The separate apartments of Portland Prison. (Joshua Jebb, 1850, Report on the Discipline and Construction of Portland Prison, London, Houses of Parliament)

Figure 2.23. The 'Punishment Block', Spike Island. Completed by 1860, it housed the prison's most dangerous prisoners. (Richard Tuffin, 2018)

on that pursued in England (Figure 2.23).[101] Under it, convicts served the first portion of their sentence in separate isolation, prior to incarceration in a public works prison, before progressing to the less strict regime of an intermediate prison and then conditional release under a Ticket-of-Licence (much like the Ticket-of-Leave used in colonial Australia).[102]

At Port Arthur, proposals to convert the mill had first arisen in 1848, the year of Portland Prison's completion. In August a plan had been drawn up by the Acting Commandant, L.F. Jones, to convert the structure to house 232 cells, 9 ft (2.70 m) × 7 ft (2.10 m).[103] Concerns about modifications to load-bearing elements within the building led to a counter-proposal by John Hampton, the Comptroller-General, for a building that combined separate cells on the ground floor, a mess room above and a dormitory for associated

---

101 R.S.E. Hinde, 'Sir Walter Crofton and the Reform of the Irish Convict System, 1854–61 – Ii', *Irish Jurist*, Vol. 12, No. 2, 1977, pp. 295–338, pp. 308–10.

102 R.S.E. Hinde, 'Sir Walter Crofton and the Reform of the Irish Convict System, 1854–61 – I', *Irish Jurist*, Vol. 12, No. 1, 1977, pp. 115–47, pp. 140–41.

103 G.H. Courteney, Superintendent, to J.S. Hampton, Comptroller General, 2 August 1848, MM62/1/24, A1122, no.10759, TA.

accommodation at the top.[104] The eventual conversion five years later adhered almost completely to Hampton's early outline.

According to historian James Kerr, Hampton was an advocate of the Pentonville style of incarceration.[105] It is also clear that he was familiar with the styles of prison increasingly advocated by Jebb. In this he was joined by Civil Commandant James Boyd, who had originally been employed at Pentonville, but from the early 1840s had been part of the administrative apparatus of Van Diemen's Land. Boyd took over as Civil Commandant at Port Arthur in 1854, therefore overseeing the bulk of the penitentiary's conversion work. Together, Hampton and Boyd were responsible for the inception and the execution of the plan.

A dwindling convict population, coupled with the intensive works taking place on Port Arthur's separate prison, meant that the mill conversion had not taken place in 1848. Impetus was once again provided when, in May 1852, Hampton proposed to relocate convicts from the ultra-penal settlement of Norfolk Island (1,500 km off the east coast of New South Wales) to the Tasman Peninsula.[106] He indicated that, if this relocation were to take place, Port Arthur required new separate cells to facilitate the required classificatory regimes and resurrected the idea of converting the mill.

By this time, work had begun on another large-scale penal project. Situated in the colony of Western Australia, Fremantle Prison was begun in 1852 and completed in 1859 (Figure 2.24). Like Port Arthur's penitentiary, it clearly reflected the influence of Jebb in its design and adoption of the mixed styles of accommodation – although unlike the penitentiary, it had been constructed on a greenfield site. Fremantle Prison was first occupied in 1855, making it near contemporaneous with Port Arthur's converted penitentiary.

At Port Arthur, significant delays in receiving assent for the removal of prisoners from Norfolk Island meant that work on the conversion did not begin until late 1853. These works were unspecified, but likely involved the

---

104 G.H. Courteney, Superintendent, to J.S. Hampton, Comptroller General, 2 August 1848, note by J.S. Hampton, 4 August 1848, MM62/1/24, A1122, No. 10759, TA.
105 Kerr, *Design for Convicts*, p. 160.
106 J.S. Hampton, Comptroller General, to William Denison, Lieutenant Governor, 12 May 1852, Enclosure No. 1, in: William Denison, Lieutenant Governor, to Earl Grey, Secretary of State, 12 June 1852, *Convict Discipline and Transportation*, British Parliamentary Papers, London, 1852–53, (1601) (1677), p. 86.

Figure 2.24. Fremantle Prison, Western Australia. (Richard Tuffin, 2018)

large-scale modifications to flooring and internal walls necessitated by the new prison's design.[107] Despite these early works, Boyd reported that the conversion really only got underway from September 1854.[108]

During the process of conversion, there were overt references to the authorities' aspirations to replicate the philosophies of British penal design. In November 1853 William Denison, Lieutenant Governor, reported that the 'new penitentiary and separate apartments … are now in the course of being erected', with the plans in 'accordance with those adapted in England'.[109] A requisition for prison furniture forwarded in October 1853 from the Royal Engineers specified that 'The description of the Articles to be similar to those used in Pentonville Prison England'.[110] These articles included: locks, inspections panes, a clock for the proposed clock tower, fluted glass [prismatic glass] panes, lead sheets and taps for baths, washing basins, ventilation grates, bell pulls and hoisting machines (Figure 2.25). Delays were experienced in the supply of the required materials due to indecision about the future of Norfolk Island, and it was not until June 1854 that the order to ship the articles was given.

---

107 William Denison, Lieutenant Governor, to Secretary of State, 21 November 1853, CO280/310, reel 725–26, no. 249, TA.

108 James Boyd, Commandant, to J.S. Hampton, Comptroller General, 4 January 1855, Enclosure No. 3, in: J.S. Hampton, Comptroller General, to William Denison, Lieutenant Governor, 4 January 1855, *Convict Discipline and Transportation*, British Parliamentary Papers, London, 1854–55 (1916) (1988), p. 25.

109 William Denison, Lieutenant Governor, to Secretary of State, 21 November 1853, CO280/310, reel 725–26, No. 249, TA.

110 'Supplementary Demand of Stores and Materials Required for Convict Services to Be Carried on by the Royal Engineer Department in Van Diemen's Land during the Year 1854–55', Royal Engineers' Office, 5 October 1853, in: Secretary of State to Sir Charles Trevelyan, 23 June 1854, CO280/310, reel 725–26, No. 249, TA.

Figure 2.25. Cell identification number in the separate prison, similar to the prison fittings imported from Britain and used in the penitentiary. (PAHSMA 2020)

A converted space

The conversion of the mill saw the structure gutted of its former apparatus and flooring. In its place were added the separate cells, dormitory, mess hall, chapel and library. The bakehouse and cookhouse were in a newly built structure added to the former mill's west. As well as housing the necessary spaces of incarceration, the new penitentiary by necessity had work and service areas. The ovens of the kitchen and bakehouse fuelled the day-to-day work of the convict, while the library and chapel provided fuel of a different ilk. With the addition of the ablutions and laundry areas, the penitentiary became the place where convicts underwent the rigours of Port Arthur's punishment regime, at the same time as witnessing the mundane, everyday aspects of their lived experience.

The conversion of the building meant that its shell became host to a purpose for which it had never been intended. The archaeological investigations found evidence of the process, both in the form of additions to the building and precinct, as well as the impact upon the fabric of the mill and granary as redundant mill fittings, internal walls and levels were removed. All of this went unremarked in the historical record. As indicated in the historical overview, the process was likely a staged one, carried out after 1848 when it became apparent the mill was doomed to failure. The creation of a massive mortar and dolerite raft below the separate cells and clocktower removed much of the flooring treatments of the treadwheel, mill house and granary space, leaving little evidence of the original composition of the spaces – or even the level of the internal ground surface. Similarly, the addition of the new four-storey layout saw original windows covered and wall surfaces and treatments hidden.[111]

The large-scale archaeological investigations of the ablutions and laundry proved fundamental to understanding how this area was adapted to its new penal use. At the time of the conversion, this space between the converted mill and the Champ Street retaining wall was the only feasible location for these important functions. Buildings already existed to the west and east of the mill, while the area to the north was undergoing the process of reclamation.

Squeezed into an existing area, the spatial solution was always going to be a compromise. Defined by high walls on three sides, the addition of the laundry building was to completely close off the area's western end. Within this zone the authorities erected further architecture that mirrored the classification being sought inside the penitentiary building. The ablutions area was divided into three main spaces (two yards and a central ablutions building), with each yard subdivided into two separate halves.

Issued their towel and small allowance of soap, prisoners washed at the troughs or basins before being mustered in the yard at the front of the penitentiary. The prisoners were required to wash again each evening, immediately after being assembled after their workday. Those convicts working around the settlement, or excused from gang duty, would also have used the ablutions yard throughout the day. Sundays, the day of rest, would have been even busier.

This concentration of activity in the morning and evening would have been difficult to properly manage during Phase I. If we were to only refer to the ca. 1856 historical plan, the impression is of a space that would facilitate good management: big yards, heated by well-sited fireplaces and with plenty of shelter from the elements. The centrally placed ablutions block housed

---

111 G. Jackman, *Penitentiary/Flourmill Archaeological Interpretation – Preliminary Notes*, Port Arthur Historic Site Management Authority, Port Arthur, 2009.

the toiletry and washing facility requirements, as well as a partitioned-off inspection walkway for the guards.

However, the archaeological investigation showed that the yards were actually fitted with fewer fireplaces than planned. Surfaced with freshly broken brick and hemmed in by the masonry of the penitentiary, yard walls and Champ Street, these would have also been uncomfortably bright and hot places to spend any time during the summer. Downpours of rain caused immediate puddling in the yards and, as mentioned, the overflow of some of the drains.

In the central ablutions block, 15 privies and eight urinals were required to service the needs of the nearly 350 convicts who slept in the penitentiary's dormitory, as well as over 136 men kept in isolation. This meant a ratio of one privy for every 32 men. The space was arranged to encourage anti-clockwise movement, with men entering from the west to circulate past the privies, urinals and wash troughs before heading out the eastern exit. With so many men using it morning and evening, the ablutions block would have been a bottleneck. Equally impossible would have been any form of efficient circulation through the 27 wash stations secreted away behind the laundry.

As well as illustrating the difference that existed between planned intention and built reality, the archaeological record also suggested that there was a certain indecisiveness on the part of the authorities as to how the spaces would be designed and used. For example, although evidence of drainage associated with the central structure was encountered, supportive of its Phase I use as an ablutions block, this drainage was added *after* the construction of the central building and the dividing wall in the eastern yard.

This indicated that the drainage requirements – and therefore the hygiene needs of the prisoner population – were not fully considered until after the major elements of the ablutions yard had been decided. Similarly, the historical evidence suggested that the fireplaces flanking the central structure had gone out of use after Phase I, but archaeological evidence suggested that they were in fact reused as part of the heating added to the newly configured day room.

The wholesale conversion of the ablutions yard and the associated modification of the laundry structure that took place as part of the penitentiary's second phase of occupation therefore had its genesis in the inadequate design of the first phase. The conversion saw the ablutions facilities

Figure 2.26. Historic plan detail of latticework. (Unknown author, untitled plan of penitentiary Port Arthur, ca .1863, PWD 266/1/1779, Tasmanian Archives)

removed to the flanking yards, which became a combination of washing and toiletry areas, as well as for exercise. The central structure became a day room, heated by the two repurposed fireplaces. The yards once again became mirror images of each other, fitted with shelters covering lavatory basins, urinals and privies. The extension of the laundry added room for the new hot water boiler and its associated chimney.

This remodelling, which took place around 1862, at one stroke improved the ability to manage the prisoners' routine. Although the entrance to the penitentiary remained an unavoidable bottleneck, the separation of washing and toilet functions into separate areas facilitated a more efficient process in the mornings and evenings. The provision of latticework frontage to the lavatory and toilet shelters, as recorded in the historical plan, would have allowed for a certain level of privacy, while still allowing observation by the guards (Figure 2.26).

As with the first phase, there were discrepancies in the recorded design of areas during the second. Archaeological investigation demonstrated that the two large shelters in both the east and west yards were larger than depicted in the plan, with different construction techniques indicative of their separate uses. The configuration of the day room was also different to that recorded, with fireplaces on either side of the space reusing chimneys from the first phase yards.

There is also a question of whether the conversion actually improved the supervisory conditions in the area. Although it was cramped and noisome, the ablutions shelter during the first phase had a walkway that facilitated inspection. The triangular designs of the four yards and the lack of enclosed structures also allowed guards to observe activity from a yard's entrance. The conversion introduced new structures to each yard, the new posts, screens and walls hampering the ability to observe activity in either yard. This meant that total observation could only be achieved by closer supervision. In 1864 it appears the authorities began to use the elevated position of Champ Street (Plate 2.8) to effect observation, with watchmen placed on the wall when prisoners were in the yards.[112]

As well as a design response to a space that failed to work, we also need to consider if the conversion was a response to the station's ageing population. With no transportees arriving in the colony after 1853 and prisoners convicted in the colonies increasingly funnelled into other institutions, the 'old lags' slowly began to account for a growing percentage of the population. A population becoming increasingly aged and infirm was not capable of the hard labour it had once carried out.

As the probation system wound down after 1853, many of the male convict populations of existing establishments were redirected to Port Arthur. As already discussed, this is when the Norfolk Island prisoners were transferred to the station. The 1855 closure of the Cascades timber station resulted in many prisoners being brought to Port Arthur, reinvigorating the dormant timber industry.[113] When the peninsula station of Impression Bay closed in June 1857, having been an invalid station since 1848, its population of some 238 invalids and 74 lunatics were all transferred to Port Arthur.[114]

This influx of invalids was housed in the old 1835 prisoners' barracks. Prior to the availability of the purpose-built 1863 paupers' dormitory and the 1868 asylum (Figure 2.27), these old barracks were the only facilities for the housing and care of the weakest of the prison population. In 1860 the barracks building was described as:

> A long weatherboarded house fitted up with iron stretchers … [the] beds, consisting of a mattress, abundance of blankets, and a rug. Several fireplaces were in the building, and a blazing fire in each, imparted a feeling of warmth and comfort throughout. The invalids

112 John Heywood, 14 July 1864, p. 916. Port Arthur Court Record Book 1861–1865, R.2007.60. Tasmanian Museum and Art Gallery (TMAG).

113 Tuffin, 'The Evolution of Convict Labour Management'.

114 The Impression Bay station was first used as an Invalid station from late 1846 through to mid-1847, when it was occupied by convicts transferred from Norfolk Island. R Lord, *Impression Bay: Convict Probation Station to Civilian Quarantine Station*, Richard Lord and Partners, Hobart, 1992, pp. 27–29.

Figure 2.27. The Paupers' Mess (foreground), with the Asylum in the background, 1890. ('Photograph, Asylum at Port Arthur', 1890, PH30/1/4521, Tasmanian Archives)

themselves are allowed a full ration of meat and bread besides tea and sugar and extras.[115]

There is no evidence to suggest that invalids were housed within the penitentiary. Until the late 1860s, the penitentiary was still housing the class of convict known as 'effective' – those capable of labour and therefore the riskiest segment of the population. The penitentiary housed mainly those convicts in the 'quarry gang', 'wharf gang' and 'ordinary labour' classifications, with invalids taking up mainly special occupations. With classification a paramount concern, the paupers and invalids in the prisoners' barracks and, later, in the paupers' depot and asylum, would have been kept separate from those in the penitentiary.

Without a large invalid population in the penitentiary, the ca. 1862 conversion of the ablutions and laundry areas was therefore likely not due to any overarching benevolent concerns about the welfare of the more vulnerable prisoners. The overall character of the prison population was

---

115 *Hobart Town Advertiser* 22 August 1860, in: M Morris, *Invalids, Paupers & Lunatics – Port Arthur, New Norfolk and other Peninsula Stations*, report prepared for PAHSMA, 2002, p. 58.

changing, getting older and increasingly infirm, which may have been a factor. However, the conversion occurred at a time when both the dormitory and separate cells of the penitentiary were fully occupied and the rigid system of classification still in force. Hence, the conversion was likely a localised response to logistical pressures, rather than a reaction to population dynamics or wider penal philosophies.

Local and global influences

The story of the 1854 conversion is therefore one of response to the immediate requirements of the local situation, as well as to the more esoteric influences exerted by penal philosophies adopted elsewhere. The Port Arthur station was established at a time of great change, as old systems of penal confinement and coercion were giving way to regimes based on classification and attempted reform. The partial adoption of the principles of separation in 1833 demonstrates that, although the antipodean penal settlement was far from the centres of imperial power, it was still shaped by the grand ideas permeating British penal philosophy at the time.

What is clear is that the penitentiary that eventuated between 1854 and 1857 incorporated ideas about regimented separation and controlled association into its design. In this way it copied the public works prisons, like that at Portland, which had appeared in Britain's penal landscape from the late 1840s. In its replication of Pentonville, it sought to import the ideal of rigid separation. However, it is important to recognise that the penitentiary operated as part of a unit at Port Arthur. Replicating the greater penal cycles, such as those found in Ireland, it operated in tandem with the separate prison to create a closed system based on separation, classification and displays of reformation. Together, the two buildings were a penal system in miniature, creating a hierarchical system through which the convict progressed: from their introduction to the settlement, to their removal to the less-strict penitentiary. Within the penitentiary itself, gradations of accommodation based on separation and associated labour allowed for further systems of classification and movement through them.

This principle continued in the ablutions and laundry areas. Excavations revealed an area initially constructed to reflect the classificatory infrastructure present within the penitentiary. It had the capacity to divide and classify the penitentiary's prisoner population, using the confined space to create areas of enclosure and control. However, these same spatial confines led to the failure of the first phase infrastructure, and the authorities were forced to completely adapt the area only six years after it was first built. This improved design facilitated the better movement of prisoners through the area – albeit at the expense of neatly subdivided yards. In the next chapter, we bring together archaeological and historical narratives to attempt to understand the experiences of those who used these yards.

Plate 0.1. Port Arthur, former penal station and now World Heritage historic site. The penitentiary is in the centre of the image. (Hype TV for PAHSMA, 2017)

Plate 0.2. The Port Arthur penitentiary building (1842–77). (PAHSMA 2020)

Plate 1.1. Illustration of Port Arthur in 1863, looking from the northern side of Mason Cove. By this time much of the cove had been reclaimed. (Unknown author, 'Port Arthur', ca. 1860, W.L. Crowther Library, Tasmanian Archives)

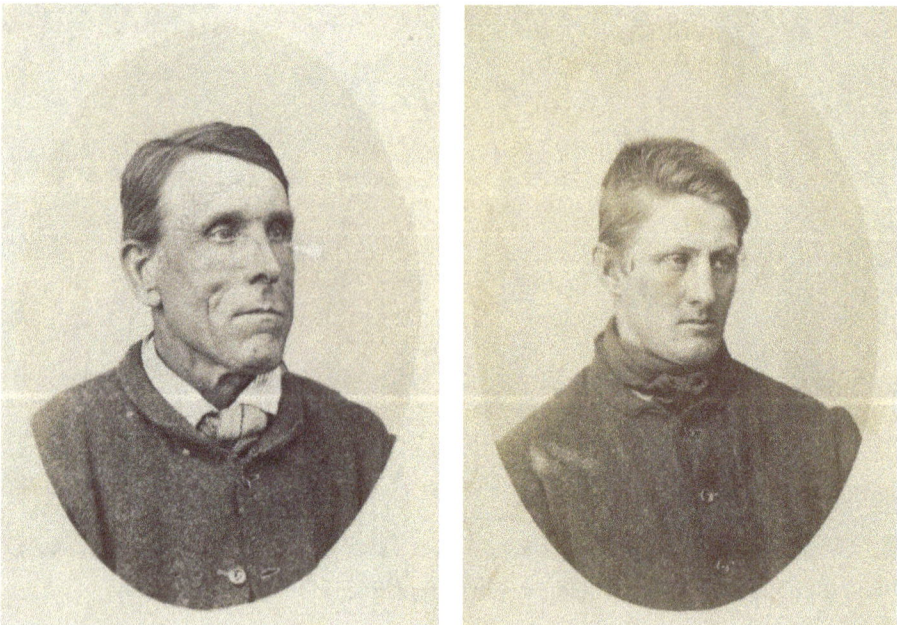

Plate 1.2. In 1874, members of Port Arthur's prisoner population were photographed. At left is Thomas Francis (transported on the Lady Franklin) and on the right is John Gregson (a native of Van Diemen's Land). (Thomas Francis, 1874, PIC Album 935 #P1029/14; John Gregson, 1874, PIC Album 935 #P1029/20a, National Library of Australia)

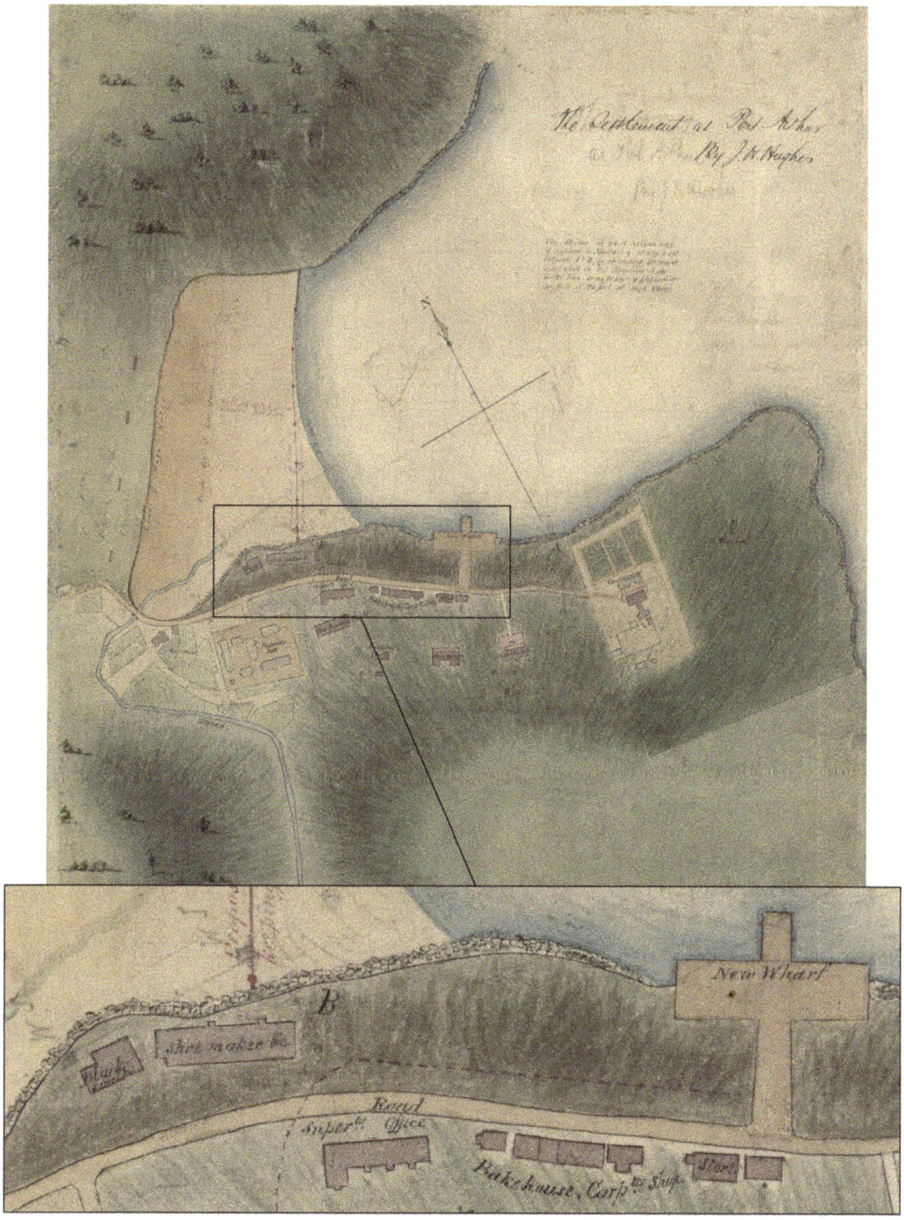

Plate 1.3. The first plan of Port Arthur, produced in 1833. The waterfront workshops are shown in the inset (left), with the wharf to the right (before the Commissariat store and boat basin were built). The lumber yards were situated between. (J.H. Hughes, 'The Settlement at Port Arthur', 1833, AF397/1/7, Tasmanian Archives)

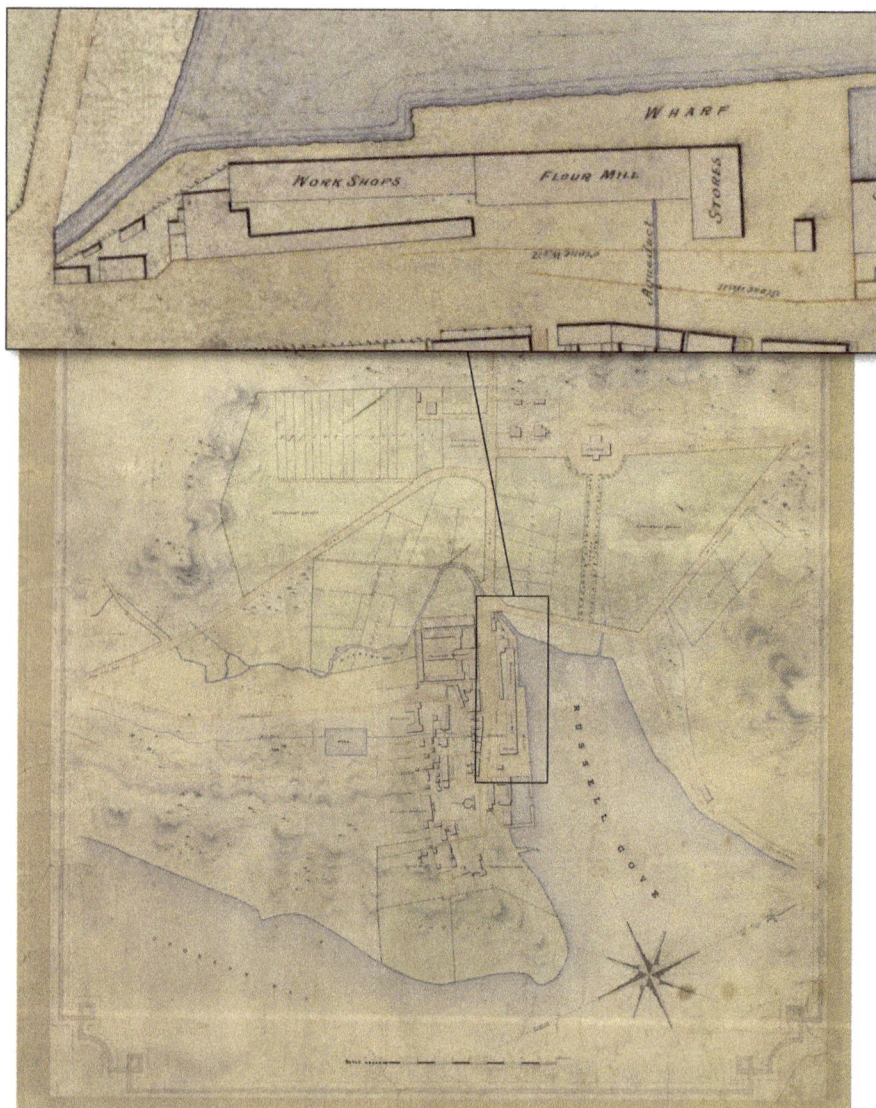

Plate 1.4. Map by J.R. Hurst of Port Arthur in 1846. (J.R. Hurst, 'Plan of the Penal Settlement of Port Arthur', 1846, AF397/1/8, Tasmanian Archives)

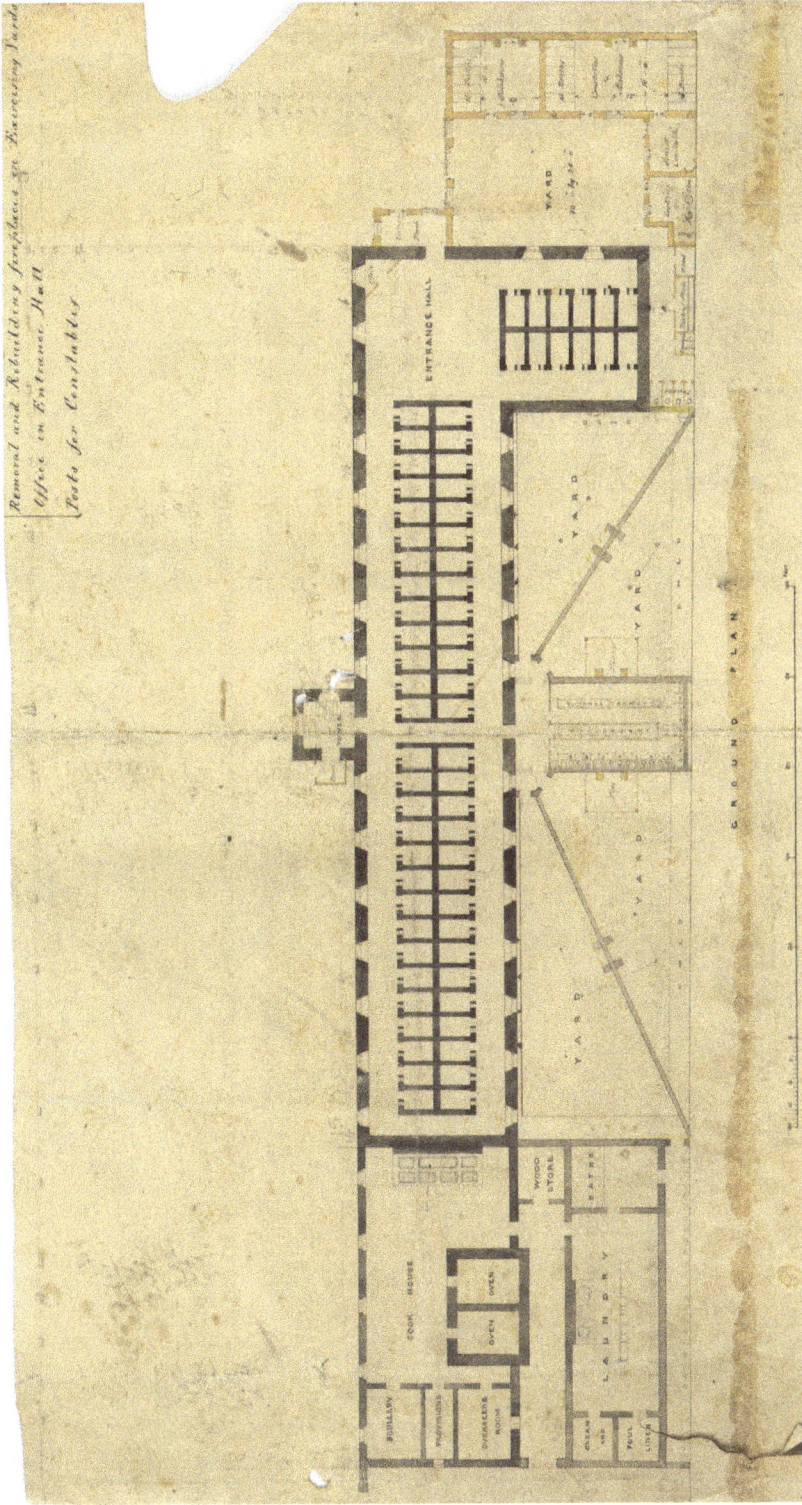

Plate 1.5. Plan of the penitentiary and its ancillary structures and areas in about 1856. (Plan of Port Arthur penitentiary, ca. 1856, PXD 52, Mitchell Library, State Library of New South Wales)

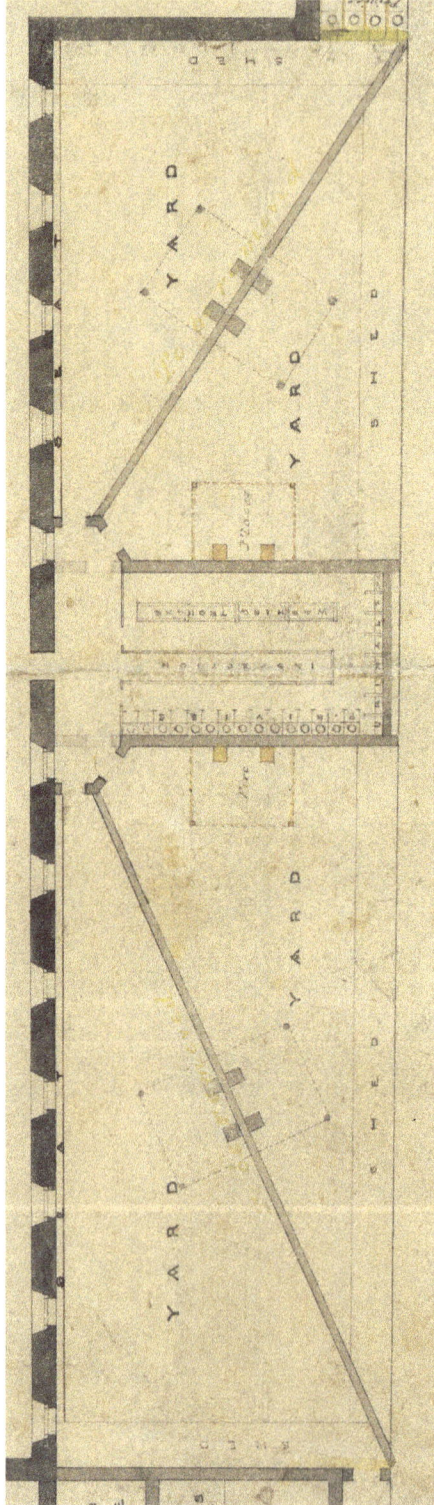

Plate 1.6. Detail of the ca. 1856 plan, showing the ablutions area. (Plan of Port Arthur penitentiary, ca. 1856, PXD 52, Mitchell Library, State Library of New South Wales)

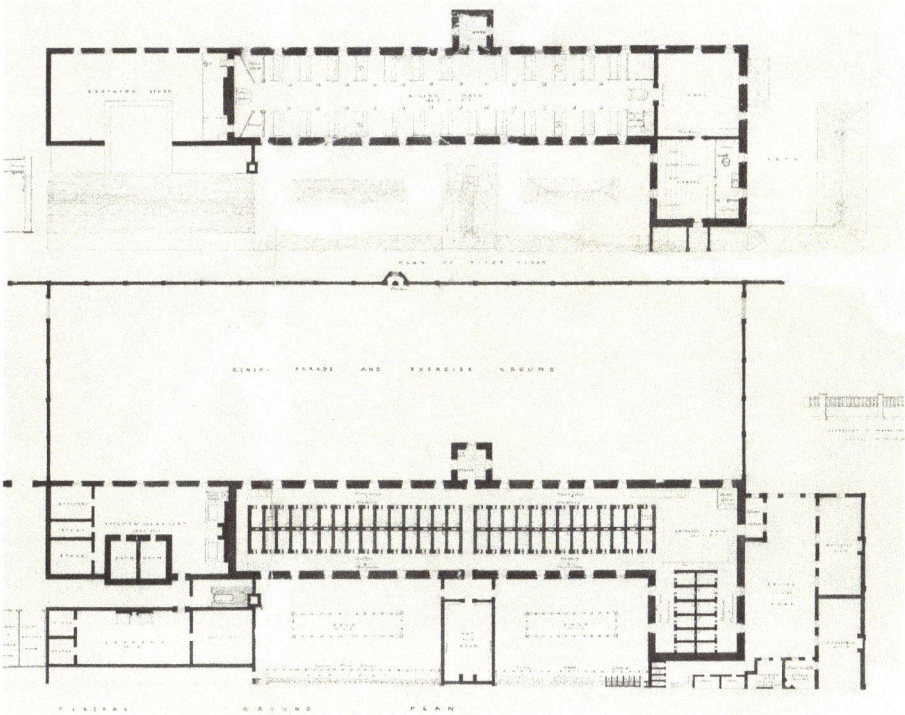

Plate 1.7. Ground (below) and first floor plans for the penitentiary, showing changes to the ablutions and laundry areas ca. 1862. (Unknown author, untitled plan of penitentiary Port Arthur, ca. 1863, PWD 266/1/1779, Tasmanian Archives)

Plate 2.1. Dolerite shore near Port Arthur. The original waterfront would have looked similar to this. (PAHSMA 2020)

Plate 2.2. A view of Port Arthur in ca. 1834. The process of clearance and settlement was well underway by this point. ('Port Arthur, Van Diemen's Land', ca. 1834 [attributed to John Russell], W.L. Crowther Library, Tasmanian Archives)

Plate 2.3. Large log of 0.60m diameter incorporated into the reclamation cribbing, found during excavations within the penitentiary footprint. (PAHSMA 2014)

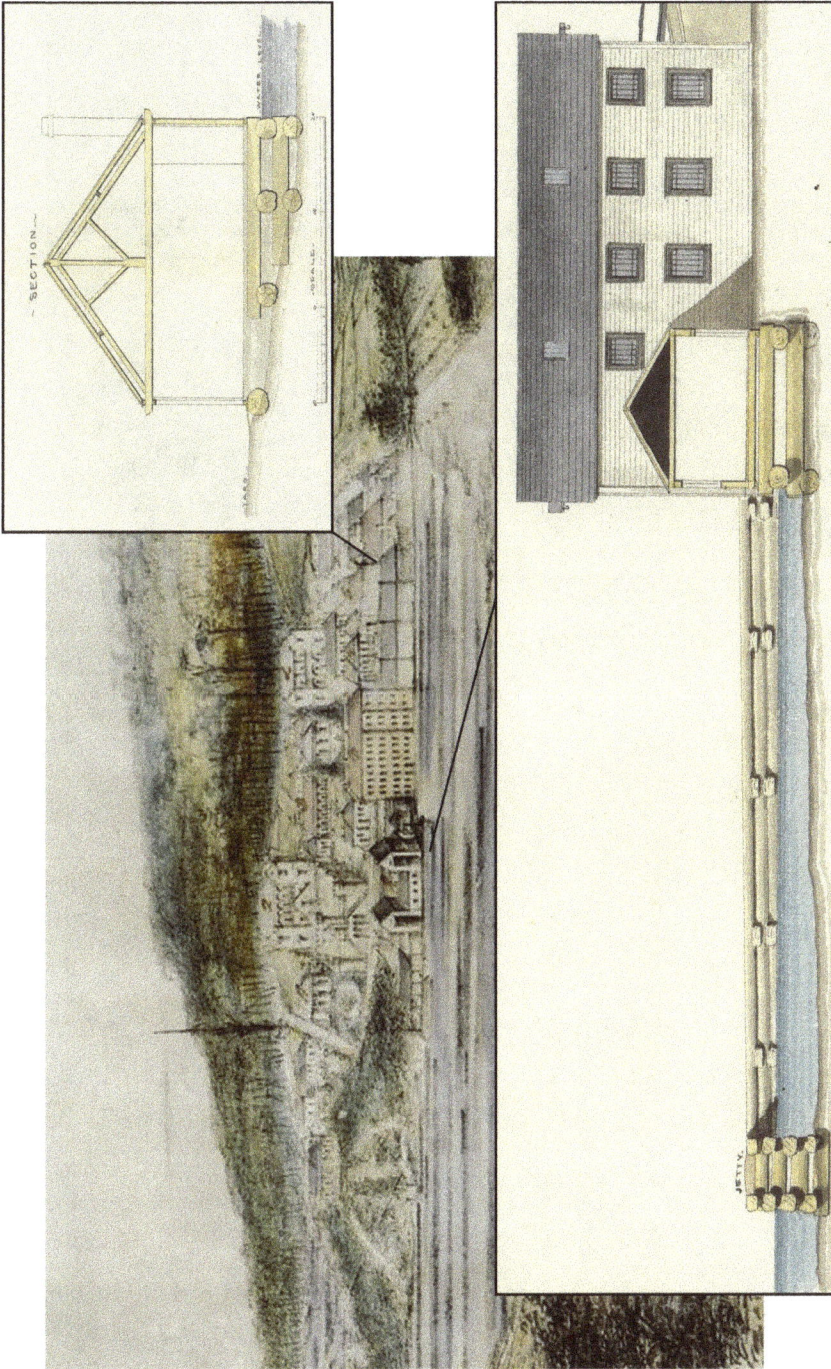

Plate 2.4. Illustration of Port Arthur waterfront in 1843. The inset illustrations are elevations by Henry Laing in 1836 showing the extent of the reclamation under the workshops (above) and the nearby Commissariat store (below). (Unknown author, 'Port Arthur, Tasmania, 1843', 1843, SV6B/Pr Arth/5, Mitchell Library, State Library New South Wales; Henry Laing, 'Commissariat Stores', 1836, CON87/1/14, Tasmanian Archives; Henry Laing, 'Artificers' Shops', 1836, CON87/1/35, Tasmanian Archives)

Plate 2.5. A convict-made pair of boots. (PAHSMA, 2020)

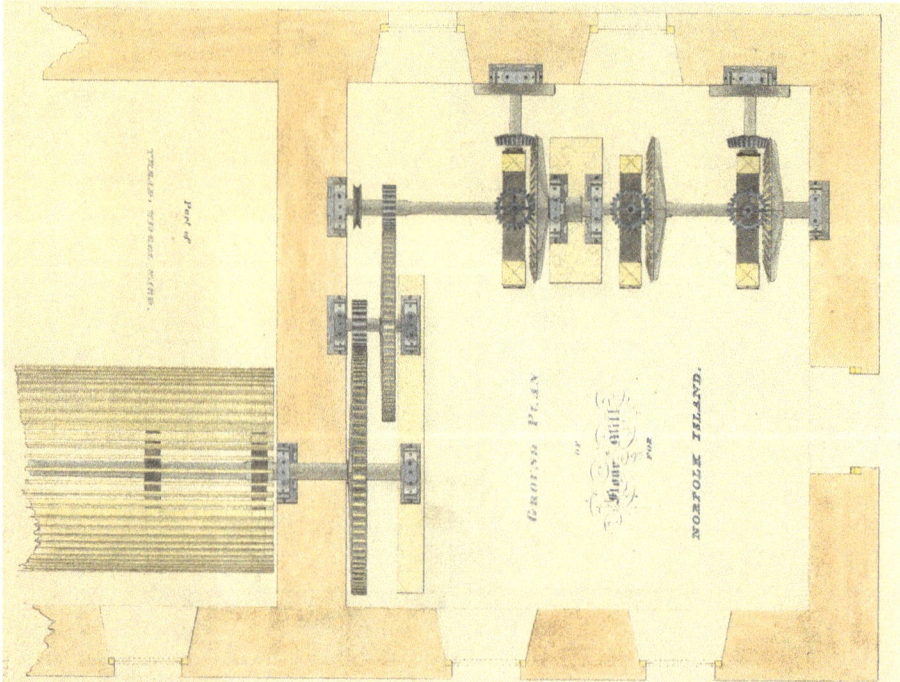

Plate 2.6. Plan of the treadwheel (left) and milling gear proposed for Norfolk Island. (J.C. Victor, 'Ground plan of flour-mill [sic] for Norfolk Island', July 1845, in: Eardley Eardley-Wilmot, Lieutenant Governor, to Lord Stanley, Secretary of State, 25 August 1845, CO 280/184, reel 536, no. 124, Tasmanian Archives)

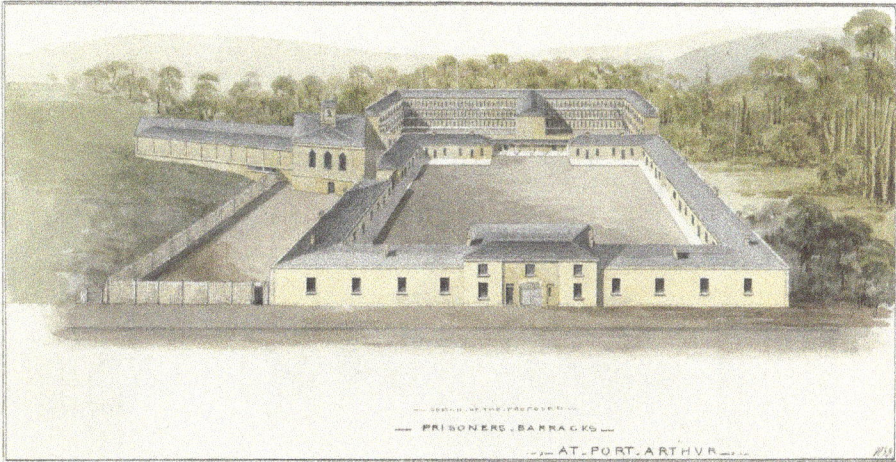

Plate 2.7. Booth's 1833 plan for the new prisoners' barracks. Note the triple-tiered range of separate cells at the back of the compound. (Henry Laing, 1833, 'Sketch of the proposed Prisoners' Barracks at Port Arthur', CSO1/584/13194, p. 47, Tasmanian Archives)

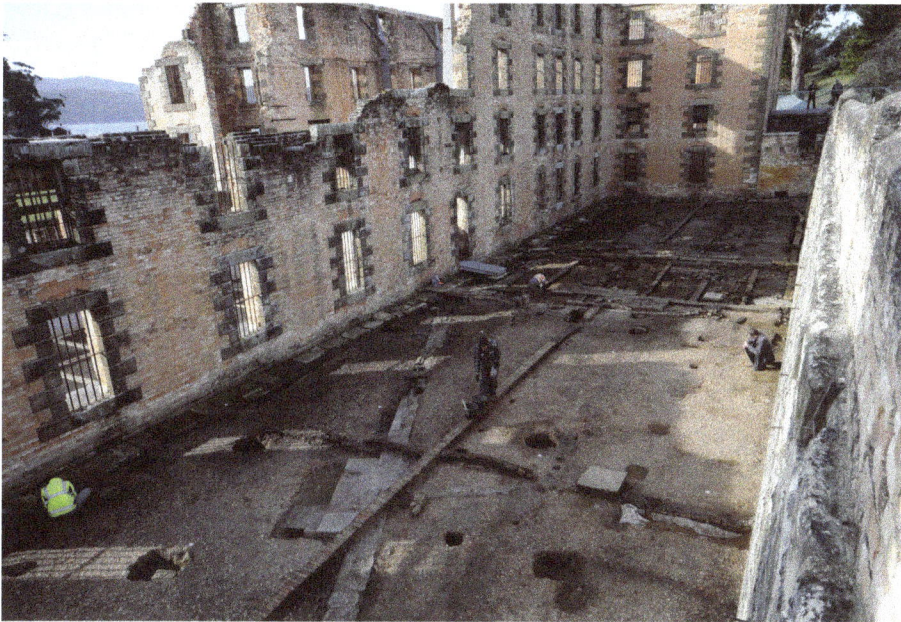

Plate 2.8. Looking down upon the excavation (with the Phase I dividing walls visible) from Champ Street. (David Roe, 2016)

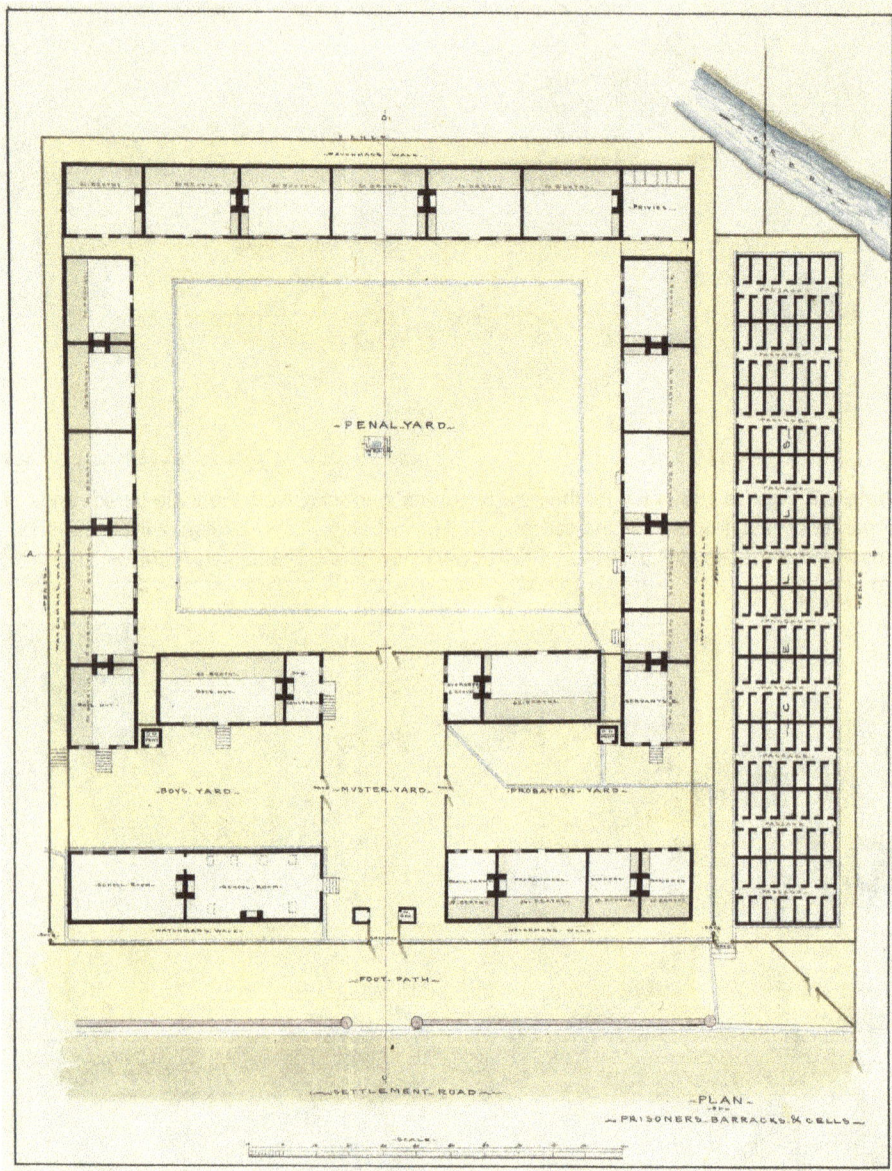

Plate 2.9. Plan of the 1835 prisoners' barracks. (Henry Laing, 1836, 'Plan of Prisoners' Barracks & Cells', CON87/1/38, Tasmanian Archives)

Plate 3.1. Some of the clay tobacco pipes recovered during the 2016 excavation. The two commemorative pipes are visible. (PAHSMA)

Plate 3.2. Lead tokens found during the excavation of the ablutions area. (PAHSMA)

Plate 3.3. A cluster of tokens was found in the topsoil, over the footings of the wet yard's central shelter. (PAHSMA 2016)

Plate 3.4. A selection of buttons found during 2016. The four-hole bone button at the front has had a cross inscribed upon it. (PAHSMA 2020)

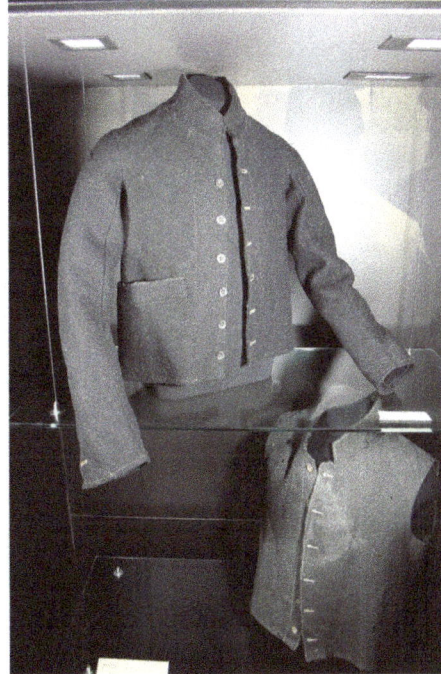

Plate 3.5. Convict uniforms held in the Port Arthur collection. Parti (left) and grey (right). The grey jacket has iron sew-through buttons, with bone sew-through buttons used on the waistcoat below. (PAHSMA)

Plate 3.6. A selection of bottles (clockwise from left: beer, gin and aerated water), with some of the fragments found during 2016. (PAHSMA 2020)

Plate 4.1. The laundry and ablutions areas before excavation commenced in 2016. (PAHSMA 2015)

Plate 4.2. The laundry and ablution areas taken during the excavations. (PAHSMA 2016)

Plate 4.3. The ablutions and laundry area, situated between the penitentiary (left) and Champ Street retaining wall (right). (PAHSMA 2016)

Plate 4.4. Mid-excavation shot of the ablutions block/day room, showing the area gridded for artefact recovery. (PAHSMA 2016)

Plate 4.5. This 1851 painting by Ludwig Becker shows the timber cribbing used for building the two boat slips of the Port Arthur dockyard. (Ludwig Becker, 1851, Port Arthur [östl Ende], Tasman's Peninsula, VDL, 19 December 1851, courtesy of Menzies Fine Art Auctioneers and Valuers)

Plate 4.6. The diagonal sandstone dividing wall of the west yard during excavation. Also visible are the back-to-back fireplaces and yard gravel. The brick footing is from the later Phase II shelter. (PAHSMA 2016)

Chapter 3

PRIVATE LIVES IN PUBLIC SPACES: UNDERSTANDING THE CONVICT EXPERIENCE

Where were the people in all of this? We've caught glimpses of the administration, as it sought to confine and coerce an unfree population. We've seen how the labour of the convicts was appropriated, and how spaces were constructed to manage and confine this labour. Yet, apart from a few examples, the convicts and their captors are missing.

This is where historical archaeology is at its strongest, using its access to the written and material record to recover lives lost to time. Artefacts, in particular, provide us with strong links to people and their past actions. Archaeologists are skilled at taking the artefact and extracting a story: of the mundane, the ephemeral, the illicit. Objects speak to us of society, wealth, power, labour, race and gender. Through careful excavation and painstaking analysis we try to extract these stories, make sense of them and share what we have learned. We build upon the work of others, and our work will be built upon in turn. What results is a better understanding of the past.

In this section we will seek to understand more about the convicts and their administrators. We will delve into the documentary record to recover the intent, actions and even the names of the individuals who used these spaces. We have already demonstrated how the archaeological record can in part recreate the environment that the men were forced to negotiate on a daily basis. We will now explore in more detail the artefacts that create that vital link between people, space and action. We will start with a short overview of the quantity, type and location of the artefacts we found. This is followed by an historical and archaeological analysis, as we seek to understand more about the people behind the walls.

Overview of the artefacts

During the 2013–16 archaeological investigations we found 33,874 artefacts (Figure 3.1). Further analysis estimated that these represented a minimum of 18,251 objects. This is due to the fact that once-intact objects fragment before or upon entering the archaeological record – meaning we often find multiple pieces from the same object.[1] Of these, we determined that 10,563 of the objects related to the convict period, with the remainder recovered from post-1877 deposits. The majority of these objects came from the excavation of the ablutions (5,715) and laundry (3,224) areas.

When the artefacts were catalogued we categorised them according to their presumed function. This meant that we were able to derive a coarse understanding of what activities were represented: clay tobacco pipes represented 'recreation'; buttons 'clothing', and so on. Of course, such analysis is only based upon what we know about the type of object. It cannot always take into account secondary functions for which an object was used: pipes may have acted as currency in a black-market economy; buttons may have been used as gaming tokens. Many objects that enter the archaeological record have such hidden lives. In most cases such uses will remain hidden forever. Occasionally, however, we are able to recover some historical information that hints at the alternative lives of objects.

The excavation and monitoring program during 2013–15 recovered 1,624 artefacts from convict period deposits, shown in Table 3.1 and provided evidence of activity during the 1830–54 period and the flour mill's conversion. Shells (165) comprised the largest number of finds within the 1830s reclamation, possibly having been mixed in with the reclamation or deposited during tidal events. Otherwise the reclamation deposits had only small amounts of bottle and window glass, a single clay tobacco pipe, nails, three buttons and pieces of iron strapping. Of note was the preservation

---

1 The artefact counts provided from this point on are expressed in terms of Minimum Number of Items (MNI).

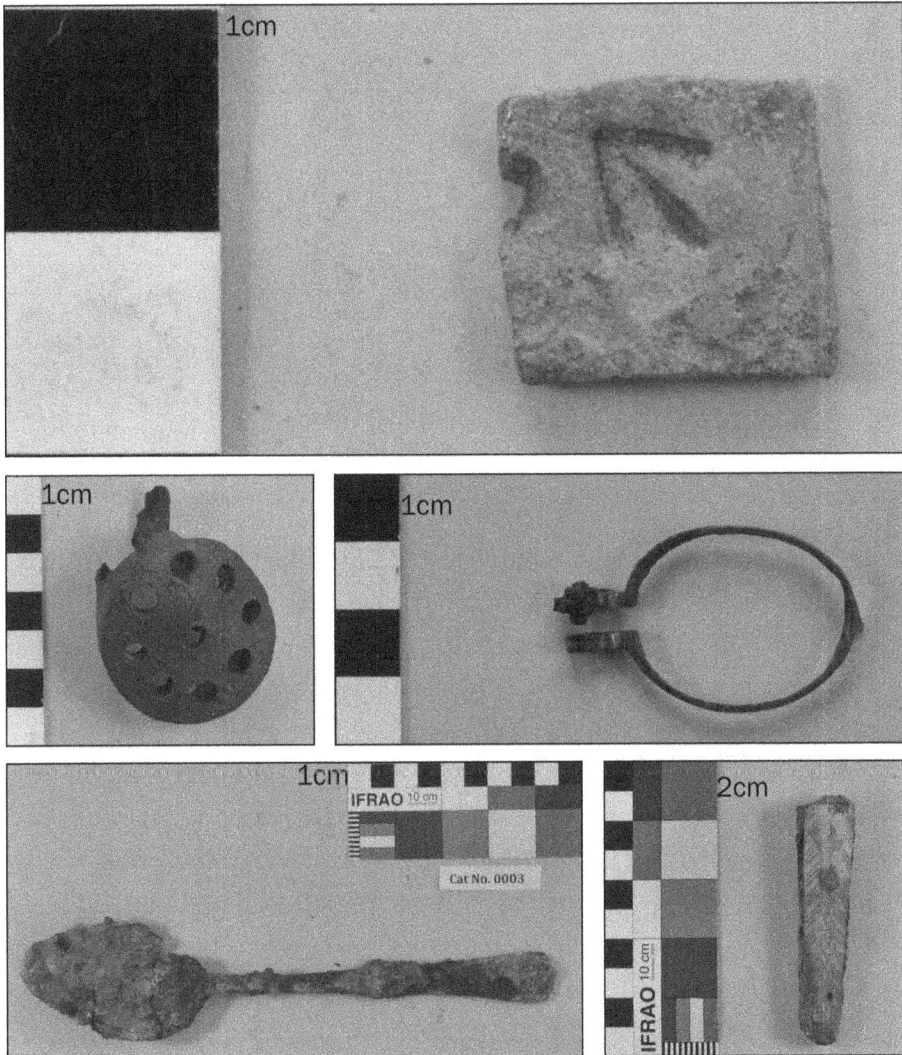

Figure 3.1. Some of the objects found during the 2013-16 investigations. From top (clockwise): a piece of lead with the broad arrow stamp, spectacle frame, carved bone handle from a knife, spoon, water reticulation fitting. (PAHSMA 2016)

of 16 timber offcuts and two shingles (short timber boards used as roofing tiles) within the clays, derived from the industrial nature of the waterfront. A similarly small number of artefacts were retrieved off some gravel surfaces from the 1830s or 1840s, predominantly nails (33).

Artefacts related to the occupation of the workshops during the 1830s were more varied. These included objects related to the industrial functions carried out within the complex: hooks, a knife and handle, file, rasp, saw

Table 3.1. Artefacts recovered from convict period (1830–77) deposits during the 2013–15 excavations.

Phase	Activity	Number (MNI)
1830–54	Reclamation, 1830s	227
1830–54	Waterfront surface, 1830s	42
1830–54	Workshops deposit	555
1830–54	Flour mill construction	17
Penitentiary – Phase I	Penitentiary conversion	783
	Artefacts recovered from monitoring	469

blade, iron strapping, washers and 33 metal offcuts (copper alloy, lead, iron, wood). The majority of the finds were retrieved from a single deposit from a trench within the footprint of the bakehouse. Relating to the workshops just before the bakehouse was constructed, the deposit contained 438 artefacts – of which 307 were nails.

Only a small number of artefacts related to the construction and occupation of the flour mill and granary (scattered nails, bottle glass and shells). A larger number derived from the period of conversion. This portion of the assemblage was not markedly different, although it comprised more window glass (37), iron strapping (27), nails (398), and flashing (4) – reflecting the construction-related nature of the deposits. Buttons (15), bottle glass (13) and clay tobacco pipes (13) were also found throughout.

While the types of artefacts found during the 2016 excavations of the ablutions and laundry area were not substantially different from those found in 2013–15, their quantities, concentrations and variety were. This was undoubtedly due to the different scales of the investigations, as well as the different activities that were carried out in the investigated areas. Table 3.2 shows artefacts recovered from convict period deposits in these two areas.

Of the artefacts found, nails by far comprised the largest assemblage, accounting for over 55 per cent of the total collection. They were made predominantly from iron, although 23 copper alloy nails (generally used for boatbuilding) were also found. The nails represented a variety of types and forms of manufacture – clout, brad, box and roofing. Alongside roofing

Table 3.2. Table showing artefacts (MNI) recovered from convict-period contexts during the excavation of the ablutions and laundry areas. It has been organised according to function analysis and lists the most common identities of artefacts recovered from that class (excludes low-count functions).

Function	Number	%	Dominant identities
Unidentified	4,437	49.7%	Nails (3,523), unidentified metal (204), bottle glass (116), ceramic vessels (58)
Architectural	2,226	24.9%	Nails (1,598), window glass (385), roofing slate (85)
Recreation	959	10.7%	Clay tobacco pipe (923), tokens (31), marbles (4)
Food	719	8.1%	Food remains (413), alcohol containers (163), ceramic service ware (104)
Clothing	448	5.0%	Button – bone (283), button – metal (123), shoe plates (16)
Clerical	60	0.7%	Pencils – slate and graphite (34), writing slate (22), ink bottles (3)
Utility	23	0.3%	Chimney lamp glass (13), plumbing pipe (4)
Hygiene	19	0.2%	Ceramic basin/vessel (19)
Personal	12	0.1%	Spectacle lens (7), eye glass – frame (2), comb (1), bead (1)
Currency	7	0.1%	Half-penny (4)
Industry	6	0.1%	Lead sprue (5)
Pharmaceutical	6	0.1%	Bottle - glass (4), bottle – flint (2)
Domestic	5	0.1%	Copper alloy tack (2), iron handle (2)
Sewing	3	0.0%	Pin (3)

slate, iron strapping (to reinforce brickwork) and window glass, they were recovered from deposits related to the demolition and renovation that occurred in the ablutions and laundry areas during the convict period. Some artefacts were also undoubtedly related to the post-convict period of salvage and abandonment, recovered from very mixed deposits (like in the ablutions' central structure, later the day room).

Table 3.3 shows a further breakdown of the non-architectural artefact types according to the area in which they were found. The ablutions area

Table 3.3. Showing key artefact functions and use classification (not including architectural) and the breakdown between those found in the ablutions and laundry areas (MNI).

Function	Use	Total	Ablutions	% of total	Laundry	% of total
Clerical	Writing	59	49	83%	10	17%
Clerical	Tool	1	0	0%	1	100%
Clothing	Fastener	429	156	36%	273	64%
Clothing	Footwear	19	10	53%	9	47%
Currency	Coinage	7	6	86%	1	14%
Domestic	Furnishing	3	2	67%	1	33%
Domestic	Laundry	2	2	100%	0	0%
Food	Food Remains	413	407	99%	6	1%
Food	Alcohol	163	128	79%	35	21%
Food	Service	118	103	87%	15	13%
Food	Storage	12	11	92%	1	8%
Food	Beverage	8	7	88%	1	13%
Food	Unidentified	5	4	80%	1	20%
Food	Preparation	1	0	0%	1	100%
Hygiene	Ceramic vessel	19	19	100%	0	0%
Industry	Metal sprue	5	5	100%	0	0%
Industry	Shipbuilding	1	1	100%	0	0%
Personal	Eyewear	9	7	78%	2	22%
Personal	Adornment/ accessory	3	3	100%	0	0%
Pharmaceutical	Bottle	6	6	100%	0	0%
Recreation	Smoking	923	801	87%	122	13%
Recreation	Token	32	32	100%	0	0%
Recreation	Toy	4	3	75%	1	25%
Sewing	Pin	3	0	0%	3	100%
Unidentified	Hardware	3715	2095	56%	1620	44%
Unidentified	Unidentified	615	359	58%	256	42%
Unidentified	Storage	98	98	100%	0	0%
Unidentified	Tool	9	4	44%	5	56%
Utility	Lighting	14	14	100%	0	0%
Utility	Fuel	4	3	75%	1	25%
Utility	Plumbing	5	5	100%	0	0%

yielded the highest number of artefacts, and also the highest proportion of artefacts linked to writing, smoking, eating and drinking. The laundry area had the highest proportion of clothing and sewing-related items.

If we break this down further, we can begin to see patterns of use within the two areas. Tables 7 and 8 (in the appendices) show artefacts according to their distribution within the ablutions and laundry. In the ablutions area, the central structure was a focus of activity; over 55 per cent (88) of buttons, 75 per cent (408) of food remains, 47 per cent (23) of writing-related items and all (7) of the personal items were found in the ablutions area were recovered from the structure's mixed deposits. While 35 per cent (277) of the clay tobacco pipes were found within this structure, the majority were found in the adjoining yards: 20 per cent (163) from deposits relating to Phase I and 36 per cent (288) to Phase II – with the remainder coming from mixed deposits or the Intermediate Phase of occupation. Nearly 20 per cent (30) of the buttons were recovered off Phase I yards, with 22 per cent from those related to Phase II and the Intermediate Phase. The yards also had the most alcohol-related finds (68 per cent [88]): 21 from Phase I and the remainder from the later phases.

The spatial division of artefacts in the laundry area was very different. By far the largest number were recovered from deposits associated with Phase II: 84 per cent (1,982) of the non-architectural convict period finds. The greatest concentration (1,440) was from the eastern rooms of the building, which underwent modification during this phase of occupation. Of the non-hardware artefacts, buttons were predominant; 96 per cent (263) came from this area during Phase II. The eastern rooms also accounted for over 80 per cent (99) of the clay tobacco pipes found in the laundry, 74 per cent (26) of the alcohol-related objects and all of the few food remains (6).

It is clear that the excavations of 2013–16 provided us with a wealth of artefacts. Within the ablutions and laundry, in particular, the extensive scale of the investigations meant that we were able to link deposits (and therefore the artefacts within them) to particular areas and phases of occupation. In this way we were able to demonstrate that the ablutions central structure (day room) was a focus of 'recreational' activity, as were the adjoining yards. The laundry itself provided far fewer objects related to food, recreation and service – as would be expected in a space predominantly dedicated to labour.

Beyond this coarse understanding of type and spatial location, the artefacts from the penitentiary excavation have proven a challenge to understand as originating from penal use. This is because they are all distinctly *ordinary* objects. If these artefacts had been found in isolation – away from the stone, brick and iron of the penitentiary – very few (if any) of them would suggest a place of incarceration. Clay tobacco pipes, writing slate, spectacle glass and earthenware fragments are encountered on excavations of most 19th-century places: residences, inns, offices, laneways. There is nothing particularly 'penal' or 'convict' about them. Archaeologist James Garman, upon excavating Rhode Island Prison (1838–78) in the United States, noted that artefacts related to the institution were 'mundane and above all repetitive', the products of a system designed to 'create unity among a body of individuals and to stamp out any non-conformity'.[2] For all the painstaking collection, cleaning, cataloguing and analysis that has gone into our artefacts, we have to ask ourselves: where are the prisoners and their gaolers in this pile of 'things'?

Direct points of comparison in Australia are relatively few. As we discuss later in the section 'Placing the excavation in context', there have been a number of investigations of convict places: cells, chapels, barracks. However, there have been fewer examinations of the more mundane aspects of convict life: the places of work, exercise, leisure and everyday needs – particularly within the context of a colonial penal institution. Further, most of the investigations that have taken place have not been on the same scale – providing narrow snapshots through smaller test trenches – or have not yet been published.

Considering similar places internationally, the points of comparison are sparse. Historical archaeologists have spent a lot of sweat and ink on investigations of institutions, but larger-scale investigations of 19th-century prisons and places of involuntary incarceration and labour are rare. Where such work has taken place, the archaeologists have similarly faced difficulties finding the prisoner in their artefact assemblages. In the United States, excavations of the Walnut Street Prison in Philadelphia (1775–1836) found evidence of labour in prison workshops, but the general assemblage was

---

2   J. Garman, *Detention Castles of Stone and Steel: Landscape, Labor, and the Urban Penitentiary*, Knoxville, 2005, p. 203.

ambiguous in its depiction of prisoners' everyday lives.[3] Garman's work at Rhode Island was more focused on the spatiality of the institution and the insight it provided into its penal regimes. In the United Kingdom, excavations of Salford prison (1790–1868) in Manchester defined a series of cells, yards and workshops – but failed to recover artefacts.[4]

Where investigations and analysis has occurred at Australian convict institutional places, they have usually reinforced the idea that these were establishments designed to quash individualism. This was achieved through prison design, the regulation of interpersonal interactions, and the control of the flow of material culture into and out of the place.[5] Offset against this is the evidence derived from the material culture of these places. For example, many artefacts recovered from individual cells and shared barracks spaces at Hyde Park Barracks (New South Wales), Fremantle Prison (Western Australia), Ross Female Factory (Tasmania) and Port Arthur's early prisoners' barracks were interpreted as evidence of prisoners' activities.[6] Among the objects that could be definitively linked to convicts were bone buttons, writing slate and slate pencils, clay tobacco pipes, gaming tokens, partial and whole pieces of convict clothing. The latter, found at Hyde Park Barracks, comprised clear indications of convict institutional life: government-issued shirts and outer-wear, as well as a leather guard to mitigate chaffing of the ankles by irons.

---

3   J.L. Cotter, D.G. Roberts, and M. Parrington, *The Buried Past: An Archaeological History of Philadelphia*, Philadelphia, 1993, p. 178; L.A.D. Cunzo, 'Reform, Respite, Ritual: An Archaeology of Institutions; the Magdalen Society of Philadelphia, 1800–1850', *Historical Archaeology*, Vol. 29, No. 3, 1995, pp. 1–168, p. 58.

4   R. Reader, *Archaeological Excavation Report: Land Off Stanley Street, Central Salford: Plots B5/6 (New Bailey Prison)*, University of Salford, Manchester, 2015, p. 43.

5   L. Bavin, 'Punishment, Prisons and Reform: Incarceration in Western Australia in the Nineteenth Century'. Special Issue: Historical Refractions, Edited by Charlie Fox', *Studies in Western Australian History*, No. 14, 1993, pp. 121–48, pp. 131–33; E. Casella, 'Horizons Beyond the Perimeter Wall: Relational Materiality, Institutional Confinement, and the Archaeology of Being Global', *Historical Archaeology*, Vol. 50, No. 3, 2016, pp. 127–43, pp. 134–35; Kerr, *Design for Convicts*; C. D'Gluyas, M. Gibbs, C. Hamilton, and D. Roe, 'Everyday Artefacts: Subsistence and Quality of Life at the Prisoner Barracks, Port Arthur, Tasmania', *Archaeology in Oceania*, Vol. 50, 2015, pp. 130–37.

6   F. Starr, 'An Archaeology of Improvisation: Convict Artefacts from Hyde Park Barracks, Sydney, 1819–1848', *Australasian Historical Archaeology*, Vol. 33, 2015, pp. 133–36; E. Mein, 'Inmate Coping Strategies in Fremantle Prison, Western Australia', Honours, University of Western Australia, 2012; D'Gluyas et al., 'Everyday Artefacts'.

The reading of these artefacts as signs of prisoner agency relies not upon the object itself, but on the provenance in which they were found. Therefore, at Ross, small objects below a solitary cell potentially recorded deliberate acts of secretion.[7] At Hyde Park Barracks, convict agency was detected in the size of some of the artefacts, which could only have entered the archaeological record through deliberate action.[8] A homemade eating utensil found at Old Newgate Prison, Connecticut, or gaming tokens made out of ceramic plates at Cabildo Prison, Louisiana, provide an instant, individual connection to the past.[9] Whether secreted, lost or discarded, these objects represented a prisoner's ability 'to reduce pain and inconvenience, and to make the path through the penal system more tolerable'.[10]

Therefore, for us during the penitentiary investigations, sparks of intense connection were not generated by the inherent 'convict' nature of the artefacts found. The token is just a piece of chipped ceramic or clipped lead sheeting. Not even a piece of lead marked with the broad arrow, today a classic symbol of convict Australia, definitively meant 'convict' – it was just a mark of government property. But found in a small cluster, beneath floorboards, secreted in an excavated hole, such things do begin to speak of rule-breaking and individual action.

Over the following pages we will discuss some of the key artefact types that tell us the most about the prisoners and the way in which they were administered. This will take place against a discussion of the regulatory environment that defined the everyday lives of the convicts incarcerated in the penitentiary. The objects that we found were a direct result of these lives being carried out within an institutionalised setting. This means that we can derive limited understanding of the activities that led to their attainment, use and eventual deposition in the archaeological record, through the documents of control and coercion.

---

7 E. Casella, 'Archaeology of the Ross Female Factory: Female Incarceration in Van Diemen's Land, Australia', Records of the Queen Victoria Museum, Launceston, 2002, pp. 62–63.

8 P. Davies, P. Crook, and T. Murray, *An Archaeology of Institutional Confinement: The Hyde Park Barracks, 1848–1886*, Sydney: Sydney University Press 2013, p. 14.

9 Megan Gannon, 'Starving Felons, and Other Lessons from Prison Archaeology', 19 May 2015, *Atlas Obscura*, https://www.atlasobscura.com/articles/old-newgate-prison; *Archaeology at the Cabildo*, Louisiana, Louisiana State Museum, n.d., pp. 12–13.

10 Starr, 'An Archaeology of Improvisation', p. 50.

The convict as inmate

The principles of separation and classification ruled the life of the convict at Port Arthur, as the authorities strived to divide the convict population by batten, bar or ration. Designed in part to mirror the new penal philosophies, the penitentiary was meant to facilitate classification. At the time of the mill's conversion, convicts were divided into four main classes:[11]

> 4. Separate Prison: 'The worst class of criminals, on arriving at the settlement, are placed under strict treatment in the separate prison for periods varying from four to twelve months ...'
>
> 3. Quarry Gang: 'the convicts wear heavy irons, and are employed in the severest description of labour ... The usual period to be passed in this gang is six months'
>
> 2. Wharf Gang: 'light chains ... in which the labour is somewhat less severe than in the quarry gang ... The usual period passed in this stage is also six months'
>
> 1. Ordinary Labour: 'from which the convicts emerge to the depot [in Hobart] eligible for private service on wages'.

For the quarry gang, constituting 'idle and restless individuals', the work was extremely demanding.[12] In 1856 two quarry gangs, with a total of 100 labourers, were engaged in quarrying, excavating, blasting and stone-breaking.[13] In the wharf gang, 'somewhat less severe than ... the quarry gang', men were put to work burning lime and charcoal, carting and procuring saw logs. Those at ordinary labour filled the myriad of other positions: blacksmiths, carpenters, wheelwrights, coopers, sawyers, splitters, and brickmakers. Invalids, never a large percentage of the convict population prior to 1857, fulfilled the lighter positions of tailors, shoemakers, cooks, servants, wood cutters, scavengers

---

11 James Boyd, Commandant, to J.S. Hampton, Comptroller General, 19 January 1854, *Convict Discipline and Transportation*, British Parliamentary Papers, London, 1854–55 (1916)(1988), pp. 41–42.

12 James Boyd, Commandant, to William Nairn, Comptroller General, 28 July 1862, *Convict Discipline and Transportation*, British Parliamentary Papers, London, 1863, p. 69.

13 'Return showing the Employment of Convicts at this Establishment on 30th June 1856', 14 August 1856, *Convict Discipline and Transportation*, British Parliamentary Papers, London, 1856, p. 179.

and watchmen. These 'special employments' were also filled by the better-behaved from the main prisoner body, provided that they had completed one-sixth of their period of detention.[14]

When this system of classification was recorded in 1856, it was specified that those in the quarry gang were to be confined to the separate cells in the prisoners' barracks at night, their interaction with prisoners of a higher classification heavily restricted.[15] To rise to the wharf gang was to be allowed to sleep in the main dormitories.[16] With the move to the penitentiary in 1857, this system of classification continued, with convicts on heavy labour kept in the 136 separate cells on the ground and mezzanine floors and those on light labour in the dormitory upstairs.[17] Within the walls of the penitentiary, silence was meant to be enforced at all times, to minimise communication between prisoners.[18]

As we will discuss in more detail later, prisoners were clothed according to classification. Men serving less than three years and/or on their first conviction were dressed in grey. All others, consisting of the mid-rank and recalcitrant, wore the parti-colour uniform, which comprised alternating patches of yellow and black on the torso and legs (Plate 3.4).[19] A mix of uniforms would have existed in the dormitory, but in the separate cells, the dominant uniform was the parti.

One of the most important and difficult tasks for the authorities was to ensure that new prisoners were kept separate and processed away from the 'corrupting influences' of the old hands. New arrivals were shaved, bathed

---

14 Convict Department, *Rules and Regulations for the Penal Settlement on Tasman's Peninsula*, Tasmania, 1868. Reprint: PAHSMA, Port Arthur, 1991, pp. 10, 40.

15 James Boyd, Commandant ,to J.S. Hampton, Comptroller General, 19 January 1854, *Convict Discipline and Transportation*, British Parliamentary Papers, London, 1854–55 (1916)(1988), pp. 41–42.

16 James Boyd, Commandant, to J.S. Hampton, Comptroller General, 19 January 1854, *Convict Discipline and Transportation*, British Parliamentary Papers, London, 1854–55 (1916)(1988), pp. 41–42.

17 W. Nairn, Acting Comptroller General, H.E.F. Young, Governor, 14 August 1857, *Convict Discipline and Transportation*, British Parliamentary Papers, 1859 (August), p. 180.

18 Convict Department, *Rules and Regulations for the Penal Settlement on Tasman's Peninsula*, Tasmania, 1868. Reprint: PAHSMA, Port Arthur, 1991, p. 27.

19 Convict Department, *Rules and Regulations for the Penal Settlement on Tasman's Peninsula*, Tasmania, 1868. Reprint: PAHSMA, Port Arthur, 1991, p. 39.

Table 3.4. Hours of convict labour, ca. 1868. (Convict Department, *Rules and Regulations for the Penal Settlement on Tasman's Peninsula*, Tasmania, 1868. Reprint: PAHSMA, Port Arthur, 1991, p. 46)

Summer	November	From 5:30am to 5:30 pm, ¾ hour for Breakfast, and 1 hour for Dinner
	December	10 ¼ hours daily
	January	
	February	
Spring/Autumn	March	From 6am to 5:15pm, ¾ of an hour for Breakfast and 1 hour for Dinner
	April	9 ½ hours daily
	September	
	October	
Winter	May	Breakfast before going out. From 7:30am to 4:45pm. 1 hour for Dinner
	August	8 ¼ hours daily
	June	Breakfast before going out. From 7:45am to 4:30pm. 1 hour for Dinner
	July	7 ¾ hours daily

and had their hair cut short, and were dressed in uniform according to classification.[20] Settlement regulations for this period state that:

166. All prisoners on arrival must be at once placed in the reception-cells, until they can be searched, bathed, have their hair cut short, and clothed according to the instructions furnished from the Commandant's office. The new arrivals are to be kept apart from the other convicts until classified by the Commandant and the Surgeon.[21]

This likely applied to the separate prison, in which most new intakes were first incarcerated. However, on removal to the penitentiary, they would have

---

20 Convict Department, *Rules and Regulations for the Penal Settlement on Tasman's Peninsula*, Tasmania, 1868. Reprint: PAHSMA, Port Arthur, 1991, p. 39.
21 Convict Department, *Rules and Regulations for the Penal Settlement on Tasman's Peninsula*, Tasmania, 1868. Reprint: PAHSMA, Port Arthur, 1991, p. 26.

undergone a similar process, with the ablutions block sometimes referred to as a 'receiving room'.[22] With a laundry for the issue of clothing and, particularly during the first phase, yards for the further segregation and classification of the prisoners, the ablutions and laundry space offered a controlled area for the reception of new arrivals.

A daily routine

The routine for convicts incarcerated within the penitentiary was largely the same for those in separate or dormitory accommodation. Convicts in the dormitory began the day by getting their sleeping places in order and then attending to their morning ablutions. On Saturdays all convicts were required to have a more thorough bath.[23]

Breakfast, consisting of gruel (oatmeal and molasses) and bread, was had by the dormitory class in the dining hall.[24] It is likely that the prisoners undergoing separate confinement ate in their cells, although this is not specified in the historical sources. After breakfast, all convicts were mustered in front of the penitentiary to be split into their respective gangs. From here they were marched to the place of work, the strictest silence being observed at all times.[25]

Having laboured throughout the day, the convicts were returned to the penitentiary, where another general muster was held and dinner commenced.[26] Again, it is presumed that those in separate confinement ate in their cells.[27] An edifying reading from the Bible accompanied both the morning and

22 James Boyd, Commandant, to J.S. Hampton, Comptroller General, 4 January 1855, *Convict Discipline and Transportation*, British Parliamentary Papers, London, 1854–5 (1916)(1988), p. 25.

23 Convict Department, *Rules and Regulations for the Penal Settlement on Tasman's Peninsula*, Tasmania, 1868. Reprint: PAHSMA, Port Arthur, 1991, p. 47.

24 Convict Department, *Rules and Regulations for the Penal Settlement on Tasman's Peninsula*, Tasmania, 1868. Reprint: PAHSMA, Port Arthur, 1991, p. 57.

25 Convict Department, *Rules and Regulations for the Penal Settlement on Tasman's Peninsula*, Tasmania, 1868. Reprint: PAHSMA, Port Arthur, 1991, pp. 42.

26 Convict Department, *Rules and Regulations for the Penal Settlement on Tasman's Peninsula*, Tasmania, 1868. Reprint: PAHSMA, Port Arthur, 1991, p. 57.

27 The 25 tables, postulated to seat up to 10 prisoners, could only accommodate 250 of over 480 convicts. See also: K. Pearce, *The Features, Function and Significance of the Port Arthur Penitentiary*, PAHSMA, Port Arthur, p. 29.

evening meals in the main mess hall.[28] For those deemed receptive enough, schooling was available after dinner.[29] Divine Service was carried out twice every Sunday, accompanied by a general muster in the morning with the Civil Commandant and Medical Officer in attendance.[30]

The precise hours that convicts spent in the ablutions yard are unknown – during either Phase I or Phase II. Access to the area was granted in the early morning before work commenced, and in the evening.[31] Sunday would have seen increased activity, with the convicts enjoying a modicum of free time to use the exercise yards. It is known that on Saturday all convicts were required to return to the penitentiary early at 4 pm for 'bathing purposes'.[32] Those convicts employed in the specialist occupations of laundrymen, watchmen, cooks, etc., who were attached to the penitentiary full time, would have had more opportunity to use the facilities than those in the work gangs.

At night, access was obviously restricted. Six 'portable closets' served the needs of those in the dormitory.[33] The men undergoing separate accommodation would have been provided with a slops bucket, like those held in the separate prison (Figure 3.2).

> The cells are to be swept, and, with the furniture, properly scoured; and the slops are to be handed out as soon as the bell is rung in the corridor and the doors opened for that purpose.[34]

A bending of rules

Although the settlement was governed by the written rule and the watch clock, a certain fluidity could exist in its administration and regulations,

---

28 Convict Department, *Rules and Regulations for the Penal Settlement on Tasman's Peninsula*, Tasmania, 1868. Reprint: PAHSMA, Port Arthur, 1991, p. 13.

29 Pearce, *The Features, Function and Significance of the Port Arthur Penitentiary*, p. 29.

30 Convict Department, *Rules and Regulations for the Penal Settlement on Tasman's Peninsula*, Tasmania, 1868. Reprint: PAHSMA, Port Arthur, 1991, pp. 5, 14.

31 P. Priestley, *Victorian Prison Lives: English Prison Biography, 1830–1914*, London, New York, 1985, p. 83.

32 Convict Department, *Rules and Regulations for the Penal Settlement on Tasman's Peninsula*, Tasmania, 1868. Reprint: PAHSMA, Port Arthur, 1991, p. 47.

33 No author, 'Penitentiary, Port Arthur', n.d. [ca. 1863], PWD266/1/1780, TA.

34 'Rules and Regulations for the new Separate Prison at Port Arthur', 7 February 1852, *Convict Discipline and Transportation*, British Parliamentary Papers, London, 1852–53 (1601)(1677), p. 26.

Figure 3.2. The confines of a separate prison cell, much like those used at the penitentiary. (PAHSMA 2020)

especially towards the close of settlement as the population in the penitentiary thinned markedly. Prisoners deemed well behaved immediately upon arrival could find themselves bypassing the separate prison stage of confinement and working in a skilled occupation.[35] There is also evidence to suggest that those in the penitentiary's separate cells were able to mix with the prisoners from the dormitories. In 1865, in a response to a series of questions, Civil Commandant Boyd remarked on the 'partial' classification available in the penitentiary, admitting that inter-mixture did occur at 'labour, exercise and chapel'.[36]

Boyd's admission raises many issues that relate to the function of the ablutions. For example, did the unavoidable association at exercise occur in the yards at the rear of the penitentiary? The divisions of the yards during the first phase suggests that some form of classification was intended. With the penitentiary housing convicts assigned to both heavy and light labour, it is likely that the divided yards allowed the retention of classificatory regimes while the convicts were at exercise or undertaking their ablutions. Documented references in 1861 to 'no. 1' and 'no. 2' yards behind the penitentiary support this assertion.[37] Classification of the yards may have helped navigate the prisoners through their daily routines, such as when the hundreds of men from the dormitory and separate cells needed to use the ablutions area at morning and evening.

The layout of the yards also suggests a purpose other than ordering the daily regime. Compared to the enclosed wedges of the separate prison exercise yards, which were largely bereft of fixtures, the penitentiary yards, with their fireplaces and shelters, provided more welcoming spaces. Until about 1862, even with no day room, the sheltered and heated yards would have presented a chance to escape uncomfortable weather. During the working week, only those convicts engaged in penitentiary duties would have had access to the yards, the remainder of the penitentiary workforce using the yards on a Sunday.

The completed ablutions area was asymmetrical in design, with the west yard 4 m longer than the east (Figure 4.21). This may have been a

35 Pearce, *The Features, Function and Significance of the Port Arthur Penitentiary*, p. 24.
36 'Interrogatories ... Penal Settlement, Pauper and Lunatics' Depot, Port Arthur, Tasman's Peninsula, 15 November 1865, CO 280/369, reel no.1966–67, p. 89.
37 Edward Cunningham, 9 December 1861, p. 144. Port Arthur Court Record Book 1861–1865, R.2007.60. TMAG.

practical response to existing design features. The portal and abutting ablutions structure were located in line with the entrance leading from the penitentiary. The position of this entrance was in turn governed by the need for a corridor leading directly from the penitentiary's clocktower entrance to the ablutions entry.

However, the reverse is also possible: that the design of the yards may have influenced the position of the passage and clocktower. This, in turn, may have been a response to the classification requirements. If occupied at capacity, the population of the dormitory was 2.6 times that of the separate accommodation. Translating this ratio into space, of the total yard area (485 square metres), about 130 square metres would be required for the men in separate confinement – which is the area provided by the southernmost of the western yards. Although this is not documented, it is possible that spatial calculations such as this were made prior to the conversion, informing the two very different sizes of the east and west yards and in turn affecting where the entrances to the penitentiary were placed. Just as feasibly, the yard sizes may not have been based on rigid calculations, but rather on a general desire to create one or two smaller yards (the eastern) for the reception of the separately confined men.

As discussed, the ca. 1862 conversion changed how convicts interacted with the space (Figure 4.53). The central structure stopped being where prisoners were forced to carry out ablution rituals in public, but rather an area where a measure of free time and relaxation could be had. With the removal of the ablution fixtures to the yards, there was an obvious improvement to the sanitary infrastructure. Originally, with 22 privies and urinals crammed into a small space, the environment of the ablutions block must have been highly unhygienic – particularly considering that waste was collected for use at the station's farm. The 27 lavatory basins packed behind the south of the laundry would have been no better, considering their lack of light and ventilation.

Fronted by timber latticework screens (Figure 2.26), the new facilities of Phase II were open to the air and, while no doubt colder and more exposed, would have provided more space and privacy, and most likely better sanitation

– although the waste was still being collected.[38] Regulations from this period stipulated that

> 169. The bath-room, lavatory, and latrines must be thoroughly cleansed daily, and the latter purified in warm weather[39]

Although the lattice-work did not allow complete privacy, the layout of the fixtures was an improvement upon the original ablutions block, the enclosed nature of which, combined with the constant supervision, stripped the prisoners of any semblance of privacy.

With the conversion of the central building to a day room, prisoners were given the space and opportunity to sit, read and smoke. Settlement regulations stated:

> It is his [the Station Officer's] duty to see that the prisoners, when not at labour, are placed under proper supervision to ensure their orderly conduct; public reading being carried on in each yard or in the day room whenever practicable.[40]

Evidently, the relaxation of the convict, and his betterment through reading, were actively encouraged when he was not at labour. Books for this purpose would have been made available from the penitentiary library, with convicts perusing works such as *Goldsmith's Grammar of Geography* and *Murray's English Grammar Simplified*, or taking in the fortifying words of the Holy Bible.[41]

Clay tobacco pipes

It was understood that a pipe to puff on neatly complemented the contemplative task of reading. The day room was one of the few places where

---

38   'Interrogatories … Penal Settlement, Pauper and Lunatics' Depot, Port Arthur, Tasman's Peninsula, 15 November 1865, CO 280/369, reel no. 1966–67, p. 87.

39   Convict Department, *Rules and Regulations for the Penal Settlement on Tasman's Peninsula*, Tasmania, 1868. Reprint: PAHSMA, Port Arthur, 1991, p. 27.

40   Convict Department, *Rules and Regulations for the Penal Settlement on Tasman's Peninsula*, Tasmania, 1868. Reprint: PAHSMA, Port Arthur, 1991, p. 20.

41   In 1874 a list of nearly 3,500 books held by the government at Port Arthur was forwarded to the Colonial Secretary's office. 'Catalogue of Reading Books of a Religious and Secular Character Belonging to the Government, at Port Arthur Tasman's Peninsula, 27 April 1874, CSD7/1476, TA.

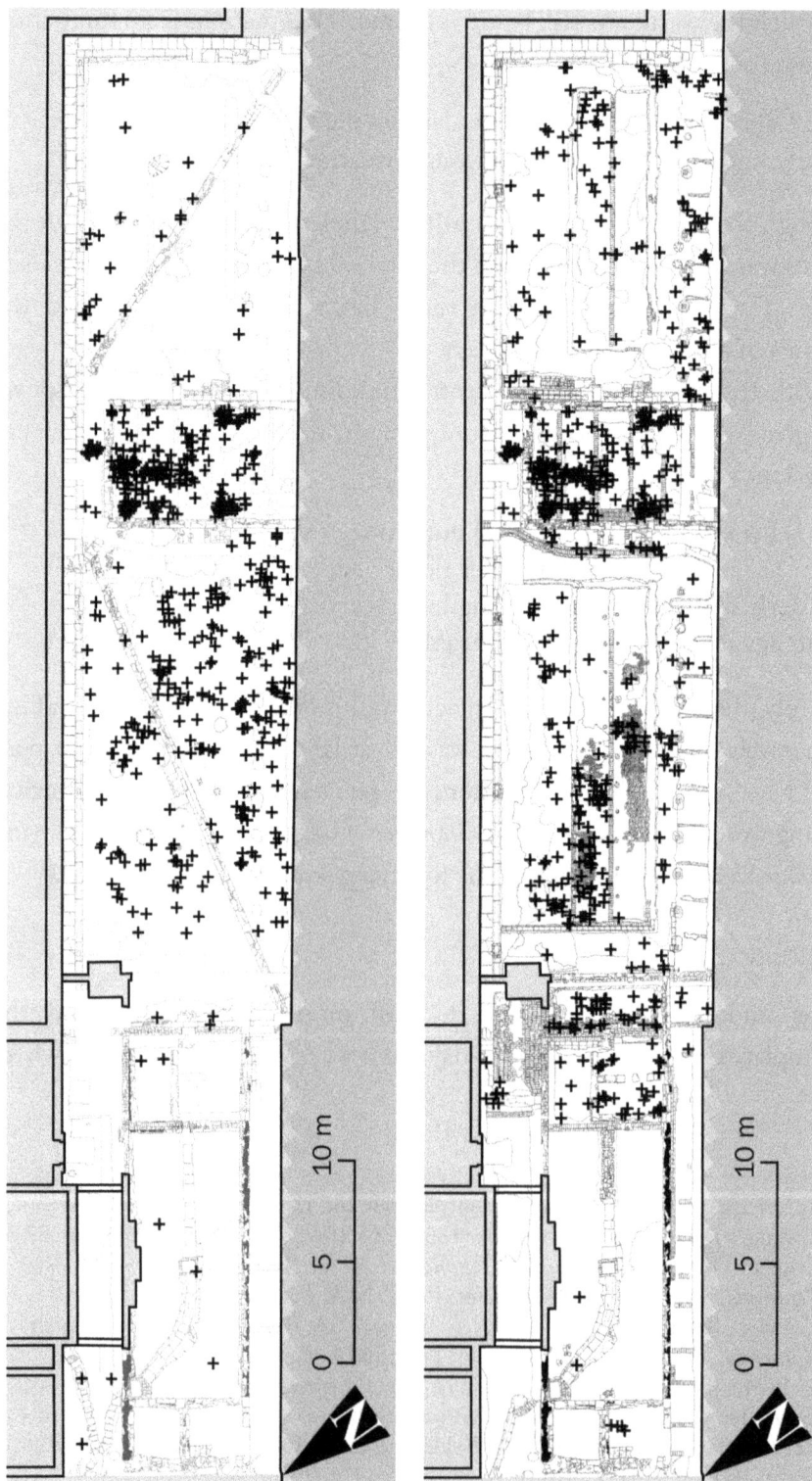

Figure 3.3. Distribution of clay smoking pipe finds during Phase I and Phase II. Excludes finds recovered from sieving.

the smoking of tobacco – only given to those convicts assigned to productive labour – was permitted.

> 315. smoking is not permitted in any part of the penitentiary except in the yards or day-room.[42]

Regulations of the period stipulated that convicts at hard and light labour were allowed 4 drams (7 grams) of tobacco (just enough to fill two pipe bowls) a day, seven days a week.[43] During the course of the excavation we recovered a large number of the kaolin clay tobacco pipes that were used to smoke this ration. All of these were fragments, comprising pieces of the stem or bowl. In total the convict-period deposits contained 1,972 pipe fragments, representing at least 923 individual pipes. As discussed at the start of this chapter, by far the largest number of fragments were recovered from the surfaces and deposits of the ablutions area, supporting the idea that in the 1850s through the 1870s smoking was not an illicit activity for prisoners to be engaged in.

As would be expected, prisoners took advantage of shelter and congregated around features like fireplaces, with concentrations of pipes found near these features in both phases of occupation. Although smoking in the laundry building was expressly against regulations, many pipe fragments were found in the eastern space of the laundry building, suggesting that the prisoners, at least during Phase II, had smoked tobacco while at work indoors (Figure 3.3). This raises the possibility that the small number of men took advantage of their position of trust to contravene the regulations. That, or the men working in this space were permitted the indulgence.

The manner by which convicts came by pipes and tobacco is interesting. As indicated by the high number of pipe fragments found, the clay pipe was a semi-disposable item, mass-manufactured and relatively easily replaceable. Archaeologists of 19th-century Australian history are well used to finding stems, bowls and – occasionally – entire pipes in their excavations.[44]

---

42   Convict Department, *Rules and Regulations for the Penal Settlement on Tasman's Peninsula*, Tasmania, 1868. Reprint: PAHSMA, Port Arthur, 1991, p. 46.

43   Convict Department, *Rules and Regulations for the Penal Settlement on Tasman's Peninsula*, Tasmania, 1868. Reprint: PAHSMA, Port Arthur, 1991, p. 56.

44   D. Gojak and I. Stuart, 'The Potential for the Archaeological Study of Clay Tobacco Pipes from Australian Sites', *Australasian Historical Archaeology*, Vol. 17, 1999, pp. 38–49, p. 38.

At Port Arthur we know that tobacco was a highly valued luxury item for at least the first two decades of settlement. Issued to convicts occupying skilled or trusted positions, it was withheld from most of the prisoners undergoing hard labour or punishment. Even the provision of tobacco to the 'deserving' few was stripped away in the early 1840s, when probation introduced much more stringent regulations that forbade its issue to prisoners. New regulations issued in 1843 stipulated 'Tobacco and every other luxury are strictly prohibited'.[45] However, by the time the flour mill was converted, changes to the station's regulatory environment evidently meant that the tobacco ration had been extended to include all but prisoners undergoing punishment.

This meant that the extent to which the station's authorities punished convicts for the possession of tobacco and the illicit smoking of pipes depended entirely on the period. This can be tested by looking at the records of the station's magistrates, who were responsible for hearing charges against prisoners and awarding punishments. We examined a sample of 4,600 individual charges brought against convicts who came before the magistrate between 1830 and 1850.[46] This showed over 250 cases of tobacco possession and over 80 involving smoking. Samuel Henderson was one such man, charged with 'Having tobacco improperly in his possession', receiving five days solitary confinement in 1838.[47] George Saxon was arraigned for receiving tobacco from the crew of the cutter *Charlotte* when it visited the station in 1835.[48] Joseph Smith received two days' solitary in 1839 for 'Smoking contrary to orders'.[49]

The regulated provision of tobacco to the majority of the convict population from the 1850s saw the number of prisoners brought before the magistrate on tobacco and smoking-related charges markedly decline. A sample of offence records from the period 1857–77 indicates that, of 503

---

45   'Regulations for the First stage of Convict Probation in Van Diemen's Land', October 1843, in: Eardley Eardley-Wilmot, Lieutenant Governor, to Lord Stanley, Secretary of State, 31 October 1843, *Convict Discipline and Transportation*, British Parliamentary Papers, London, 1845 [659], p. 12.

46   R. Tuffin, 'Port Arthur Conduct Record Offences, 1830–1868: Collective and Non-Collective Prisoner Offences', Armidale, 2020. https://hdl.handle.net/1959.11/29249.

47   Conduct record of Samuel Henderson, #371, *Claudine*, CON37/1/8, TA.

48   Conduct record of George Saxon, #591, *Woodlark*, CON37/1/8, TA.

49   Conduct record of Joseph Smith, #725, *Medway*, CON37/1/8, TA.

individual charges, the illegal possession of tobacco was recorded in only one instance, with two further charges related to smoking indoors.[50] In 1868 George Wilson was charged with smoking in the cells, while Thomas Fleming was caught doing the same in the dormitories in 1870.[51]

Tobacco could be issued as part of the ration, or acquired illegally from officers, military personnel and visitors. William Thompson, who served time at both Port Arthur and Coal Mines in the 1840s, recalled that for taking on private shoemaking work for the overseers he would get paid in tobacco.[52] George Saxon, mentioned above, got his 'fig of tobacco' from a visiting ship's crew. What is less clear is how prisoners received pipes. It is likely that pipes were treated the same as 'slops' (the clothing issued to prisoners) and were given out at set times during the year. The frequency of the issue is unknown, but the disposable nature of the pipes – as opposed to more hard-wearing boots or shirts – suggests that it probably occurred more often than clothing.

The disposability of the pipe evidently had its limits. From the 923 identified pipes, a small number (18, or 1.95 per cent) showed signs of having been reworked around the mouthpiece. This occurred when the stem of the pipe had broken, and instead of throwing the pipe away the smoker had tooled away the jagged edge of the break to form a new mouthpiece. Such a response, indicating a lack of available replacements for broken pipes, has also been noted at other prison sites.[53] However, the very small proportion of these reworked items suggests that supply at Port Arthur was generally frequent enough to replace broken pipes.

This supply was a matter for the Commissariat, which had charge of consumables at convict stations. When such goods were required, the Commissariat placed notices of tender in the local newspapers.[54] In one such 1856 advertisement, alongside the foodstuffs, oils and alcohol, was a request

---

50   CON94. Transcribed by Steve Torley for PAHSMA.
51   Conduct record of George Wilson, #227, CON94/1/1, TA; Conduct record of Thomas Fleming, #76, CON94/1/1, TA.
52   J. Clark, ed., *The Career of William Thompson, Convict*, Port Arthur, 2009, pp. 83, 86.
53   G. Hewitt, 'Defiance of Authority at Melbourne Gaol: Clay Tobacco Pipes Reworked, Curated and Then Discarded in Haste?', *Australasian Historical Archaeology*, Vol. 37, 2019, pp. 87–90.
54   *The Mercury*, 11 March 1865, p. 2. http://nla.gov.au/nla.news-article8831589.

Table 3.6. Distribution of artefacts (MNI) in the ablutions area derived from convict period deposits.

Maker	Number	%
William Murray, Glasgow	117	46%
Duncan McDougall, Glasgow	94	37%
David Miller, Liverpool	29	11%
Leonard Dobbin, Cork	7	3%
Thomas Whyte, Edinburgh	4	2%
J.G. Jones, Liverpool	1	0.40%
Thomas Davidson, Glasgow	1	0.40%
William Bearnelts (Willem Barends), Gouda	1	0.40%
William C. Wood & Sons, Glasgow	1	0.40%

for 'pipes, per gross' (a gross equating to 144 pipes).[55] Such orders indicate that pipes were imported to the settlement in large lots, brought down in the holds of vessels and stored until required.

The ultimate origin of 255 of the pipes was evident in surviving makers' marks (Table 3.6). All the makers were operational during the time the penitentiary was occupied, with the dominant pipe-making cities of Glasgow, Edinburgh and Liverpool well represented.[56]

Six pipe fragments recovered during the excavation supported the mass acquisition of pipes by a process of tender. These were found in association with the 1860s construction layers of the Phase II central shelter in the west yard and the day room, as well as a Phase II surfacing deposit in the east yard. The fragments were inscribed with the name of a Hobart tobacco retailer 'R.J. Edwards', as well as the name of his shop 'Honey Dew House', which was located in Liverpool Street (Figure 3.4). Edwards was listed in 1860 and 1861 as a successful tenderer to the convict department and was

---

55　'Objects – Clay tobacco pipe', *Sydney Living Museums*, https://sydneylivingmuseums.com.au/taxonomy/term/18636#object-109216.

56　Gojak and Stuart, 'The Potential for the Archaeological Study of Clay Tobacco Pipes from Australian Sites', p. 40.

Figure 3.4. Historic advertisement for R.J. Edwards' establishment in Hobart. ('R.J. Edwards, Wellington Bridge, Hobart Town', n.d., Tasmanian Archives)

by far the largest supplier. Edwards' supplied provisions including tobacco at 4 shillings 3 pence per pound and pipes at 1 shilling 10 pence per gross.[57]

The fact that tobacco pipes were issued from a centralised store suggests that they – like a prisoner's jacket or mess utensils – were non-tailored items attained through a process of random selection. Yet, as anybody who has seen these pipes knows, they were often highly decorated objects that could be used to carry overt (and sometimes covert) political and social messages through the motifs embossed on the pipe's bowl. At a penal station where hierarchies were supposedly set by the authorities, uncontrolled access to such accessories may have given the prisoner the ability to signal status or particular affiliations.

During the excavation we recovered fragments from 225 different clay pipes that retained signs of decoration (Plate 3.1). The majority of these were from the bowl of the pipe, which was commonly where the decoration was situated. These decorated bowl fragments accounted for just over half of the total number of bowl fragments recovered (434). This tells us that decorated pipes were relatively common at Port Arthur.

A variety of styles of decoration were found, from maritime-themed pipes, depicting a ship or an anchor, to stylised vegetation, faces or figures.

---

57   *The Hobart Town Daily Mercury*, 3 March 1860, p. 4.

Figure 3.5. Pipes bearing the British and American flags. (PAHMSA 2016)

The largest number were generic fluted pipes, with the bowls marked by a series of ridges. A number related to specific places, such as the three-legged triskelion motif of the Isle of Man, or the pipes recovered bearing the Union Jack on one side and the American flag on the other.

This latter design can be dated with some certainty to the period from 1862 (Figure 3.5). Although neither of the flags on these pipes is historically accurate, the American flag most closely represents the 15-star 'Star Spangled Banner' design in use between 1795 and 1810, while the British flag aligns with the 'Kings Colours' of the Kingdom of Great Britain (1707–1801). This suggests that the pipes may have commemorated the 50th anniversary of the War of 1812 – a conflict between the United States and the United Kingdom, its American colonies (later Canada) and its Native American allies. Similarly, a number of pipes were recovered which bore the heads of Britain's great hero – Arthur Wellesley, the Duke of Wellington – and his French nemesis – Napoleon Bonaparte – on opposing sides of the bowl. These pipes were issued to mark the 50th anniversary, in 1865, of the Battle of Waterloo.

Pipes were likely imported to the settlement as mixed lots, and decorated pipes were probably not an uncommon sight. While they included an array of different motifs, none of the pipes represented designs that would have been considered overtly threatening to the established order – as for example

Irish motifs or slogans would have. This was also noted in an assemblage from a 1970s excavation of the Port Arthur prisoners' barracks.[58] Pipes may have been sorted upon delivery, ensuring that any controversial messages did not get through to the prisoners. However, if a prisoner or group of prisoners wished to attach value or meaning to a certain style of pipe, there was little that the authorities could do – other than restrict their access to it.

Tokens

We have somewhat surprising evidence for prisoners attaching illicit meaning to what were effectively everyday objects through another class of artefact. Excavation in the ablutions and laundry areas found 70 tokens scattered across the yards and in the subfloor deposits of the central structure (Plate 3.2). Fashioned from lead, copper alloy and ceramic, these tokens were either square or circular, with the vast majority of the metal ones having a cross or saltire inscribed on one face. In a neat subversion of the government mark, a number of small lead tokens bore the broad arrow stamp.

While we can't be sure what these tokens were used for, it is evident that they were manufactured by the prisoners from materials acquired at the station. The ceramic tokens were made from sherds of plates and bowls sourced from the rubbish pits of the officers, filed down to form rough circles and squares. The lead and copper was likely pilfered from the nearby workshops and cut down to size using a pair of similarly purloined shears. We found several rolls of lead in the deposits of the ablutions central structure, from which such tokens may have been clipped.

Eight of the tokens (both lead and ceramic) were recovered from the mixed deposits within the central structure, with a further 12 predominantly from the Phase II deposits of the east yard (Figure 3.6). The remainder were from the western yard, of which the majority were found in the topsoil layers covering the site. Found in discrete concentrations, it is possible that these tokens had been secreted in the timber superstructure of the yard's central shelter (Plate 3.3). Upon the shelter's demolition, the tokens fell to the ground and were covered by silt and rubble.

---

58   A. Dane and R. Morrison, *Clay Pipes from Port Arthur 1830–1877: A Descriptive Account of the Clay Pipes from Maureen Byrne's 1977–78 Excavations at Port Arthur, Southeast Tasmania*, Canberra, 1979.

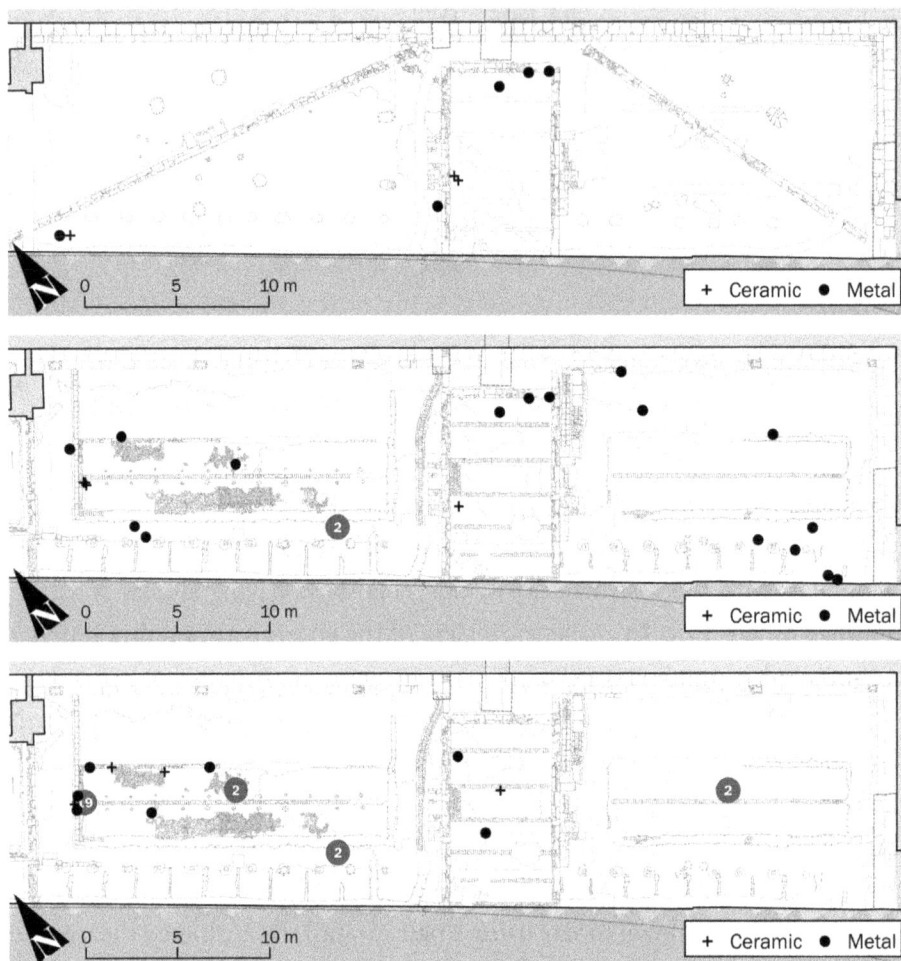

Figure 3.6. Distribution of tokens during Phase I (top), Phase II (middle) and recovered from post-1877 deposits (bottom). Circled numbers denote finds recovered during sieving.

What the tokens suggest are activities centred around gaming or gambling, both of which were in direct contravention of the settlement's rules and regulations. One of the games the men might have played was Nine Men's Morris, a game dating back to prehistoric times (Figure 3.7). Handily the board can be scratched onto any surface. The board could also be drawn on linen, the perfect medium for men trying to keep their activity secret; the bag could be whipped up, tokens and all, at the first sign of a guard.

Evidence of gaming may also be found in the buttons that were found scattered across the yard surfaces, with at least one bearing an inscribed cross like the metal tokens (Plate 3.4). These items may have been lost off prison

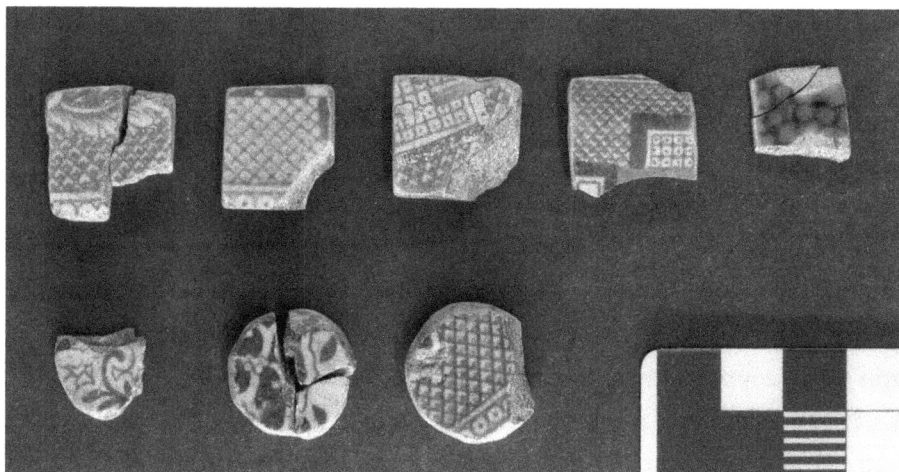

Figure 3.7. A number of ceramic tokens recovered from the excavation. (PAHMSA 2016)

uniforms before rolling underneath the timber floors of the ablutions buildings or being lost in the gravel of the yard. However, such items could easily have been repurposed to serve as tokens in lieu of their ceramic or lead counterparts.

Offence records from the 1860s and 1870s contain a number of examples of convicts being arraigned for gambling. Prisoners Michael Langley and Thomas McCranny both received an additional four months' hard labour for gambling in 1866.[59] Another convict, John White, was charged in May 1865 of strong suspicion of gambling with fellow prisoner Michael Murphy.[60] Found in a locked shed in the workshops, Murphy was searched and six copper tokens were found in his possession.[61] In 1863 William Smith was sentenced to hard labour for attempting to obtain tobacco by trading five imitation coins he had made by filing down metal buttons.[62]

---

59   Michael Langley, #116, CON 94/1/1, p. 116, TA; Thomas McCranny, #138, CON 94/1/1, p. 138, TA. Transcribed by Steve Torley for PAHSMA.

60   Conduct record of John White, #814, *Eliza*, CON37/1/8, TA; Conduct record of Michael Murphy, #2566, Fairlie, CON37/1/9, TA.

61   John White, *Eliza* (4), 11 May 1865, Port Arthur Court Record Book 1861–1865, R.2007.60. TMAG, p. 1109.

62   William Smith, #2496, *Emerald Isle*, 3 December 1863. Port Arthur Court Record Book 1861–1865, R.2007.60. TMAG, p. 775.

Buttons

What of the humble button? During the excavation of the ablutions and laundry areas we found 426 buttons (156 in ablutions; 270 in the laundry). In the ablutions area the buttons were predominantly recovered from the yard surfaces (from all phases of penitentiary occupation), as well as from the mixed deposits of the central structure (Figures 4.61 and 4.72). In the laundry the overwhelming number (263) were found in the eastern rooms of the structure. The buttons were made from a variety of materials: bone (279), iron (115), copper alloy (7), wood (5), shell (5) and porcelain (3).

Previous analysis of buttons recovered from convict sites (including Port Arthur) indicates that most of the buttons we recovered were 'government issue' – that is, they derived from pieces of uniform issued to the convicts during their time at the penal station.[63] These types are identified as bone, copper alloy and iron sew-through (three- and four-hole), as well as copper alloy shanked. In total, 332 (78 per cent) buttons were identifiable as government issue: in the ablutions, 95 (61 per cent of the total buttons found), and in the laundry, 227 (84 per cent). A number of iron buttons in the ablutions (37, or 24 per cent) and laundry (14, or 5 per cent) were unidentifiable due to corrosion.

These buttons had been attached to the jackets, trousers, shirts and waistcoats that had been issued to convicts when they first arrived at Port Arthur. The slops (uniform) that they wore were an important part of the classification system, allowing the authorities to deduce from a glance the status of the convict. As discussed, from 1833 all newly arrived convicts wore a yellow uniform, with well-behaved men provided with grey or blue outfits (Plate 3.5).[64] Men sentenced to work in chains wore the yellow uniform, but with the word 'Felon' stamped upon it. By the late 1830s the parti-coloured

---

63 S. George, 'Unbuttoned: Archaeological Perspectives on Convicts and Whalers' Clothing in Nineteenth Century Tasmania', Honours Thesis, LaTrobe University, 1999.

64 'Standing Instructions for the Regulation of the Penal Settlement on Tasman's Peninsula', January 1833, CSO1/639/14383, TA.

(yellow and black) uniform was being issued to convicts working in chain gangs.[65] These men were generally worked at the hardest forms of labour.

During the probation period (1840s) the convicts' clothing began to be marked with their prisoner number.[66] A visitor to Port Arthur in 1842, David Burn, recalled seeing the men ranked up in church in 'their yellow raiment (or half-black, half-yellow), with P.A., and their respective numbers stamped in various parts'.[67] Men continued to be issued with yellow or parti-coloured uniforms upon arrival, with the grey later given to men who had satisfactorily served 2/3 of their sentence.[68] Every six months they would be issued a new jacket, trousers, waistcoat, shirt, pair of boots and cap.[69] This arrangement continued until the close of the settlement, with regulations from 1857 and 1868 stipulating that the convict had to be dressed according to their class:

> all first convicted men are to be dressed in grey, and also such men as may be under sentences not exceeding 3 years; all others are to wear yellow or parti-colour ...[70]

Settlement regulations made it clear that the convict was responsible for the care of his uniform. As early as 1831, punishment awaited those who 'shall

---

65   'Questions and answers relating to the Condition of Convicts in Van Diemen's Land', 1837, Enclosure No. 2, *Copy of a despatch from Lieut.-Governor Sir John Franklin, to Lord Glenelg*, British Parliamentary Papers, London 1837–38, [309], p. 28; M. Forster, Chief Police Magistrate, to J. Montagu, Colonial Secretary, 14 January 1839, British Parliamentary Papers, *Secondary Punishment*, London, 1841 [412], p. 83.

66   'Regulations for the First stage of Convict Probation in Van Diemen's Land', October 1843, in: E. Eardley-Wilmot, Lieutenant Governor, to Lord Stanley, Secretary of State, 31 October 1843, *Convict Discipline and Transportation*, British Parliamentary Papers, London, 1845 [659], p. 15.

67   Burn, *An Excursion to Port Arthur in 1842*, p. 17.

68   'Regulations for the Penal Settlement of Port Arthur', 1845, in: E. Eardley-Wilmot, Lieutenant Governor, to Lord Stanley, Secretary of State, 3 October 1845, *Convict Discipline and Transportation*, British Parliamentary Papers, London, 1846 [402], p. 29.

69   'Regulations for the Penal Settlement of Port Arthur', 1845, in: E. Eardley-Wilmot, Lieutenant Governor, to Lord Stanley, Secretary of State, 3 October 1845, *Convict Discipline and Transportation*, British Parliamentary Papers, London, 1846 [402], p. 30.

70   Convict Department, *Rules and Regulations for the Penal Settlement on Tasman's Peninsula*, Tasmania, 1868. Reprint: PAHSMA, Port Arthur, 1991, p. 39; Convict Department, 'Rules and Regulations', 15 December 1857, in: CO280/341, reel 746, no. 77, TA.

wilfully destroy, waste, damage, lose through neglect, or make away with without leave, any Article of Clothing'.[71] From 1845 the regulations stated that convicts were expected to 'appear as clean in his person and dress as circumstances will admit', with punishment for those who damaged, gave away or exchanged clothing articles.[72] Such requirements carried through to the last years of settlement, with order 275 of the 1868 regulations specifying that prisoners were to keep their clothing 'clean and repaired'.[73]

Convicts undoubtedly experienced difficulty in keeping their uniform in good order, given the nature of the labour they were forced to do. William Thompson, when sent to Coal Mines in the 1840s, recollected:

> The clothing also was not sufficient for the rough work we had to do
> ... most of us were indecent in appearance, and it was laughable to
> see us on muster in the square in front of the chapel. We were truly
> a ragged army.[74]

Clothing was supplied by the ordnance department, who had it shipped from Britain. The quality and regularity of the supply could be variable.[75] In 1840 Commandant Booth reported the state of the convicts' uniforms was 'very bad' due to supply delays, with 600 men in need of trousers and another 497 of jackets.[76] At the boys' reformatory of Point Puer, they got around this problem by making their own clothing.[77] This was not immediately replicated at Port Arthur, with convict tailors predominantly repairing

---

71 'J. Mahon, Commandant, 23 August 1831, CSO1/553/12027, TA.
72 'Regulations for the Penal Settlement of Port Arthur', 1845, in: E. Eardley-Wilmot, Lieutenant Governor, to Lord Stanley, Secretary of State, 3 October 1845, *Convict Discipline and Transportation*, British Parliamentary Papers, London, 1846 [402], p. 30.
73 Convict Department, *Rules and Regulations for the Penal Settlement on Tasman's Peninsula*, Tasmania, 1868. Reprint: PAHSMA, Port Arthur, 1991, p. 40.
74 Clark, *The Career of William Thompson, Convict*, p. 79.
75 C.J. La Trobe, 'Copy of a Despatch from C.J. La Trobe Esq., Acting Governor of Van Diemen's Land, to Earl Grey', 31 May 1847, *Convict Discipline and Transportation*, British Parliamentary Papers, London, 1847–48, (941), pp. 36, 44.
76 Charles O'Hara Booth, Commandant, to Comptroller General to Matthew Forster, Acting Colonial Secretary, 16 May 1840, CSO5/240/6220, TA.
77 W. Champ, Comptroller General, to E. Eardley-Wilmot, 1 August 1846, *Convict Discipline and Transportation*, British Parliamentary Papers, London, 1847, [785], p. 121.

uniforms, or making clothing for the officers.[78] From the 1860s, however, the men appear to have been more involved in the manufacture of their own uniforms, producing and repairing all manner of clothing items: jackets, trousers (including with a button fly for fitting chains), shirts, braces, caps, belts and even ankle pads for wearing chains.[79]

Like the uniforms themselves, the raw material for such manufacturing had originally been supplied from Britain. During the probation period there were increasing calls to support and grow local manufacturing. By 1850 women in the Female Factory, Hobart, were manufacturing cloth that was being used to make uniforms for the male convicts.[80] However, buttons appear to have continued to be imported from Britain, with no evidence that the convicts were ever involved in the manufacture of these items.

Punishing convicts for improper and unkempt uniforms had a twofold purpose: to ensure that the prisoner population was visually classified and to damp down the illicit trade networks inside the station. Access to spare clothing, through theft either from stores or from other people, provided the prisoner with a means of barter and, sometimes, income. As the examples above indicate, even innocuous items like buttons could be used for gambling or trade. Prisoners could therefore receive seemingly harsh punishments for contravening these regulations. In July 1849 two men, John Lee and John Press, received time in the solitary cells for altering their clothing.[81] William Bigbee was sentenced to hard labour in February 1851 for the same offence.[82] William Thompson, placed in the shoemakers' and tailors' shop at Coal Mines, managed to maintain a steady income of tobacco by taking apart black and yellow trousers:

---

78 Charles O'Hara Booth, 17th February 1842, 'Yearly Return of Work performed by Mechanics and Laborers at Port Arthur Tasman's Peninsula from the 1st December 1840 to 30th November 1841', CSO49/1/8, TA.

79 For example see: Report of the Civil Commandant, 30 July 1863, Enclosure E, 'Return showing the number and description of all articles of clothing made during the year ending 30th June 1863', CO280/360, no. 83, reel 2977, TA.

80 W. Denison, Lieutenant Governor, to Earl Grey, Secretary of State, 31 January 1850, *Convict Discipline and Transportation*, British Parliamentary Papers, London, 1850, [January], p. 96.

81 John Lee, *Anson*, John Press, *Lord Goderich*, 16 July 1849. Port Arthur Police Court Records 1847–51, D17, Mitchell Library, State Library of New South Wales (ML), p. 425.

82 William Bigbee, #7548, *Moffat* (3), 10 February 1851. Port Arthur police court records 1847–51, D17, ML, p. 536.

making the black cloth into black trousers, and the yellow into yellow ones, and by using an old red coat of the soldiers … he would have a pair of good regimental trousers … These would be sold to the soldiers.[83]

Alcohol

Another offence that appeared in the records was drunkenness – among both the free constabulary of the station and the prisoner population. As with smoking and gambling, drinking by convicts had attracted censure since the earliest days. Although alcohol was a prohibited item for the prisoners, the fact that free officers and military personnel had access to it meant that it entered the station's black-market economy. Prisoners employed in positions of trust, such as those working in the stores or at the hospital, also had increased access. As such, a number of prisoners were brought before the magistrate during the 1830s and 1840s for being drunk.

In a sample of charges brought against convicts during this period, only 13 related to drunkenness – from over 4,700 separate arraignments. This would suggest that, while it was not unknown at the settlement, stringent regulations and their enforcement kept alcohol consumption at a low level – or, at least, out of sight of the authorities. The same could not quite be said of the 1860s and 1870s, where out of only 500 arraignments, 15 related to drunkenness.

The record of the Port Arthur magistrates' bench book between 1861 and 1865 similarly recorded alcohol-fuelled behaviour. Prisoner James Squires drank a bottle of cider and was found drunk near the penitentiary.[84] John Sullivan, when charged with being under the influence of liquor, claimed a soldier had given him a glass of beer.[85] Other men, when admitted back into the penitentiary after a day's work, similarly blamed members of the military for the provision of liquor.[86]

That the prisoners had access to alcohol was reflected in the number and distribution of alcohol-related objects in the ablutions and laundry areas. Over

---

83 Clark, *The Career of William Thompson, Convict*, p. 86.
84 James Squires, 10 April 1862, p. 294. Port Arthur Court Record Book 1861–1865, R.2007.60. TMAG.
85 John Sullivan, 3 February 1862, p. 212. Port Arthur Court Record Book 1861–1865, R.2007.60. TMAG.
86 James Bridge, 17 February 1863, p. 589; Daniel Connors, 27 June 1863, p. 681. Port Arthur Court Record Book 1861–1865, R.2007.60. TMAG.

160 such objects were identified (from over 720 fragments) and included pieces of beer, wine, gin, ginger beer and even champagne bottles (Plate 3.6). These were scattered throughout all the convict-period layers relating to the occupation of the penitentiary and were situated in all the significant spaces – both open yard areas and enclosed structures. All of these objects entered the archaeological record through breakage, with none found intact.

We should be cautious, however, about immediately associating such material with the act of drinking. In 1862, prisoner John Springall was charged with giving away lamp oil.[87] As part of the evidence it was stated that another prisoner had provided Springall with an empty bottle sourced from a 'dirt heap' (rubbish pile). Such evidence does indicate that bottles that had once held alcohol may have been routinely reused for such purposes, reminding us that we should always be careful when using material culture as absolute evidence of an activity – particularly when that activity was considered illicit. Of course, it also went the other way too, with evidence that alcohol was secreted in less suspicious bottles.[88]

Archaeology of the unexplainable

What, therefore, should we make of these artefacts? Of the yard-trampled fragments of clay tobacco pipe, or the accumulations of buttons in the laundry? What of the presence of alcohol containers throughout the laundry and ablutions areas? From what we know of the history, we simply would not expect to find these objects in such abundance. Our challenge is to understand and explain not *what* they were, but *why* they were deposited in the first place.

Some artefacts can be more readily explained than others. We can understand the reason for the deposition of timber and leather offcuts within the reclamation fills, or the accumulation of architectural debris within deposits associated with construction and reconstruction. Go to any work site today and you will see the same patterns of discard occurring. The high

---

87   John Springall, 15 April 1862, p. 306. Port Arthur Court Record Book 1861–1865, R.2007.60. TMAG.
88   John Robinson, 1 January 1863, p. 558. Port Arthur Court Record Book 1861–1865, R.2007.60. TMAG.

number of buttons and the presence of sewing paraphernalia in one of the spaces of the laundry could be linked to the loss of working materials – either accidental or deliberate.

The presence of high numbers of other types of artefacts in supposedly controlled areas, particularly the exercise yards, shelters and ablutions area day room is more challenging to understand. At the start of this chapter and throughout this book we have mentioned the clay tobacco pipes, food and drink containers, clothing and personal items that ended up broken and scattered across the surfaces and within spaces. What processes led to such patterns of deposition, particularly in the restricted setting of a prison within a prison? As Australian archaeologist Denis Gojak points out, such environments are 'not generally conducive to the retention of unauthorised archaeological evidence'.[89]

At Port Arthur the established rules and regulations tried to create an environment that discouraged the accrual and survival of material culture. One way this was done was by heavily controlling the acquisition, possession and use of material things:

> 187. Prisoners are not to have in their possession any article or thing whatever, either of food, clothing, or otherwise, except such as shall have been properly issued to them, or sanctioned by the Commandant.[90]

Documentary records indicate that this attempt to control extended to the convicts' interactions with station and non-station personnel, the tools and raw materials used in their labour, the products of that labour, and even the convicts' interaction with the natural environment. However, these same records also speak of the porosity of these regulatory barriers, revealing a constant flow of non-sanctioned goods trafficked between prisoners and between the prisoners and their guards.

Such documented activity perhaps explains how convicts may have attained the lead or ceramic to make their gaming tokens. What eludes our analysis is the act that led to the object's deposition and the environment

---

89   D. Gojak, 'Convict Archaeology in New South Wales: An Overview of the Investigation, Analysis and Conservation of Convict Heritage Sites', *Australasian Historical Archaeology*, Vol. 19, 2001, pp. 73–83.

90   Convict Department, 'Rules and Regulations', 15 December 1857, in: CO280/341, reel 746, no. 77, TA, p. 40.

that permitted it to remain in a situation for us to recover it. We are not looking wholly at simplistic explanations of loss or discard. This was a penal environment, where everyday objects took on new meaning and significance. As we have shown, the presence of smoking paraphernalia had different meaning depending upon what phase of occupation they related to: are clay tobacco pipe fragments evidence of illicit or licit behaviour? In the archaeological record the presence of the non-regulated smoker is near-impossible to separate from that of the licit smoker. Similar questions surround the alcohol containers and buttons. Can they all be the discarded evidence of the everyday? Are they all evidence of subaltern lives? Clearly, neither is the case, but we will always be missing the explanatory link between the historic act of deposition and the entry of such objects into our records and reports.

In examining the exercise yards of the ablutions area, we have looked at the distribution of clay tobacco pipes and buttons to suggest that prisoners may have congregated near shelters. This rather obvious statement tells us little about the lives of the convicts – other than that they liked being near a warm fire and under a roof. Similarly, the concentration of artefacts in the Phase 11 day room indicated a similar penchant for heat and shelter. Such functional analyses become more challenging when we begin to question why these objects were there in the first place.

As we have already suggested with the buttons, the loss or discard of objects was freighted with additional consequences of censure and punishment at Port Arthur. Does the scattering of such items across the exercise yards and within the day room subfloor deposits indicate indifferent attitudes toward the power of the authorities? Does it represent wilful acts of uniform sabotage? Did all such buttons become tokens for gaming or gambling? Or are we seeing evidence of accidental loss en masse? We simply don't know.

Historic evidence suggests that, if nothing else, the convict system was tidy. Prisoners labouring as 'scavengers' cleaned buildings, cleared drains, swept yards, emptied fireplaces. Their role was enshrined within rules and regulations, with laxity attracting the censorious notation of 'neglect of duty' in magistrate bench books. Regulations issued in 1857 stipulated that the station must be kept 'clean and tidy', with officers in charge of the penitentiary charged with enforcing 'habits of order and cleanliness' in all areas – including the yards and ablutions buildings.[91] Scavengers daily scoured the penitentiary itself, which was 'swept and dusted' every Sunday.

Given such cleaning regimes were in place, why do we see what is effectively rubbish scattered in such quantities in all phases of the penitentiary's occupation? Over 430 fragments of clay tobacco pipe were found on the Phase I surfaces of the west and east yards in the ablutions area. Over 300 fragments were found on the looser gravels from Phase II. In both phases the pipe fragments were accompanied by hundreds of fragments of glass (window and bottle) and hardware components (predominantly nails).

While construction, reconstruction and abandonment events may explain the presence of hardware and architectural elements (particularly due to the exposure of the site post-1877), it is more difficult to explain the presence of objects like the clay tobacco pipes. That their deposition resulted from the use of these spaces is clear, but their continued presence on actively used surfaces is enigmatic. It suggests a failure of the regulations that guided the lives of the prisoners, with yards slowly accumulating the detritus of day-to-day usage. Is this the 'yawning gulf between the rhetoric of institutions and what actually transpired'?[92]

It is therefore the circumstances and survival of these objects which give us the greatest pause. They are common objects that, by the very act of their being, suggest to us much deeper stories than the historical or archaeological record allows. We can theorise about the reasons they made it to the archaeological record – lax supervision, or even wilful acts of mass uncleanliness – but we are surprised by their prevalence. Just as convicts can occasionally be glimpsed in the surviving illustrations and photographs of Port Arthur's penitentiary, so too do the artefacts and the spaces created by and for the convicts allow us a brief – if often enigmatic – insight into lives and labours otherwise lost to time.

---

91   Convict Department, 'Rules and Regulations', 15 December 1857, in: CO280/341, reel 746, no. 77, TA, pp. 19, 30.
92   P. Crook and T. Murray, *An Archaeology of Institutional Refuge: The Material Culture of the Hyde Park Barracks, Sydney, 1848–1886*, Sydney: Historic Houses Trust of New South Wales 2006.

Chapter 4

ILLUSTRATED SUMMARY OF THE ARCHAEOLOGICAL INVESTIGATIONS

The following section provides a detailed summary of the archaeological excavations that took place within the penitentiary precinct between 2013 and 2016. Alongside the historical research, these investigations provided the foundation upon which the preceding discussion about the precinct's development and use was built. This illustrated summary can be read in association with the preceding discussion, or as a standalone account of the archaeological investigations.

The archaeological results and interpretation are described in chronological fashion, starting with the earliest features encountered during the excavations and ending with the post-1877 impacts upon the site. The discussion necessarily concentrates on the features and deposits that were encountered, linking these to the narrative of the area's development. The artefacts are broadly characterised throughout, but are discussed in more detail in 'Private lives in public spaces'.

Why the excavations were needed

Archaeological engagement with the penitentiary precinct first dates back to 1976, when Maureen Byrne excavated two trenches to locate the footings of the former waterwheel (Figure 4.1).[1] Since that time, the investigations in the area have primarily been associated with conservation works in the area of the separate cells, along the front of the building and in the area of the watchmen's quarters. Limited research excavations were carried out in 2003 and 2004 in the area of the ablutions, workshops and muster ground. In all cases the trenches were only excavated to the first appearance of the convict-era stratigraphy.

What these four decades of archaeological investigation proved was the potential of the area to yield new and relevant information on the development of Port Arthur and the lifecourses of its unfree and free inhabitants. As demonstrated by the historical outline, it is clear that we already knew a lot about Port Arthur and the penitentiary area thanks to a rich documentary archive. Through wider studies into the history of convict Australia, we were also able to situate Port Arthur within its colonial and British context, helping us understand why and how the penal station and the Tasman Peninsula developed as it did.

The catalyst for the excavations from 2013 was the need to stabilise the penitentiary building following the results of structural tests indicating it had significant weaknesses.[2] However, the excavations were no mere mitigation exercise. While recognising that the impact of stabilisation works would impact subsurface deposits, the program of excavation was devised to capitalise upon an opportunity to conduct a research and interpretation project. The 2013 excavations responded primarily to research imperatives and not mitigation ones. The mitigation works carried out in 2014 were, to some extent, insurance, but in general monitored features that would have been unsafe to investigate without the full apparatus of safe building techniques: shoring, scaffolding and the like. Favouring research over reactive monitoring provided us with a real opportunity to engage with little-studied and under-interpreted aspects of the penal station's past. The research value of the investigations was therefore

---

1   A. Matic, D. Roe, S. Szydzik, A. Waghorn, N. Corbett, and E.J. Harris, 'Technical Report. Archaeological Investigations and Monitoring. Penitentiary Precinct Conservation Project, 2012–2014', Port Arthur: PAHSMA, 2019, p. 42.

2   R.D. Barnes, G. Lume, J. Scott, and L.Burke-Smith, *Stabilisation of an Icon: The Penitentiary Precinct Conservation Project, Port Arthur, Tasmania, Australia*, Port Arthur: PAHSMA, n.d.

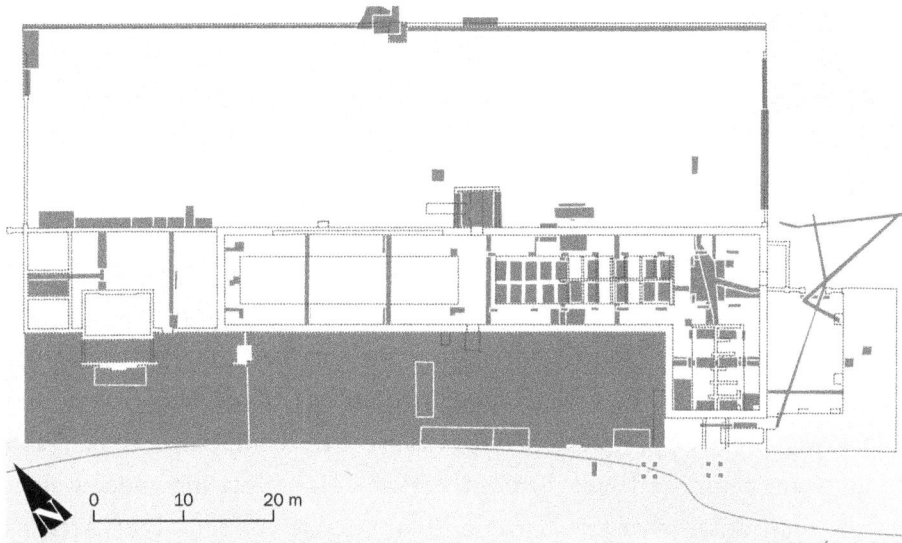

Figure 4.1. Map showing locations (shaded areas) where archaeological investigations have been carried out between 1976 and 2016.

placed at the foreground of the program, undertaken well in advance of critical path conservation works, and guided by a series of research objectives.

These objectives were centred upon six key questions concerning the development of the penal station, its place in the colonial transportation project and the effect that it had upon the lives of its unfree and free inhabitants. These six areas of enquiry were:

- the modification of the pre-1830 environment and landforms

- the presence and condition of pre-1842 subsurface features and deposits

- the development of the Mason Cove waterfront during the convict period

- the structural evolution of the flour mill and granary/penitentiary structure and what it suggests about convict labour regimes

- how the designers of the penitentiary used space to impose surveillance regimes.

With historically documented occupation of the area dating to the early 1830s, the area contained the potential to demonstrate how the waterfront was adapted to the early and ongoing needs of settlement. In particular, how the natural topography was modified as the area's use changed during the 1830s and 1840s. This aspect of early settlement is little demonstrated at Port Arthur, with later reclamation works from 1854 having erased much evidence of the original waterfront. Much early evidence of landscape adaptation and modifications on Settlement Hill have similarly been lost to the later convict period development.

The precinct also contained the potential to tell us more about the development and form of the mill, granary and treadwheel. No plans or detailed descriptions exist demonstrating the internal arrangement of the complex, particularly how waterwheel, treadwheel, machinery, stores and offices were situated. Even external depictions of the complex are limited and contain only minimal detail; there is therefore a risk of placing undue weight on the illustrations that are available. Like evidence of early Port Arthur's waterfront, the form of the mill complex was largely overprinted by later modifications. With the building largely telling the precinct's post-1854 story, archaeological evidence of transformation processes would similarly bolster our limited understanding of how the large retrofitting task was carried out.

Archaeological investigation also promised to provide insight into the hidden stories of Port Arthur. While the excavations of 2013–15 were by necessity targeted investigations that provided discrete windows into the past and focused on structural changes rather than behaviour, a different strategy of investigation was adopted for the 2016 excavations of the ablutions and laundry. Here the deposits of two complete areas were excavated and spaces were uncovered in their entirety: the rooms and yards where prisoner and overseer spent their days. The material record of these spaces, including artefacts and the structure of the spaces themselves, potentially contained evidence that speaks to the experience of its inhabitants and especially the illicit and/or secretive behaviours that are hidden to the historical record. They could tell us also about the more mundane aspects of unfree life – the drudgery of work, the boredom of incarceration, the daily routines – not often touched upon by history or modern interpretation.

Placing the excavation in context

Port Arthur has a long tradition of archaeological investigation. Maureen Byrne's 1976 investigation of the penitentiary waterwheel pit was one of the first times that archaeological methodology had been applied to a convict site in Australia. Byrne followed this up the following year with a larger-scale excavation of the Port Arthur prisoners' barracks.[3] Situated alongside excavations carried out on historic sites by the University of Sydney, these investigations at Port Arthur were some of the first historical archaeological excavations in Australia.[4]

The role of historical archaeology in understanding Australia's convict past continues to this day. As archaeologists we occupy a privileged position, able to use the written record, but party to forms of evidence that made it nowhere near the page. For us, the document is often a marker of *intent*, while the physicality of space and material record demonstrates the *actuality*.[5] From the items lost and discarded two centuries ago we can learn about the everyday patterns of life perhaps deemed too trivial to record: diets, health and welfare, the action of trade and exchange networks, the products and processes of labour, or even ephemeral and undetected acts of agency. Combined with the study of the space within which the material culture is found, we can also begin to look at the relationship of people to space and place: who was using what space, for what purpose and when. This becomes particularly interesting when looking at the supposedly controlled confines of penal places, where the convicts (and even the free) had limited influence on the objects, spaces and people they interacted with.

---

3   D'Gluyas et al. 'Everyday Artefacts', p. 130.
4   I. Jack, 'Historical Archaeology, Heritage and the University of Sydney', *Australasian Historical Archaeology*, Vol. 24, 2006, pp. 19–24.
5   After S. Lenik, 'Mission Plantations, Space, and Social Control: Jesuits as Planters in French Caribbean Colonies and Frontiers', *Journal of Social Archaeology*, Vol. 12, No. 1, 2012, pp. 52, 53.

Historical archaeologists have examined many different types of convict place. Of these, sites of incarceration have been the most dominant.[6] For example, excavations of the Ross Female Factory (1848–5), Tasmania, targeted the factory's dormitory and cell spaces.[7] In New South Wales, much work has occurred on assemblages recovered from the subfloor spaces of Hyde Park Barracks.[8] Excavations have also been undertaken of the Parramatta male convict barracks (1819–33).[9] In Western Australia, a suite of archaeological work has taken place on Fremantle Prison (1855–1991), a contemporary to Port Arthur's penitentiary, as well as on a series of former convict depots.[10] Investigations of colonial institutions, such as Old Melbourne Gaol (1851–1923) and Pentridge Prison (1850–1997), Melbourne, have provided information about contemporary incarceration practices.[11] Archaeologists have also looked at the experience of convicts in

6   C. Fredericksen, 'Confinement by Isolation: Convict Mechanics and Labour at Fort Dundas, Melville Island', *Australasian Historical Archaeology*, Vol. 19, 2001, pp. 48–59; G. Karskens, 'Defiance, Deference and Diligence: Three Views of Convicts in New South Wales Road Gangs', *Australian Journal of Historical Archaeology*, Vol. 4, 1986, pp. 17–28; G. Karskens, 'The Convict Road Station Site at Wisemans Ferry: An Historical and Archaeological Investigation', *Australian Journal of Historical Archaeology*, Vol. 2, 1984, pp. 17–26; W. Thorp, 'Directed for the Public Stock: The Convict Work Gang System and Its Sites', in J. Birmingham, D. Bairstow, and A. Wilson (eds), *Archaeology and Colonisation: Australia in the World Context*, Sydney, 1987, pp. 109–22; D. Bairstow and M. Davies, *Coal Mines Historic Site Survey: Preliminary Report*, Occasional Paper No. 15, Hobart, 1987; A. McGowan, *Excavations at Lithend, Port Arthur Historic Site*, Hobart, 1985.
7   Casella, *Archaeology of the Ross Female Factory*.
8   F. Starr, 'An Archaeology of Improvisation'; P. Crook and T. Murray, *An Archaeology of Institutional Refuge*.
9   C. Lowe, *48 Macquarie & 220–230 Church Streets, Parramatta: Archaeological Assessment*, report prepared for Coombes Property Group & Drivas Property Group, Sydney, 2017, p. 66.
10   S. Winter and T. Whitley, 'The Fremantle Prison Project', *Australasian Historical Archaeology*, Vol. 33, 2015, pp. 73–77; S. Winter, *Transforming the Colony: The Archaeology of Convictism in Western Australia*, Newcastle-upon-Tyne, 2017.
11   G. Hewitt and R. Wright, 'Identification and Historical Truth: The Russell Street Police Garage Burials', *Australasian Historical Archaeology*, Vol. 22, 2004, pp. 57–70; J. Smith, 'Losing the Plot: Archaeological Investigations of Prisoner Burials at the Old Melbourne Gaol and Pentridge Prison', *Provenance: The Journal of Public Record Office Victoria*, No. 10, 2011, pp. 62–72.

non-institutional settings, such as assignees working for private settlers, or convicts and emancipists in Australia's proto-urban environments.[12]

We draw upon the work of historians, criminologists and demographers who in turn are informed by our research. They use the vast documentary archive to get a glimpse of the intent of the convict system, contextualising the Australian convict story as part of a globe-spanning system of unfree labour management.[13] They examine the methods and implications of incarcerative and punishment-oriented regimes,[14] as well as the many processes by which unfree labour was extracted and how prisoners reacted to it.[15] Prisoner

---

12 G. Connah, 'The Lake Innes Estate: Privilege and Servitude in Nineteenth-Century Australia', *World Archaeology*, Vol. 33, No. 1, 2001, pp. 137–54; S. Lawrence and P. Davies, 'Convict Origins', in *An Archaeology of Australia since 1788*. Contributions to Global Historical Archaeology, 2011, p. 28; G. Karskens, *Inside the Rocks: The Archaeology of a Neighbourhood*, Alexandria, New South Wales, 1999.

13 C. Anderson, 'Transnational Histories of Penal Transportation: Punishment, Labour and Governance in the British Imperial World, 1788–1939', *Australian Historical Studies*, Vol. 47, No. 3, 2016, pp. 381–97; B. Kercher, 'Perish or Prosper: The Law and Convict Transportation in the British Empire, 1700–1850', *Law and History Review*, Vol. 21, No. 3, 2003, pp. 527–84; A. Atkinson, 'Writing About Convicts: Our Escape from the One Big Gaol', *Tasmanian Historical Studies*, Vol. 6, No. 2, 1999, pp. 17–27; A.G.L. Shaw, *Convicts and the Colonies*, 1971 ed., London, 1966.

14 D. A. Roberts, 'Colonial Gulag: The Populating of the Port Macquarie Penal Settlement, 1821–1832', *History Australia*, 2017; P. Edmonds and H. Maxwell-Stewart, '"The Whip Is a Very Contagious Kind of Thing": Flogging and Humanitarian Reform in Penal Australia', *Journal of Colonialism and Colonial History*, Vol. 17, No. 1, 2016; L. Ford and D.A. Roberts, 'New South Wales Penal Settlements and the Transformation of Secondary Punishment in the Nineteenth-Century British Empire', *Journal of Colonialism and Colonial History*, Vol. 15, No. 3, 2014; Maxwell-Stewart, 'The Rise and Fall of John Longworth'.

15 R. Tuffin, M. Gibbs, D. Roberts, H. Maxwell-Stewart, D. Roe, J. Steele, and S. Hood, 'Landscapes of Production and Punishment: Convict Labour in the Australian Context', *Journal of Social Archaeology*, Vol. 18, No. 1, 2018, pp. 50–76; W.M. Robbins, 'The Lumber Yards: A Case Study in the Management of Convict Labour 1788–1832', *Labour History*, Vol. 79, 2000, pp. 141–61; K. Reid, '"Contumacious, Ungovernable and Incorrigible": Convict Women and Workplace Resistance, Van Diemen's Land, 1820–1839', in Ian Duffield and James Bradley (eds), *Representing Convicts: New Perspectives on Convict Forced Labour Migration*, London and Washington, 1997, pp. 106–23.

health, the processes of conviction, even the act of forced transportation are all also fruitful avenues of research.[16]

Through multiple means – historical research, survey, excavation and analysis – historical archaeologists shed new light on the penal regimes imposed upon convicts and the ways in which men and women reacted to them. Walls have spoken of convict skills,[17] artefact caches of attempts at individuality amid imposed conformity.[18] Whole sites have demonstrated the use of convict labour in post-1788 colonisation,[19] and how that labour was deployed and managed.[20] Although the past will always keep most of its secrets, through document, place and object we are given some of the tools to recreate and repopulate this past.

The work of historical archaeologists in Australia predominantly takes place in the academic, industry and government sectors. In industry, archaeologists are involved in many types of projects: inventory creations, heritage assessments, small and large-scale excavations and surveys, and collections analysis. In government, the work can be more focused upon statutory management, although at a place like Port Arthur it also encompasses many of the tasks undertaken in industry. In academia, work

---

16   H. Maxwell-Stewart and R. Kippen, 'Sickness and Death on Convict Voyages to Australia', in Peter Baskerville and Kris Inwood (eds), *Lives in Transition: Longitudinal Analysis from Historical Sources*, Montreal & Kingston, London, Ithaca, 2015, pp. 43–70; K. Foxhall, 'From Convicts to Colonists: The Health of Prisoners and the Voyage to Australia, 1823–53', *The Journal of Imperial And Commonwealth History*, Vol. 39, No. 1, 2011, pp. 1–19; B. Godfrey, 'Prison Versus Western Australia: Which Worked Best, the Australian Penal Colony or the English Convict Prison System?', *The British Journal of Criminology*, Vol. 59, No. 5, 2019, pp. 1139–60, https://doi.org/10.1093/bjc/azz012; K. Roscoe, 'A Natural Hulk: Australia's Carceral Islands in the Colonial Period, 1788–1901', *International Review of Social History*, Vol. 63, 2018, pp. 45–63; R. Tuffin, 'The Post Mortem Treatment of Convicts in Van Diemen's Land, 1814–1874', *Journal of Australian Colonial History*, Vol. 9, 2007, pp. 99–126; L. Marshall, 'A Benign Institution?: Convict Health, Living Conditions, and Labour Management at Port Arthur Penal Station, 1868–1870', *Journal of Australian Colonial History*, Vol. 18, 2016, pp. 65–94; K. Inwood and H. Maxwell-Stewart, 'Introduction: Health, Human Capital, and Early Economic Development in Australia and New Zealand', *Australian Economic History Review*, Vol. 55, No. 2, 2015, pp. 105–11.
17   Karskens, 'Defiance, Deference and Diligence'.
18   Casella, *Archaeology of the Ross Female Factory*; Starr, 'An Archaeology of Improvisation'.
19   Fredericksen, 'Confinement by Isolation'.
20   Tuffin et al., 'Landscapes of Production and Punishment'.

occurs through the provision of grants for specific projects, supervising the research of students, or linkage to one of the other two sectors. Some very effective work occurs when the latter takes place.[21]

One problem is that the research undertaken in these sectors can remain relatively inaccessible in grey literature archives, either of universities or of government bureaucracies.[22] Put succinctly: '[r]esearch which is not available for others to use does not exist.'[23] In the case of an excavation, the actual excavation component is only one small part of an archaeological program, the mid-point of a long journey in research, data collection and analysis. This journey can be years or even decades long, which makes adequate resourcing challenging. What can suffer is the sharing of results, in which case what value has all that work actually had? The answer is increasingly being found in the digital realm. The digitally native nature of much data, as well as the digitisation of reports, means that increasingly large swathes of information are being freed from inaccessible hard drives and shelves.[24]

The archaeological excavations of the Port Arthur penitentiary were therefore a chance to learn about and share an important part of Australia's convict story – one not always captured in the reports, returns and accounts. The site of the penitentiary was a place where the intents and actualities of convict management crossed over on a daily basis. Over a 47-year period, spaces of labour and incarceration were created, managed and redesigned in response to the penal aims of the convict system's administrators. These were spaces created to confine and coerce an unfree population, and their

---

21   T. Murray, 'Integrating Archaeology and History at the "Commonwealth Block": "Little Lon" and Casselden Place', *International Journal of Historical Archaeology*, Vol. 10, No. 4, 2006, pp. 385–403; Karskens, *Inside the Rocks: The Archaeology of a Neighbourhood*.

22   Gojak, 'Convict Archaeology in New South Wales', pp. 73–83; M. Gibbs, 'The Convict System of New South Wales: A Review of Archaeological Research since 2001', *Archaeology in Oceania*, Vol. 47, No. 2, 2012, pp. 78–83.

23   J.P. White, quoted in: G. Connah, 'Pattern and Purpose in Historical Archaeology', *Australasian Historical Archaeology*, Vol. 16, 1998, pp. 3–7, p. 5, http://www.jstor.org/stable/29544409.

24   See Heritage New South Wales, 'Digital Heritage Library', Department of Planning, Industry and Environment, New South Wales, http://heritagensw. intersearch.com.au/heritagenswjspui/; S. Colley and M. Gibbs, 'NSW Archaeology Online: Grey Literature Archive,' in *Archaeology of Sydney Research Group* (Sydney: Sydney eScholarship, 2011). http://nswaol.library.usyd.edu.au.

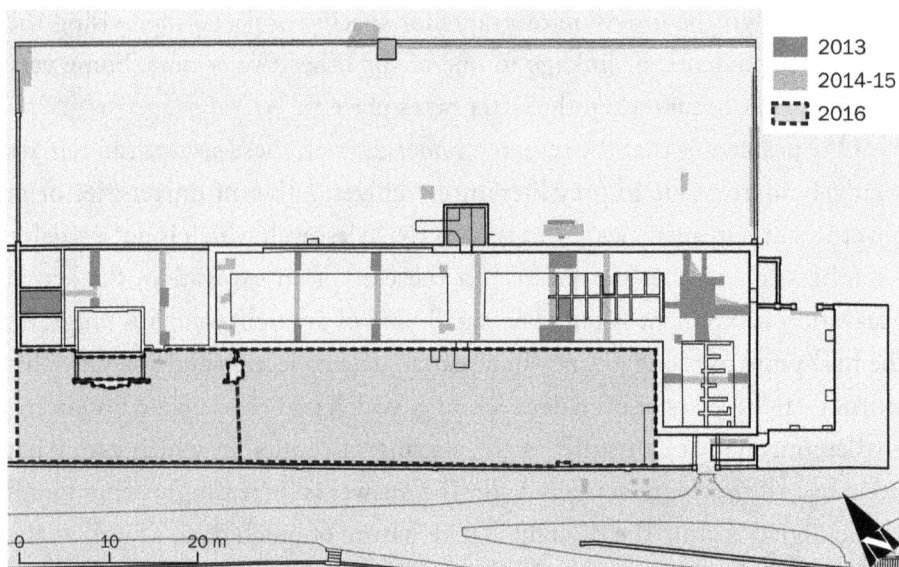

Figure 4.2. Map showing the areas excavated during 2013–16.

everyday use left behind tiny artefactual residues of their lives. They were also spaces created by the convicts; the very fabric of walls and surfaces tell us about the labour regimes imposed upon the men.

How the excavations were carried out

During 2013–15, the archaeological investigations comprised a mixture of targeted research excavations (2013) and mitigation activity in the form of monitoring of construction works and recording (2014–15) (Figure 4.2). During 2013, 22 discrete areas were excavated: 15 within the penitentiary, six within the bakehouse and one in the muster ground. Monitoring took place as and where construction occurred, both within the footprint of the penitentiary and around its periphery.

During the 2016 investigation 830 square metres was excavated, the area encompassing the zone between the former granary building and the penitentiary bakehouse (Plates 4.1 and 4.2). This comprised the ablutions (560 square metres) and laundry (270 square metres) areas (Plate 4.3). As the historical research suggested – and the excavation proved – the ablutions yard was divided into three main spaces: the west and east yards, and

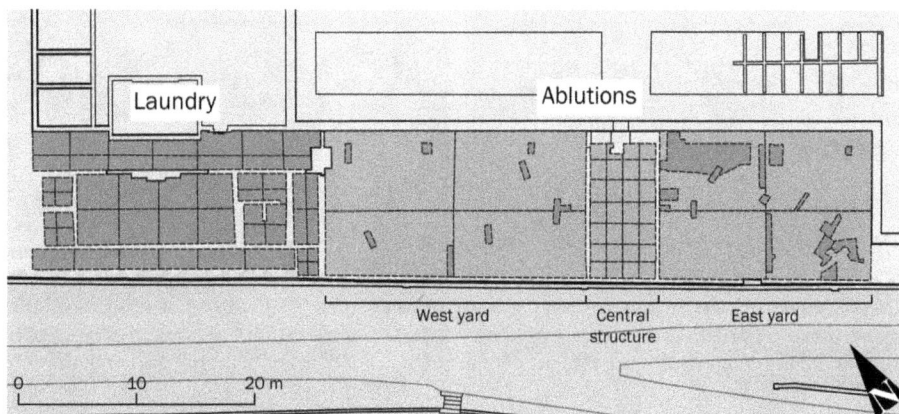

Figure 4.3. Division of the ablutions and laundry areas into areas, quadrants and spaces.

between them a central structure. The laundry comprised 11 separate spaces. During the course of the excavation the ablutions and laundry spaces were subdivided into smaller, arbitrary spatial units, providing coarse location data for artefact recovery, as well as axes for the location of drawing lines (Figure 4.3).

During all excavations, the single context system of excavation was used, with deposits, cuts and features recorded through field notes, context sheets, photographs and measured drawings (Figure 4.4). This is a favoured method of recording a historical archaeological site. It allows the archaeologist to carefully peel back the layers of a site, recording each deposit, structure or cut as a single event. When combined, these events tell us about how a place was formed, how it was used and how it eventually went out of use.

During 2016 a total station linked to a CAD program was also used, which allowed contexts to be recorded electronically in real-time. This excavation also saw photogrammetry utilised to supplement recording.[25] Photographs were processed during post-fieldwork using Agisoft Photoscan to create 3D and orthographic visualisations and records of the site. The high quality and accuracy of the photogrammetric data meant that measured hand-drawn plans were not made during 2016, but were instead generated

---

25   R. Tuffin, P. Rigozzi, D. Roe, and J. Steele, 'Old v New? Comparing the Use of Traditional Recording Methodologies with Photogrammetry in Archaeological Practice at the Port Arthur Historic Site' (Digital Cultural Heritage: Future Visions, University of Queensland, 2017).

Figure 4.4. Some of the methods used during the 2016 excavations. (PAHSMA 2016)

during post-processing. Sections, however, continued to be recorded by 1:10 and 1:20 scale measured drawing.

Finds were provenanced according to the arbitrary spatial units, with context information recorded and, if required, spot find numbers (Plate 4.4). During 2016 the 3D coordinates of artefacts from diagnostic contexts were recorded as spot finds.

All artefacts were retained, with the more sensitive objects stabilised on site through encapsulation in low oxygen, nitrogen-rich environments. All artefact processing was overseen by a specialist in historical archaeological artefact collections management, cataloguing and analysis. Following

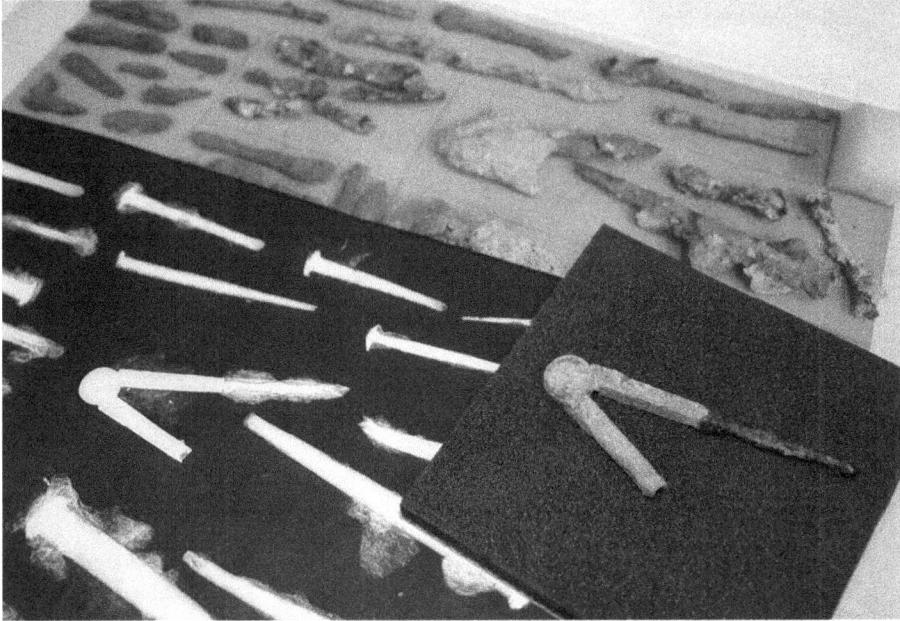

Figure 4.5. Artefacts were able to be identified through radiography. This photograph shows a scribing compass that was identified from an unidentifiable concretion. (PAHSMA 2020)

cataloguing, all artefacts have been boxed and housed in PAHSMA's collections store.

During the 2016 excavation, it was anticipated that a large amount of architectural metal artefacts would be recovered. To aid their identification and conservation, all such objects were imaged via radiography (Figure 4.5). Increasingly used in archaeology and in the study of cultural objects, radiography offers the potential to identify internal details of concreted metal objects that would otherwise be impossible through visual analysis alone.

This approach not only provided a record of unstable and deteriorating materials immediately post-excavation, but enabled the identification and measurement of 95 per cent of the 3,176 ferrous objects x-rayed, and informed later conservation priorities.

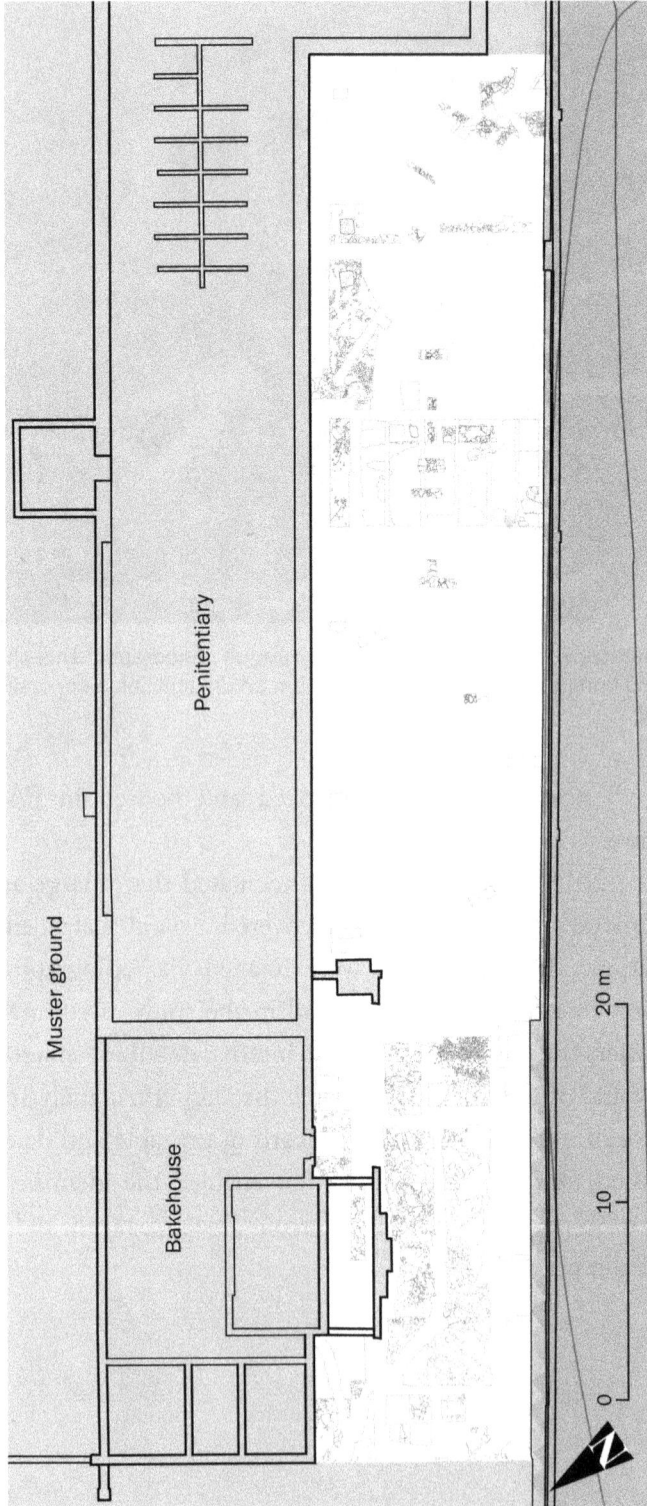

Figure 4.6. Illustrations overlaid on penitentiary plan, showing locations and layouts of ablutions and laundry areas 1830–54.

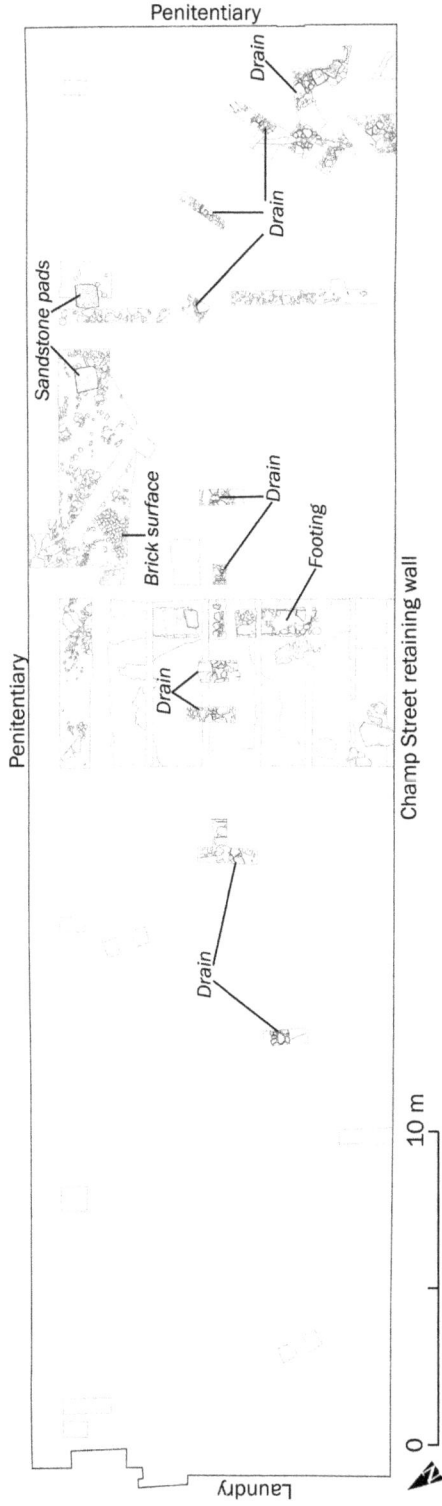

Figure 4.7. Illustration showing the series of slots cut into the ablutions area to examine features from the 1830–54 period.

Ablutions yard

Champ Street
retaining wall
(original)

Dolerite and clay fill

Penitentiary bakehouse

Champ Street retaining wall (rebuilt)

Gravel surface

5 m

0

Workshops precinct

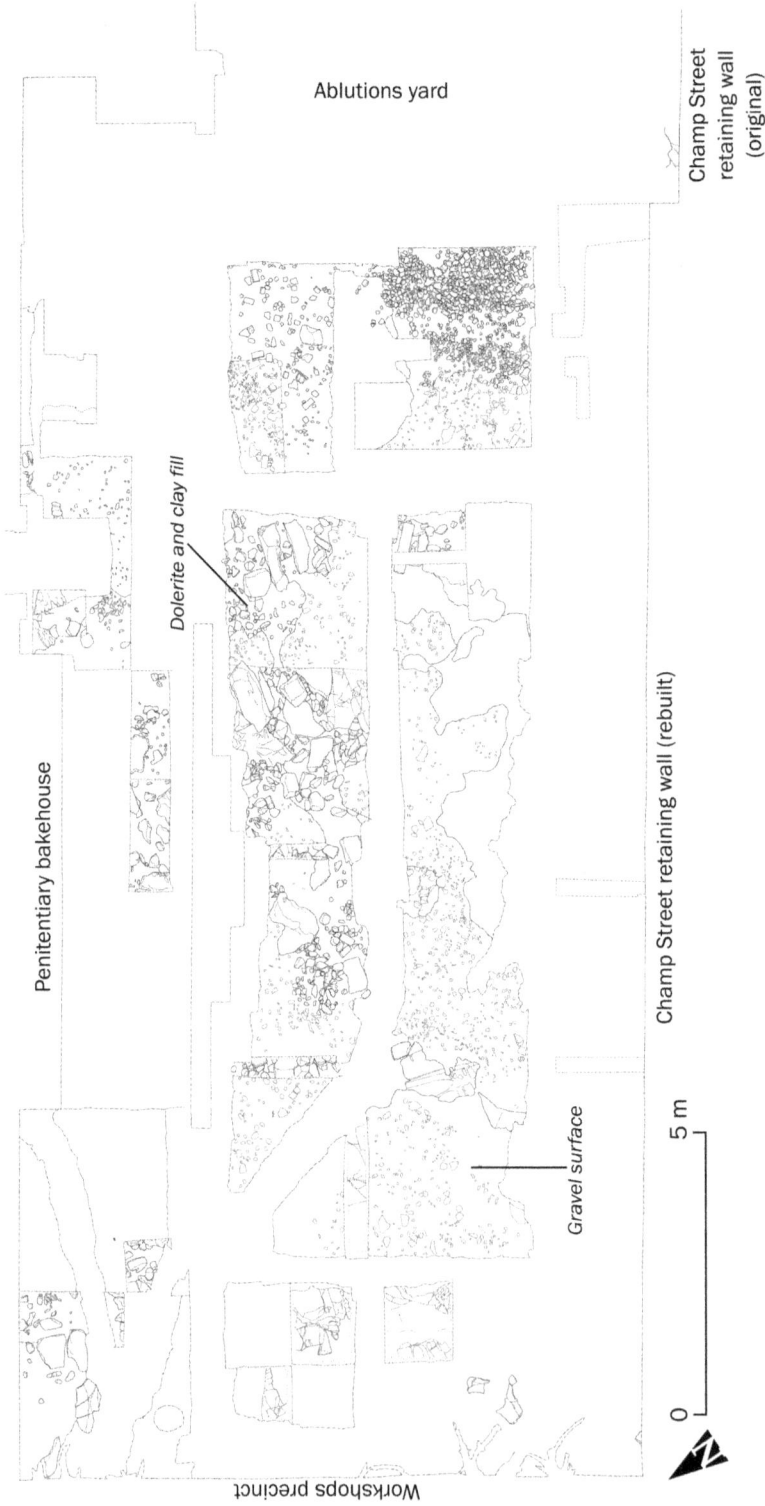

Figure 4.8. Illustration showing key features in the laundry area, 1830–54. The blank areas were unexcavated, or were where footings were present.

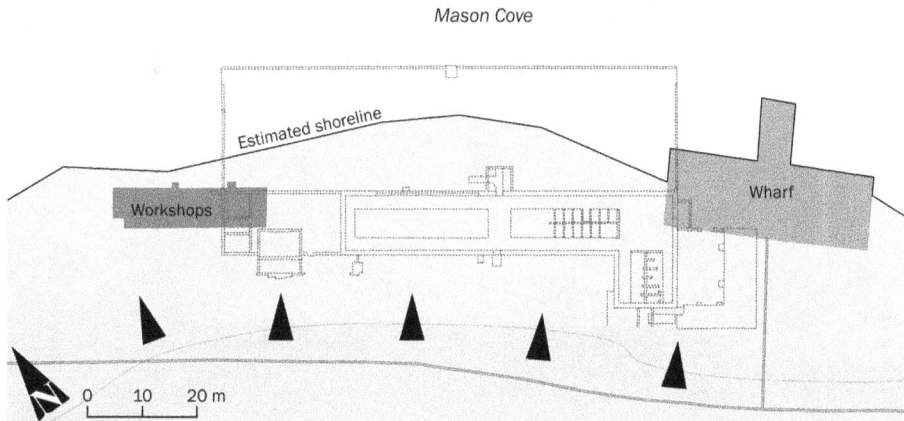

Figure 4.9. Map of the estimated line of the original waterfront in 1830, with the outline of the penitentiary overlaid. The direction of the slope is demonstrated by arrows.

Industrial waterfront phase, 1830–1854

The landscape of today's penitentiary precinct largely reflects the latter stages of convict-period settlement. By 1856, the shore of the former 1830s waterfront had been irreversibly changed by large-scale reclamation and levelling works, with much of the area overprinted by the penitentiary and its ancillary structures. Such large-scale work, which began in 1842 with the mill and granary's commencement, inevitably had a major impact upon the survival of pre-1842 features and deposits. Yet, despite this, evidence of Port Arthur's earliest decade was found during the course of the investigations. This supported a history of waterfront modification, consolidation and occupation dating from the very earliest years of settlement.

We discuss the original state and subsequent development of Port Arthur's waterfront in the section 'Settlement of a penal station'. Where it was encountered during the investigations, the original (pre-convict settlement) waterfront was formed from a dolerite bedrock overlain by clay. Dolerite bedrock outcropped close to the current ground surface, with the later Champ Street retaining wall built directly onto the stone in places (Figure 4.10). It deepened toward the north, with no dolerite bedrock encountered in a series of deep excavations against and within the foundations of the penitentiary and bakehouse (Figure 4.9). This indicated that the bedrock sloped downward toward Mason Cove.

Figure 4.10. Outcropping dolerite found during the excavation of the laundry area. (PAHSMA 2016)

Between 1830 and ca. 1842 the area was modified to accommodate workshops and a lumber yard and to formalise the waterfront. Archaeological evidence supported this record, suggesting that extensive earthworks took place in the area, accompanied by the creation of new infrastructure.

As part of these works, a large amount of dolerite-rich clay was deposited, particularly over the area where the bedrock steepened toward the former shore. This material had been imported to level the ground, the dolerite a combination of heavily weathered stones and more freshly broken pieces. In places, this clay and dolerite layer had been covered by a thinner deposit of silty clay containing a large amount of broken dolerite, brick and sandstone (quarried from elsewhere), as well as fragments of shell lime mortar and charcoal. These were gravel surfaces that had been laid down over the reclamation, with a number of buttons, iron and copper nails, a hacksaw blade, two heel plates (for shoes), wood shavings and pieces of iron strapping retrieved off their top.

The presence of these artefacts hinted at the early industrial purpose of the area, which had formerly been where the workshops, lumber yard and wharf had been situated in the 1830s (Figure 4.11). The surface followed the slope of the underlying bedrock and clay toward Mason Cove – borne out by

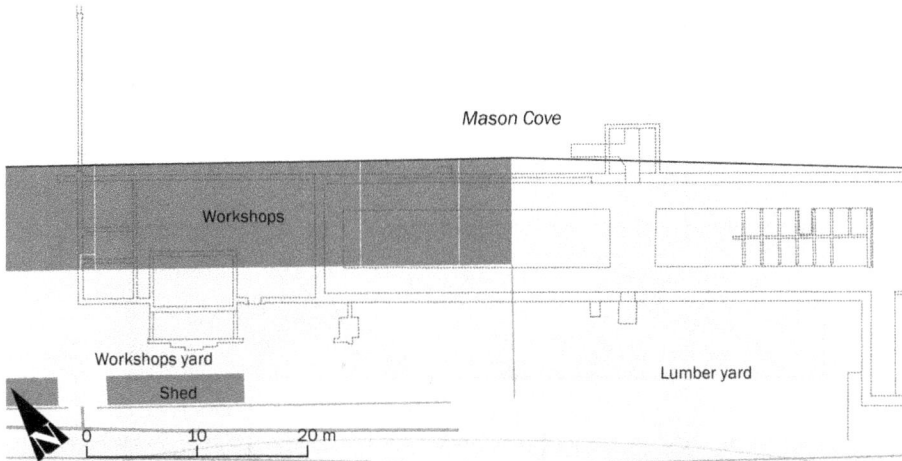

Figure 4.11. Outline of penitentiary superimposed upon the 1836 layout of the area. The open yards are indicated.

the 1833 illustration (Figure 1.3) showing the waterfront with a distinctive sloping profile.

In addition to the reclamation fill and surface, there was also limited evidence of the structures present in the area prior to 1842. A sandstone and shell lime mortar footing was uncovered in the former location of the lumber yard (Figure 4.12). Heavily affected by the later construction of the flour mill, the footing likely had supported a structure, potentially the wall shown on plans as dividing the workshops area from the Commissariat store.

Historic plans and illustrations indicate that, while the Champ Street retaining wall was not constructed until the 1840s, some form of demarcation was present by the mid-1830s (Plate 1.2). A ramp provided access from the lower waterfront level to the higher road (Figure 4.13). This ramp had been located in the southern extent of the excavation area, where the bedrock cropped close to the surface. Evidence of it had been removed during construction of the laundry in the 1850s, though a portion of the ramp's earthwork remains *in situ* today, located behind the site of the former workshops.

The 1842 construction of the mill and granary and the contemporaneous work on the Champ Street retaining wall resulted in a high level of disturbance to the earlier deposits and features across this area. This activity involved site levelling and the excavation of building footings, as well as the

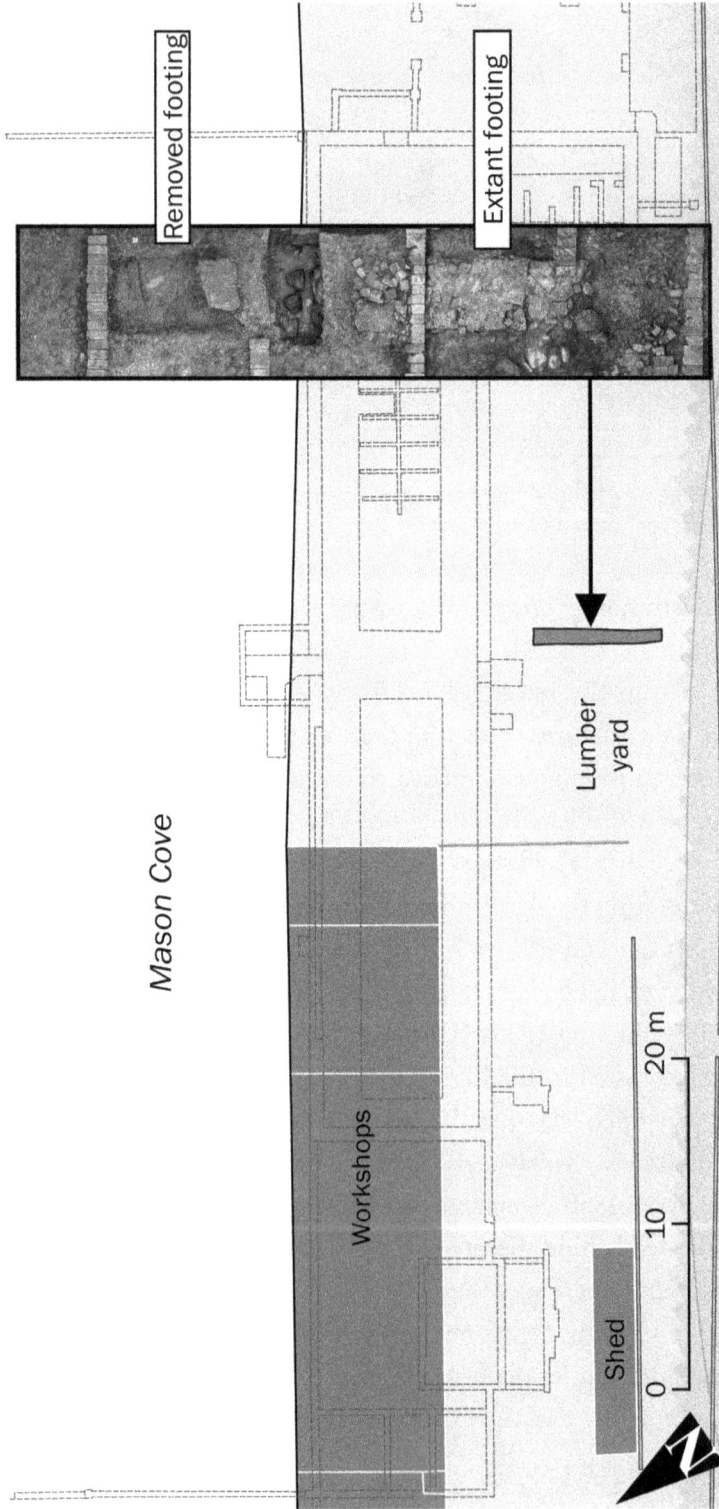

Figure 4.12. Overlay of the site in 1836, showing the location of the footing (depicted in the inset photograph).

Removed footing

Extant footing

Mason Cove

Lumber yard

Workshops

Shed

0   10   20 m

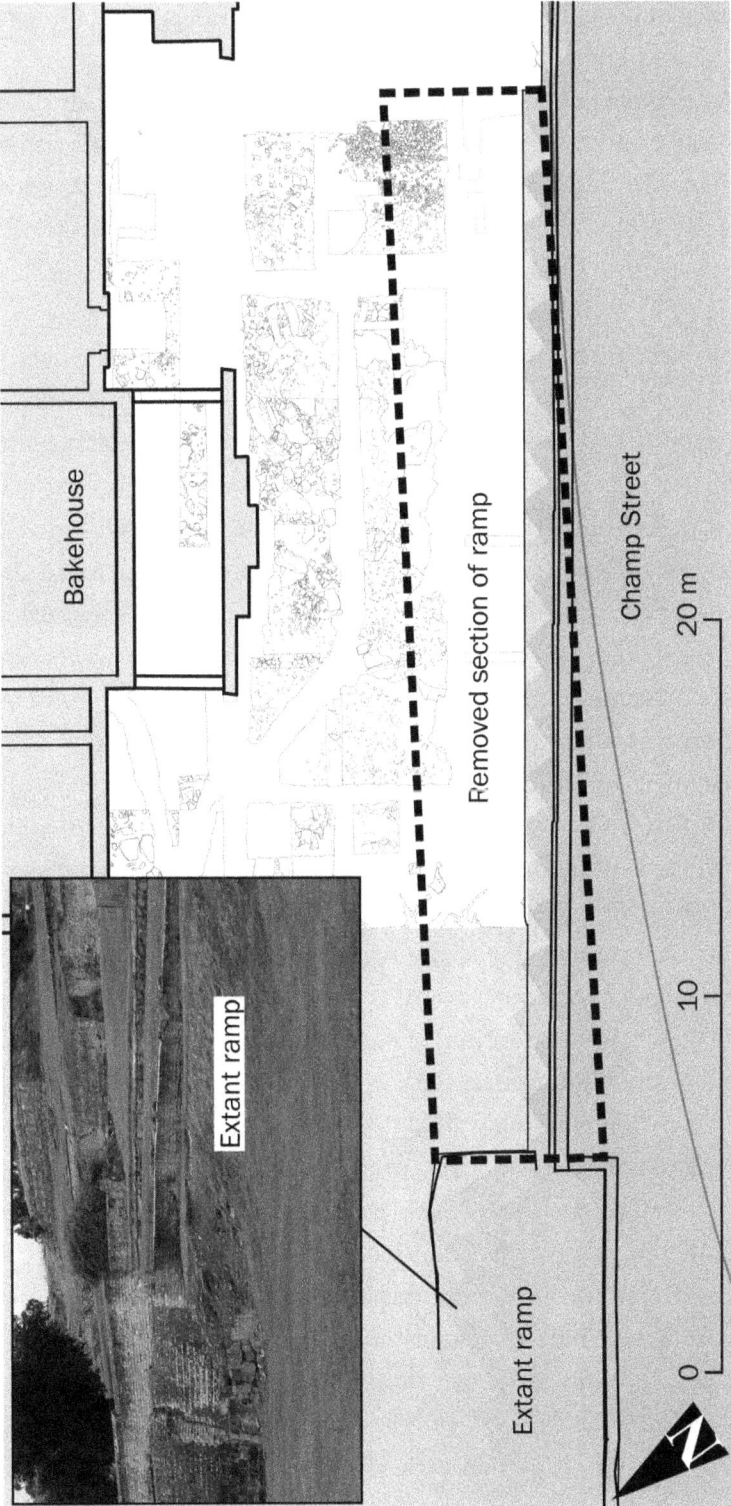

Figure 4.13. Illustration showing the estimated position of the ramp relative to the excavated area and the site's extant features. The inset photograph shows the ramp as it appears today.

importation of more reclamation material and the consolidation of waterfront infrastructure to support the mill and granary's northern frontage.

The ground was prepared prior to the work commencing on the mill. Clays and rubble were imported to build up parts of the area, with other parts levelled. At this time the bedrock was in part exposed, with the substantial sandstone footings of the Champ Street retaining wall then built directly on top. This activity resulted in the removal of much of the clay overlying the bedrock.

The construction of the mill building, granary and treadwheel ward necessitated a large amount of waterfront consolidation to ensure both structural stability and waterfront access to the new facility. A large amount of clay and stone was imported, likely sourced from the levelling activity taking place in the southern extent. This fill was then placed within a sturdy lattice of large logs. Known as cribbing, this form of reclamation had already been practised at Port Arthur, with the sections of the Commissariat Store built on such support, as well as parts of the dockyard (Plate 4.5).

Excavation found evidence of this cribbing (Plate 2.3). The *Eucalyptus globulus* (Tasmanian blue gum) logs forming the lattice were up to 60cm in diameter, having been trimmed of branches and roughly shaped before being placed in position. They were aligned running either parallel or perpendicular to the line of the mill (and therefore the waterfront). The 'cells' between the logs were infilled with a mixture of clay and stone. The logs had rotted away in a number of instances, especially where they ran perpendicular to the waterfront. Deeper excavation toward the water table found well-preserved logs still in their original positions. Excavation along the northern front of the mill and granary found that the reclaimed area had, at this time, been faced with a dolerite retaining wall.

This reclamation cribbing was probably a combination of pre-1842 waterfront infrastructure, onto which had been added further reclamation when the mill and granary were constructed. This reclamation activity had occurred contemporaneously with the construction of the mill building, which was followed by the granary and the treadwheel structure. The mill's northern footings sat above the cribbing layer, with clay and stone packed behind to provide extra stability and waterproofing (Figure 4.14). The southern footings had been excavated deep into natural and levelling

Figure 4.14. Photograph of the dolerite boulders incorporated into the reclamation material below the penitentiary. (PAHSMA 2013)

clay (Figure 4.15). Both footings were formed from squared and dressed sandstone, sitting on a rough-coursed and undressed foundation of dolerite and siltstone capped by a coarse shell lime mortar. No evidence was found that the mill had been set on bedrock. The brick of the superstructure began well above ground level.

Subtle evidence of the infrastructure built to support the building's industrial purpose was found during the excavation (Figure 4.16). Internal footings related to the treadwheel ward, mill house and granary were found, definitively delineating for the first time the composition of the structure. Although no evidence of the workings of treadwheel, mill or waterwheel were found, sections of the tailrace which collected water from the overshot waterwheel were also located (Figure 4.17). This comprised a sandstone-lined channel 1.50 metres wide, which ran from below the wheel, out through the open northern side of the building and across the reclaimed ground to the bay. Historical evidence indicated that the water had been collected for reuse, although the excavation did not find definitive evidence of this.

The 1850s conversion works resulted in the lowering of the ground floor throughout the former granary, mill house and treadwheel ward by up to

Figure 4.15. Penitentiary footings exposed during the excavation. Note the courses of dressed sandstone which have been laid atop a rougher mortar and dolerite footing. (PAHSMA 2016)

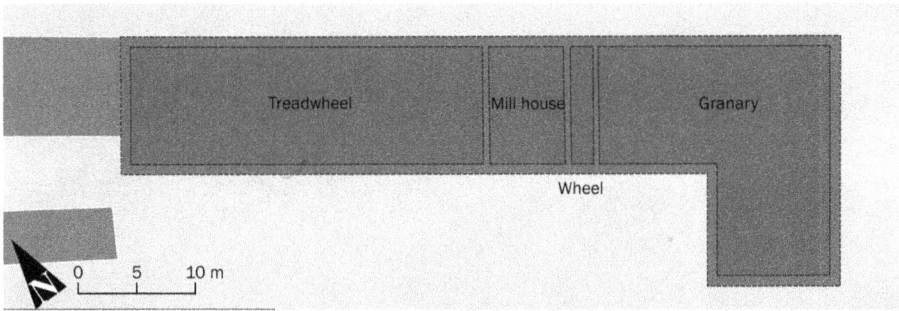

Figure 4.16. Internal divisions of the flour mill and granary, derived from archaeological investigation.

0.30 metre (one foot). This resulted in the loss of much of the evidence for original flooring levels or occupation deposits from the 1840s, as well as any machinery foundations that may have been present. The only evidence of the mill machinery and treadwheel was the presence of some enigmatic sandstone and timber inserts in the main wall and footings which had once supported the waterwheel and treadwheel axles.

At the rear of the flour mill and granary, construction activity resulted in the deposition of clay and rubble across the space (Figure 4.39). This in effect raised the area in which the ablutions yards and laundry would later be sited and created a more pronounced slope to the north-east, toward the mill.

During this time, two sandstone plinths were set in the clay (Figure 4.17). These were placed in alignment with a pillar set into the Champ Street retaining wall (Figure 4.18). The pillar, and another one set on the southern side of Champ Street, had supported the overhead flume which fed the waterwheel. Both wall and pillar were constructed simultaneously with the mill building. The two sandstone plinths had likely provided foundations for supporting structures.

At this time a subsurface drain was also established at the rear of the building, running parallel with the retaining wall (Figure 4.19). It cut through all levelling clay deposits and was constructed from a mixture of rough-rubble sandstone, rounded and angular dolerite (field and quarry stone) and occasional bricks. The drain fell toward the east, directing water and/or waste from the western extents of the area toward the south-east, where it exited through the gap between the rear of the granary structure and the Champ Street retaining wall.

191

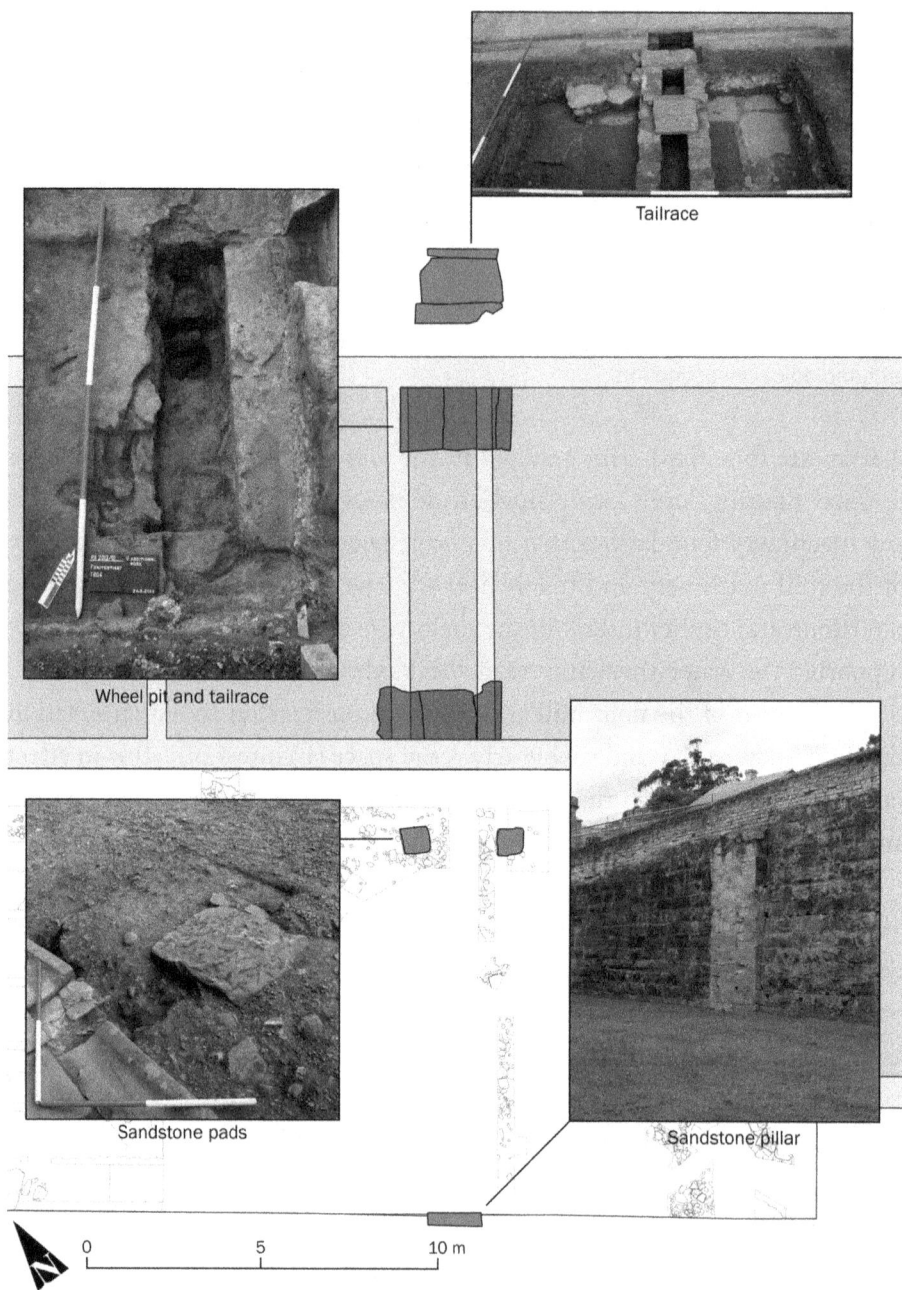

Figure 4.17. Map showing mill features.

Figure 4.18. Ablutions area, showing the pillar (lighter stone) incorporated into the Champ Street retaining wall. (PAHSMA 2016)

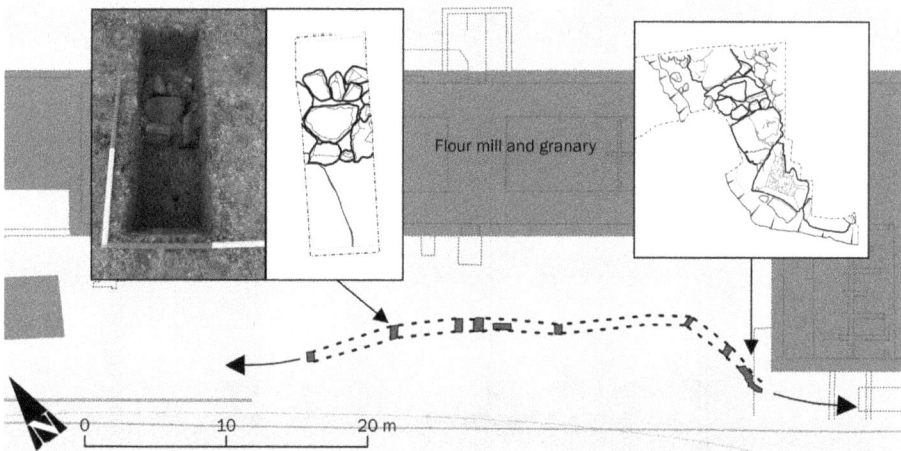

Figure 4.19. Course of the drain through the ablutions yard.

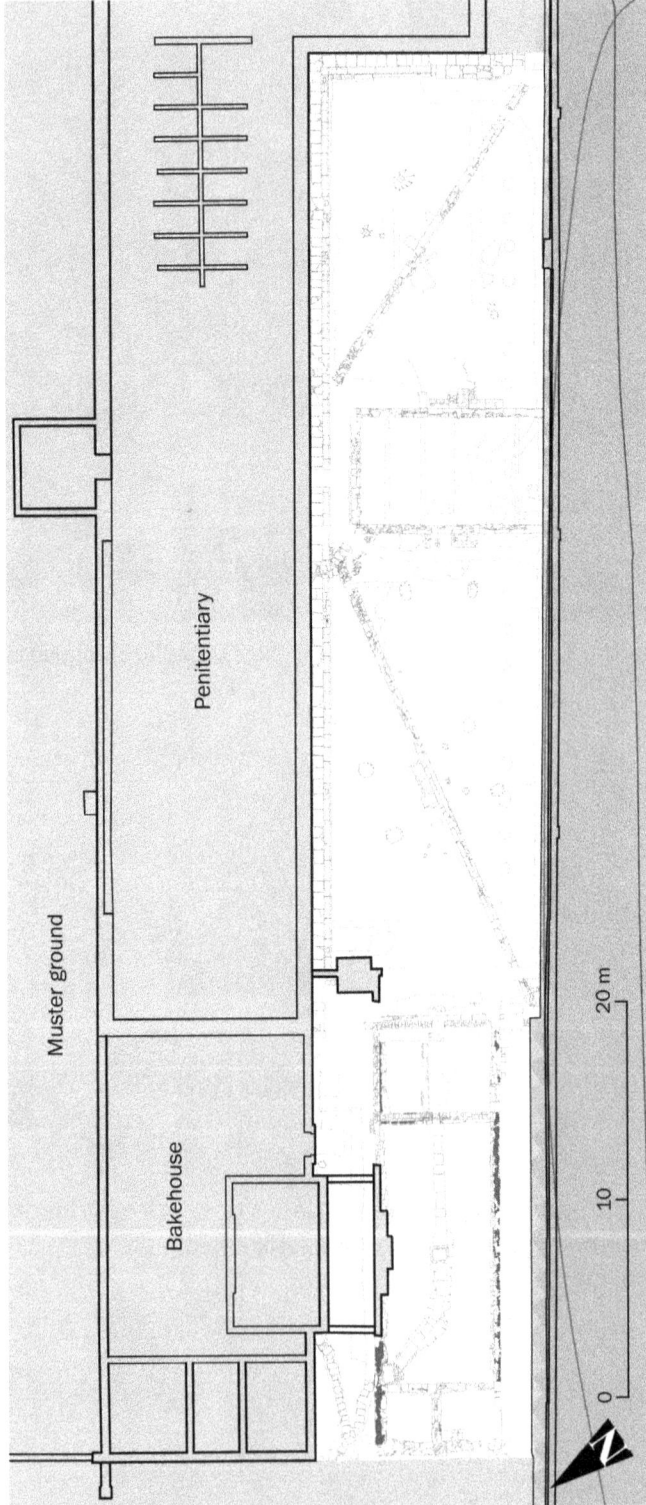

Figure 4.20. Illustrations overlaid on penitentiary plan, showing locations and layouts of ablutions and laundry areas between 1856 and ca. 1862.

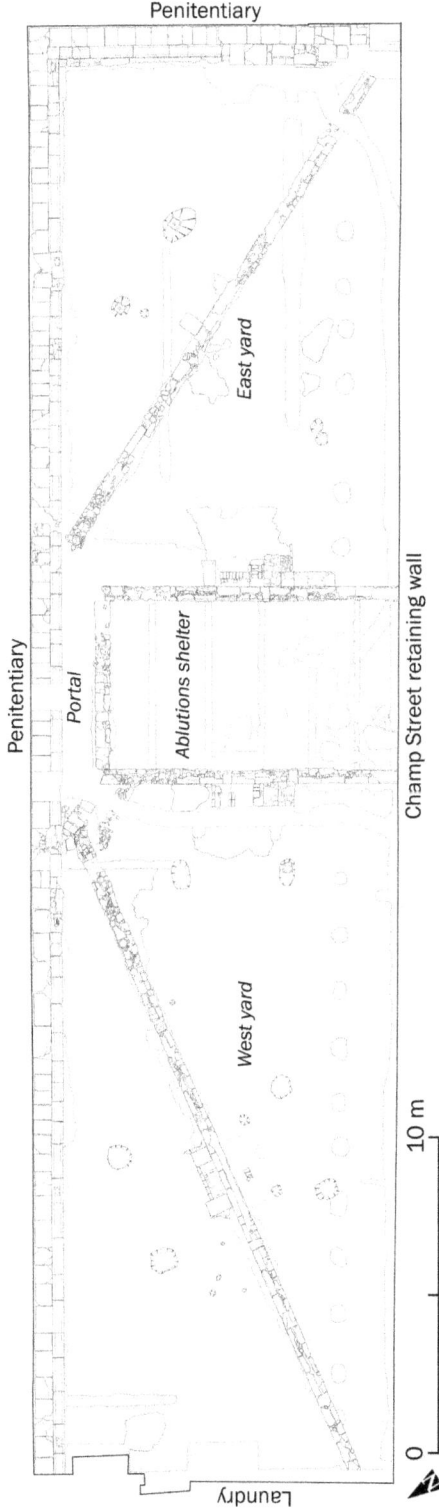

Figure 4.21. Illustration showing the ablutions area during the first phase of use, 1854 – ca. 1862.

Penitentiary

Penitentiary

Portal

Ablutions shelter

East yard

West yard

Laundry

Champ Street retaining wall

10 m

0

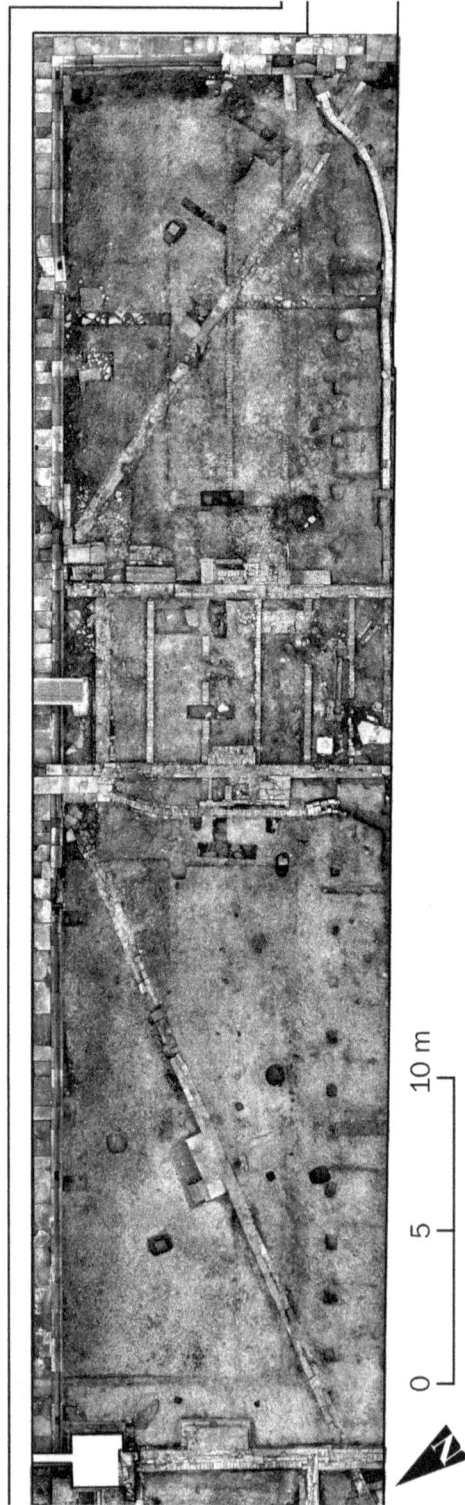

Figure 4.22. Orthophotograph of the ablutions area during 1854 – ca. 1862.

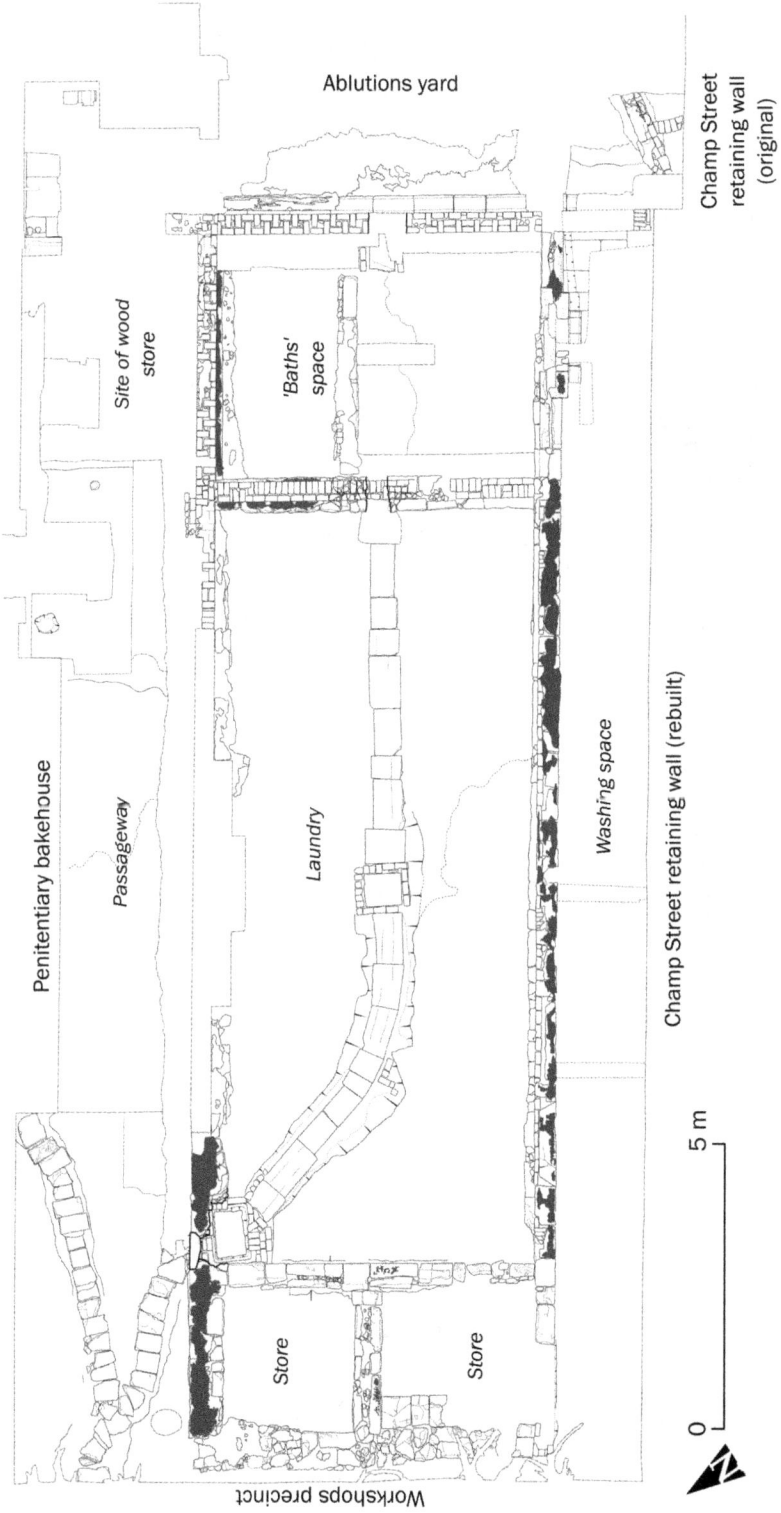

Figure 4.23. Illustration showing the laundry area during the first phase of use, 1854 – ca. 1862.

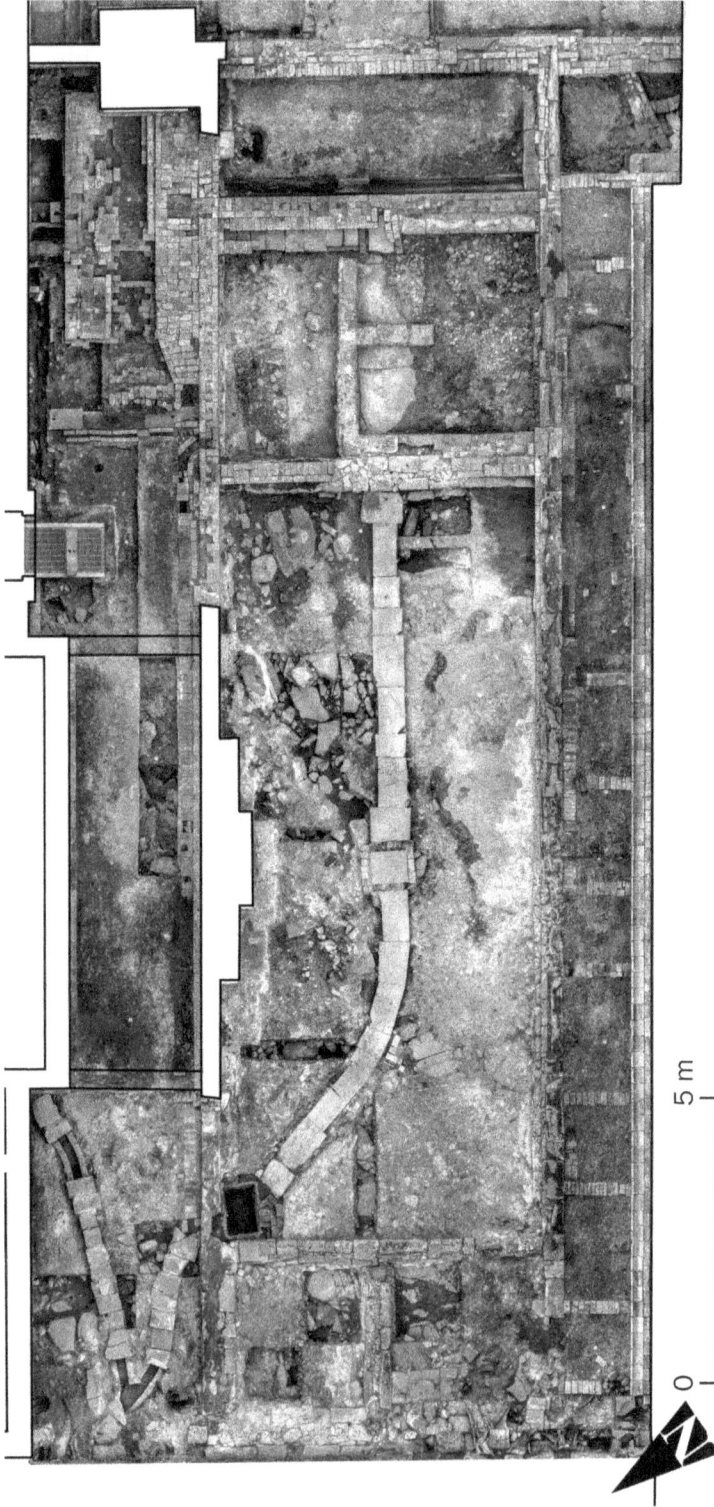

Figure 4.24. Orthophotograph of the laundry area during 1854 – ca. 1862.

0 ___ 5 m

Penitentiary conversion and occupation, 1854–77

The retrofitting of a former industrial building required a large amount of invasive work, as fittings were removed, surfaces lowered and new floors added. The building's new uses required expansion into new areas, with infrastructure and spaces created around its periphery. The works were matched by large-scale reclamation works to the front of the penitentiary, resulting in the infilling of over one-third of Mason Cove. Situated adjacent to the northern side of the penitentiary, this allowed for the construction of a large muster yard.

Today, most of the surviving structures and spaces represent those converted or constructed between 1854 and 1857. Historical and archaeological evidence indicates the penitentiary, bakehouse, watchmen's quarters and muster yard underwent very little modification after this period. The ablutions and laundry areas provide an exception to this. Although these were areas where little upstanding fabric remained, the archaeological investigation was able to find clear differentiation between three phases of occupation. The first of these (Phase I) encompassed the period 1854 through ca. 1862 and included the initial adoption of the hitherto under-utilised space for the purposes of ablutions facilities, yards and a laundry. A short period of works (Intermediate Phase) led to the second major phase of occupation (Phase II) which spanned the period ca. 1862 to the settlement close. This saw a wholesale redesign of the area, although its fundamental function was not to change.

Conversion works and Phase I, 1854 – ca. 1862

The changes to the mill/granary structures were complex and can now only be 'read' by observations of the standing fabric and the subsurface data acquired through excavation. This is particularly the case as there are no surviving 'as-built' plans of the mill and granary complex from which to measure change. An assessment of the built fabric conducted in 2009 gave an initial idea of the reconfigurations necessary to what was essentially two buildings (mill and granary structure) into a single four-level building.[26]

---

26 Unpublished notes by archaeologist Greg Jackman, Port Arthur Historic Site Resource Centre, 2009.

Figure 4.25. Excavations within the penitentiary, showing the truncation to the earlier mill house/waterwheel footings. (PAHSMA 2013)

The conversion also necessitated major changes to wall configurations and thicknesses, required to support not only the new flooring elements, but also the voids and spaces required for the new cell ventilation systems. Redundant doorways were removed from the granary and treadwheel ward areas and the massive loading bay system in the granary was filled by new brickwork. New internal walls were keyed into the existing external walls and strengthened by the insertion of hoop iron in some brick courses.

The archaeological evidence indicates that to enable these works, the waterwheel, treadwheel, associated fittings and milling gear were removed, followed by the internal walls separating the mill house from the treadwheel ward (on the west) and the granary (on the east) (Figure 4.25). These were taken down to ground level, with even the sandstone footings lifted; the L-shaped corner quoins of the north–south walls were cut through and provided the quoins for the reveals of the new windows, which were set in the gap between the granary and mill/treadwheel ward buildings. Some elements, such as the sandstone base of the waterwheel's tailrace, were retained to provide support for timber flooring.

With this done, much of the interior of the building was excavated out. Corresponding with the location of the 136 separate cells in the former treadwheel/mill house, this excavated area was then filled with dolerite broken to a standard size and capped with lime mortar (Figure 4.26). This layer was up to 0.95 metre thick, at its deepest toward the centre of the building; in total it is estimated that there is some 350 cubic metres of this material supporting the cell blocks. The upper section of this 'raft' comprised a mixture of broken dolerite and mortar, with that below largely just broken dolerite. A band of mortared dolerite ran through the middle of the deposit, presumably to seal the upper levels from tidal water ingress.

After this raft had been laid, the sandstone footings of the separate cells were constructed, followed by a thin waterproofing layer of mortar and bitumen. The sandstone plinths of the encircling footings were then cut down to accommodate the abutting floorboards, with bricks and stones placed down across the mortar base to support this flooring.

Although the construction of the bakehouse necessitated less conversion of existing elements, there was evidence that pre-existing structures in the area had been incorporated into the new structure. At least some of the bakehouse's foundation had been built atop a footing predating its construction. The foundation had likely been associated with the workshops present in the area until overprinted in the 1850s, potentially supporting the timber plate and weatherboard walls of this waterfront building. This was further supported by layers of broken dolerite and crushed brick surfacing in association with the mortar footing, potentially related to internal surfacing for the workshops (Figure 4.27).

The sandstone footings of the bakehouse were covered by a thin bitumen damp-proofing course, on which the bricks of the superstructure were built. Unlike in the penitentiary, the flooring was actually raised by the importation of clay and brick rubble, the latter bonded and sealed with mortar, placed upon the earlier reclamation clays. Some of the bricks utilised for this purpose were potentially sourced from the demolished portions of the workshops. Over this levelling layer had been spread bedding sand, on which had been placed sandstone flags. These surfaced the whole of the bakehouse structure.

At the front of the building, work got underway on the muster ground. Incorporating a small amount of reclaimed ground from the 1840s,

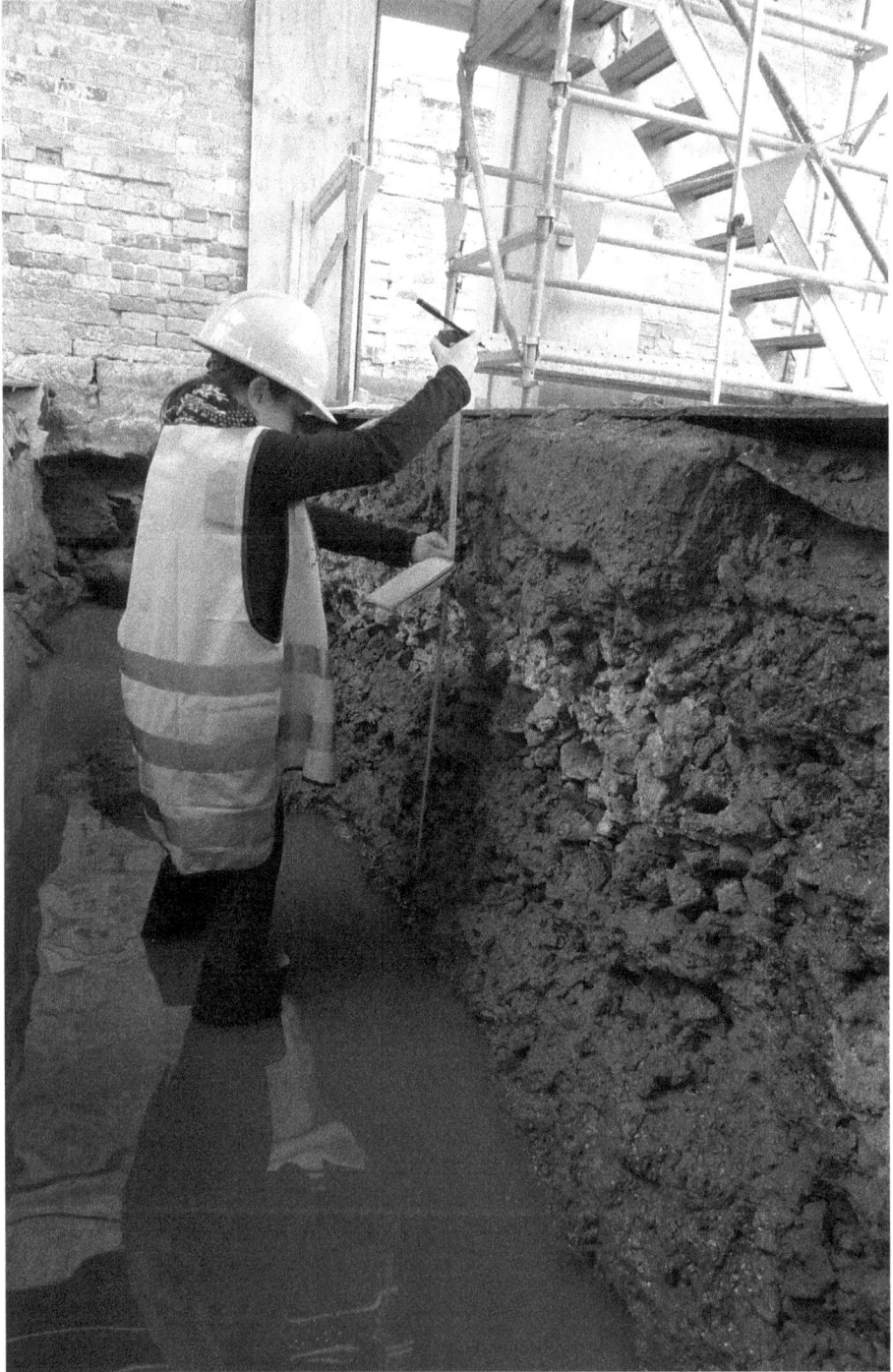

Figure 4.26. Broken dolerite raft underneath the separate cells within the penitentiary. The lighter coloured band contains mortar (PAHSMA 2014).

Figure 4.27. Broken dolerite and crushed brick surfacing, cut by the footings for the bakehouse (PAHSMA 2013)

the 1854 reclamation provided the majority of the muster ground's area, with sandstone, dolerite, earth, brick and rubbish all used in the process. Conversion of the mill likely took place at the same time. The former tailrace of the waterwheel was capped, with a new brick drain built over the top – carrying wastewater from a downpipe. A course of flagging and drainage was run around the periphery of the building, after which the level of the muster ground was raised by the importation of clay and sandstone rubble. This was capped by a surface of dolerite broken to grade, set on a bed of crushed brick and siltstone. The clocktower, keyed into the northern front of the penitentiary, was constructed at this time. It too was set on a raft of broken dolerite and mortar, like that found supporting the penitentiary separate cells.

A similar program of construction took place in the ablutions and laundry area. In the latter, the construction of the laundry building led to the removal of most of the previous structures and deposits. In the ablutions, a large amount of material was imported to change the area's profile.

Initial construction work during this phase comprised the rebuilding of the Champ Street retaining wall where it passed through the laundry area.

Figure 4.28. Champ Street retaining wall, showing the 1840s wall (lighter stone) and the section reconstructed during Phase II (darker section). (PAHSMA 2016)

Approximately 28 metres of the wall was rebuilt, creating a battered brick and sandstone wall (Figure 4.28). This covered, or completely eradicated, evidence of the original wall in this section. The ground was stripped to the shallow dolerite bedrock as part of the construction process, with the wall built atop the exposed stone.

Likely contemporaneous with the reconstruction of the retaining wall, the construction of the laundry building resulted in the laying of approximately 75 linear metres of footings, delineating seven spaces. The building's construction left an unroofed gap of about 1.60 metres between the Champ Street retaining wall and the southern footing of the laundry. These footings were laid early in the construction program (ca. 1854) and then retained through the occupational life of the building.

The laundry's footings were constructed from mortared sandstone of varying sizes and were up to two courses high (Figure 4.29). As in the bakehouse, the uppermost course of sandstone was topped by a thin layer of bitumen damp-proofing, above which was the brick superstructure of the building proper (largely removed during the post-convict period). Along the southern edge of the area, where the bedrock outcropped close to the

Figure 4.29. The former 'baths' space, showing the mixture of brick and sandstone footings. (PAHSMA 2016)

surface, some of the footings were set on bedrock and surficial (clay) deposits, with sections shaped to follow the undulations of the natural stone. Other footings had been cut into the reclamation clays and an early waterfront surface, reflecting the deepening of the bedrock where it got closer to the original shoreline.

The northern section of the laundry building comprised an elongated space linking the workshops precinct with the penitentiary's bakehouse and laundry. Surfaced with compacted rubble in the western extent, grading through to a compact mortar and brick gravel in the east, a portion of the space had likely been open to the elements. Two entrances led from the bakehouse, with one accessing an overseer's office and the other the bakehouse proper. Both were later bricked-up before, or as part of, works during Phase II. Architectural elements consistent with such construction activities were identified during excavation.

Within the laundry building, a series of surfaces reflected the different functions for which the spaces were used. The westernmost spaces, marked on plans as 'clean and foul linen' stores, had both been paved with sandstone flagging, in a fashion similar to that in the bakehouse. In the space marked

Figure 4.30. Compact crushed brick surface within the laundry space. (PAHSMA 2016)

as 'laundry', crushed sandstone, rubbly clay and compact shell lime mortar had been deposited, comprising construction waste and imported levelling fill. These were placed either side of a sandstone box drain, which bisected the space. The fill layers had been topped with a layer of crushed, compacted brick, which formed the surface of the laundry space that sat at the same level as the sandstone slabs covering the drain (Figure 4.30).

The drain commenced in the laundry's eastern spaces, fed from an inlet leading from the ablutions yard (Figure 4.31). Running through the laundry space, the drain emptied into a sump in the north-western corner of the space. Formed from an iron box edged with brick, the sump had no base, emptying directly into the doleritic clay. Covered with timber, the sump had likely been a sediment trap, collecting solids rinsed off during the washing process. The wastewater from the sump passed out of the building through a drain and into a drainage system in the workshops precinct.

In this area, immediately north of the linen stores, copper offcuts, a copper nail, a drafting compass and a bone-handled knife were identified in mixed clay and rubble deposits, likely associated with earlier workshop activities.

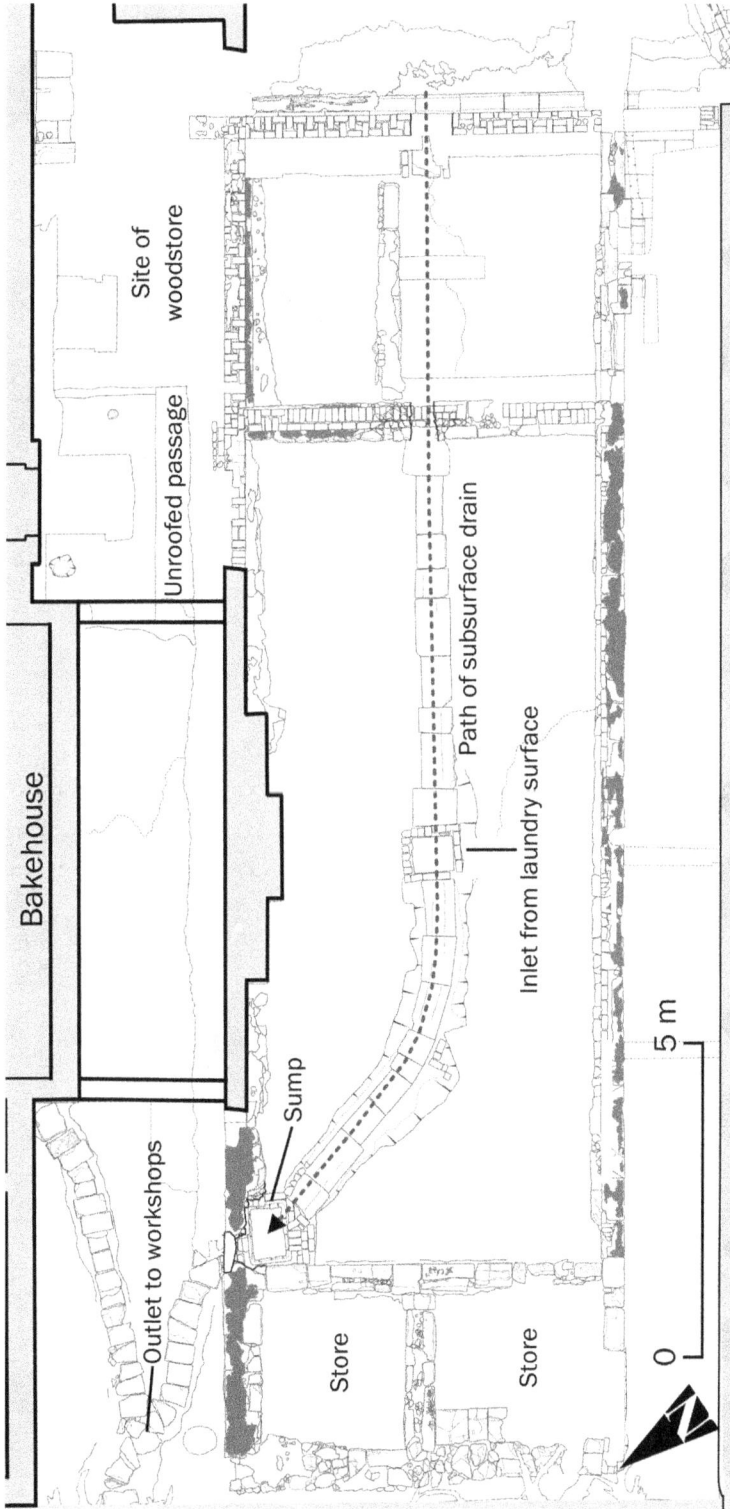

Figure 4.31. Illustration showing the course of the drain through the laundry.

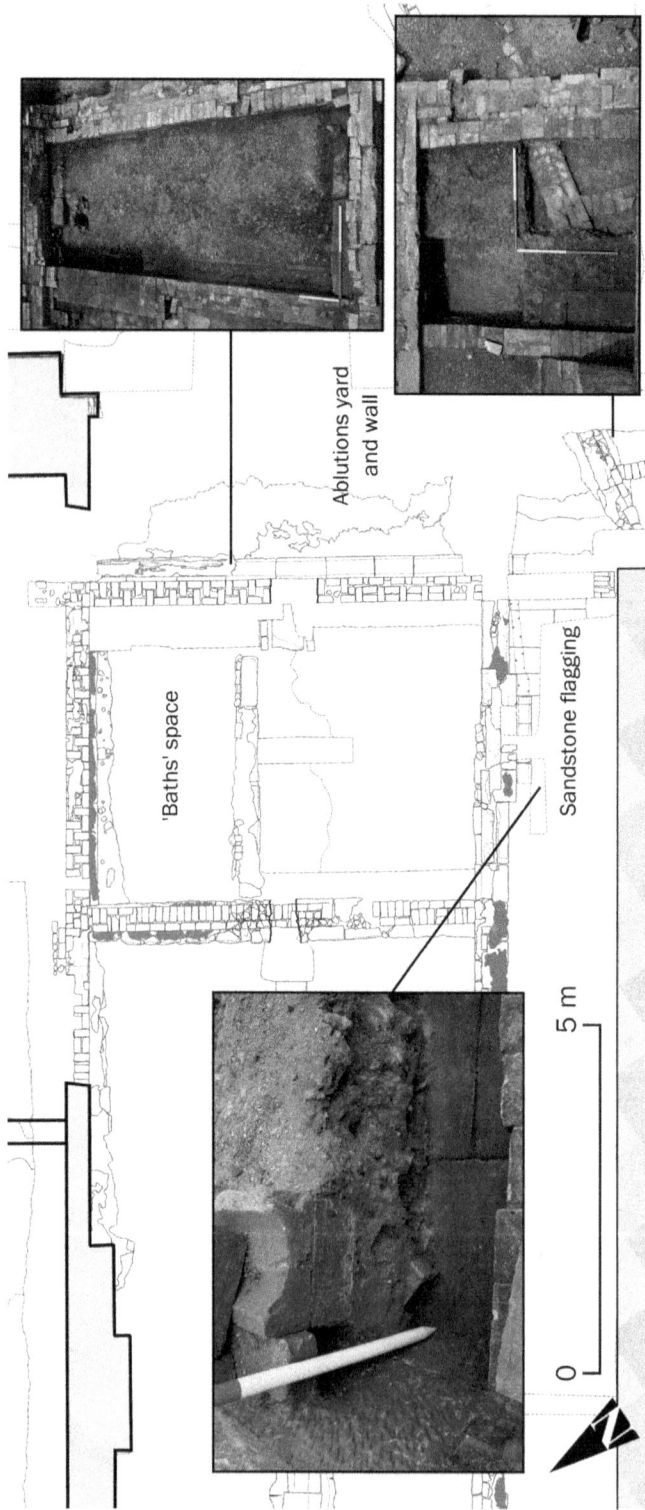

Figure 4.32. Illustration showing the features of the laundry's easternmost spaces (clockwise from left: sandstone flagging below later Phase II fills, the ablutions yard overprinted by later Phase II laundry footings, a section of dividing wall footing covered by Phase II footings).

During this phase, the two easternmost spaces were recorded as 'wood store' and 'baths'. Although the former area had been heavily modified by the later addition of a boiler base in Phase II, evidence of the original footing dividing the laundry and ablutions area was located below it. In addition, a series of organic-rich horizons encountered within the space likely represented the accumulation of bark and dust in the store from the firewood.

The 'baths' space was, at a later period, subdivided into two (Figure 4.32). This, and the extension of the building during Phase II, had greatly disturbed the deposits relating to the space. Artefacts recovered from these spaces, largely comprising buttons and clay tobacco pipes, were predominantly from mixed-phase deposits – making it difficult to definitively understand the purpose of the space. The presence of the drain running through it does support the idea it was a wet area. It had likely been covered by timber flooring, although the presence of broken dolerite surfaces also suggests that some of the space might have had a metalled surface – a strange addition for an internal area.

The narrow space between the laundry and the Champ Street retaining wall had initially been scoured down to bedrock as part of construction activity. After this, crushed brick had been laid as a surface. A passage existed between this space and the adjacent ablutions yard, paved with an apron of sandstone, with a drain which carried water into the ablutions yard (Figure 4.32). Movement from the laundry to ablutions yard required a small step down. The entrance provided access to the northernmost division of the western ablutions yard. The yard's dividing wall formed a narrow angle where it joined the Champ Street retaining wall, and a lightweight timber screen was likely erected to deter access to the less visible wall corner. Evidence in the form of a series of cuts on the upstanding section of Champ Street retaining wall shows where the series of basins shown on the plan had been fixed to the wall.

In the ablutions area, the conversion during 1854–57 resulted in the overprinting of the existing levelling layers with bedding and surfacing deposits, and the division of the area into the three spaces: west yard, central structure and east yard. These open, covered and enclosed spaces created demarcated areas for amenities, exercise and recreation. Surfaces and features relating to both yards were encountered during the excavation, with the west

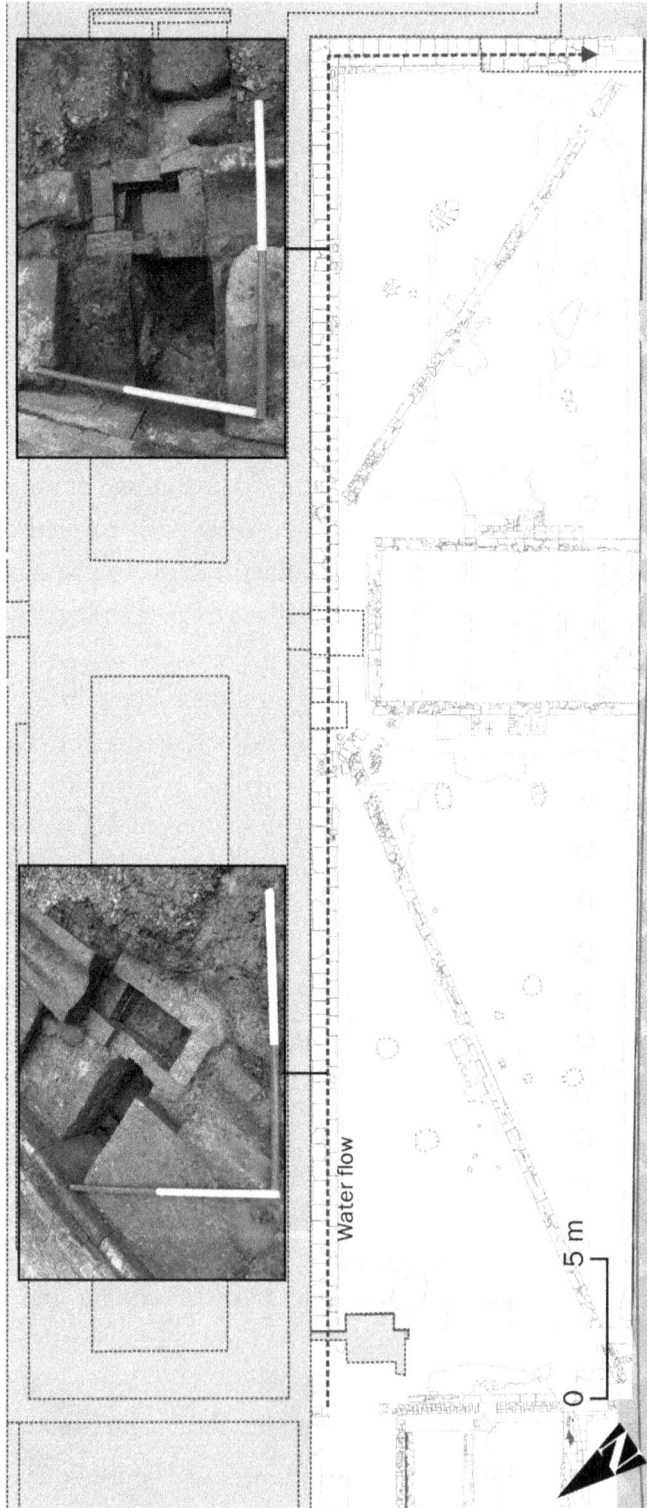

Figure 4.33. Illustration of ablutions area, showing drainage and sumps around the perimeter.

yard retaining a higher degree of intactness than its eastern counterpart. Remains of diagonal dividing walls were found in both yards. In the central structure, deposits and features relating to Phase I had suffered marked disturbance, though some elements likely to date from this period of activity did still survive.

A major element of the initial work was the laying of a spoon drain and flagging around the northern, eastern and western edges of the area, running along the base of the penitentiary and laundry buildings (Figure 4.33). This replicated the flagging and drainage laid at the front of the building on the edge of the muster yard. The laying of the flagging and spoon drain tiles was accompanied by the construction of five subsurface brick box sumps: three in the west yard and two in the east (Figure 4.33). These were accessed via grated holes cut in the drainage tiles. The drainage system was designed to direct water away from the base of the penitentiary, as well as to collect water running off the yard; the spoon drain fell toward the south-east. Water that did not collect in the sumps would have passed through the portal and day room and into the east yard, where it collected in the north-eastern corner. In the east of the east yard, a portion of the drain and flags had been covered by sandstone flagging, which would have brought it to the same level as the adjacent yard surface.

At the same time the drain and flagging were laid, work commenced on the central ablutions structure, accounting for the large number of artefacts with architectural function found within the space. Situated on sandstone footings, the structure was cut into the pre-construction levelling clays laid down in both the east and west yards (Figure 4.34). Its construction, as well as the installation of drainage infrastructure, resulted in heavy disturbance to earlier deposits and features from the industrial waterfront phase period of occupation.

Measuring 12 metres (north-east to south-west) by 6 metres, entry to the building was facilitated by a portal situated immediately after entering the ablutions area from the penitentiary (Figure 4.35). This portal was similarly constructed on sandstone footings, splaying outward from the northern termini of the central building's footings. This created an elongated space, providing the room necessary to allow passage not only to the central structure, but to each of the yards.

Figure 4.34. Detail of the central structure's shallow sandstone footings (the brick alignment belongs to a later phase of use). (PAHSMA 2016)

Although no physical evidence of the structure's form above footing level survived, substantial cuts into the Champ Street retaining wall indicated that the building had masonry – possibly sandstone – walls. These cuts also indicated that the building had a hipped roof. The plan from ca. 1863 supports this (Plate 1.6), additionally indicating that the structure was shingled and fitted with a series of skylights.

There was some archaeological evidence to support the presence of ablutions fixtures in the central structure (as indicated in the ca. 1856 plan; see Plate 1.5). Two brick box sumps and spoon drains were situated in the southern extent of the building's sub-floor area (Figures 4.36 and 4.37). These had probably been covered originally and had emptied toward the south-east, flowing into a covered spoon drain that ran along the base of the Champ Street retaining wall (Figure 4.38). It terminated at the earlier drain (Figure 4.19) leading out of the ablutions yard.

The construction of this drainage had necessitated modification of the central structure's footings, as well as that of the dividing wall in the east yard. This indicates that the presence of the drains had not been initially

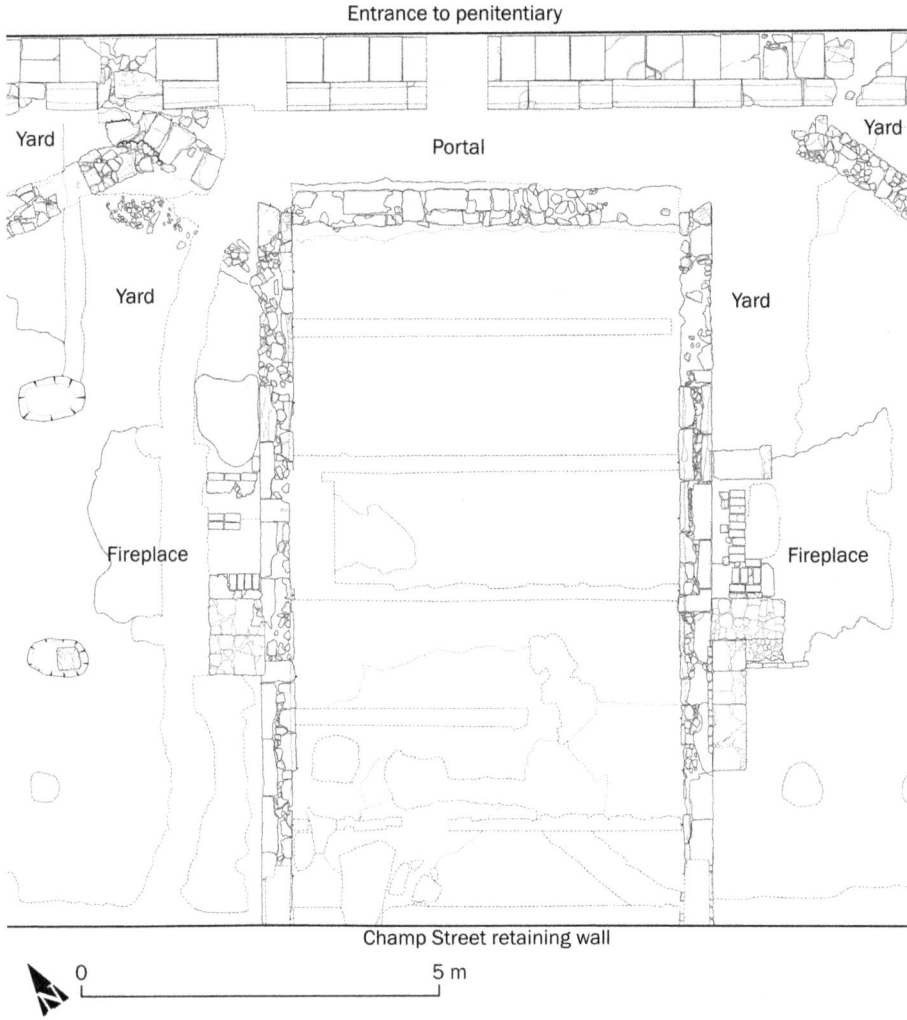

Figure 4.35. Illustration showing the central ablutions structure.

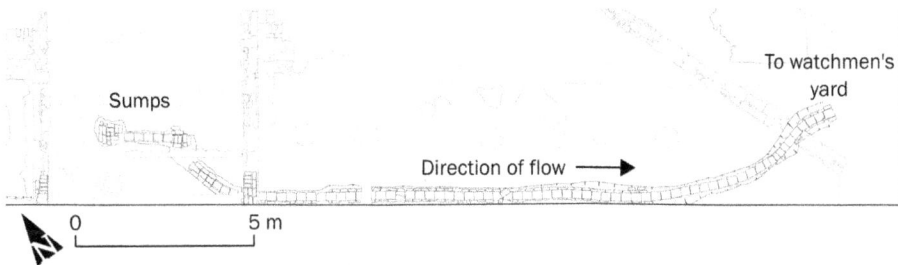

Figure 4.36. Illustration showing the position of the sumps within the central structure and the associated drain through the east yard.

Figure 4.37. The brick tile spoon drain within the central structure. (PAHSMA 2016)

planned for, and were added after major elements of the Phase I ablutions yard had already been constructed. The location of the sumps away from the location of the urinals, which were against the retaining wall, indicates that they had been placed to collect water runoff from the washing troughs.

The mixed nature of the deposits within the structure made it difficult to assign artefacts to Phase I with any confidence. Most artefacts recovered were potentially related to Phase II, and characterised by the heavy presence of items related to smoking, food consumption, clerical activities, gaming and clothing. However, from a more secure deposit associated with Phase I, a number of personal and clothing items were retrieved, which must have been lost to the sub-floor space during the use of the building for ablutions.

In the yards, the Phase I works resulted in the creation of mirrored layouts: both yards divided by a diagonal wall, outfitted with fireplaces and shelters, and surfaced with a hard-wearing compacted brick gravel. These works were also reflected by the large number of architectural artefacts scattered across the yard surfaces and in its associated deposits.

In the west yard, Phase I saw the division of the area by a dividing wall set on substantial sandstone foundations up to three courses high. Although

Figure 4.38. Section through the east yard showing the top of the brick tile spoon drain running from the central structure. (PAHSMA 2016)

the yard, which measured 22 metres by 12 metres, had a marked slope toward the penitentiary, the footing had been laid to an even level across the yard's entirety and was keyed into the portal at one end and terminated at the Champ Street retaining wall at the other. This meant that there were individual entrances leading directly from the portal to each half of the yard. Little evidence of the superstructure of the wall which once sat on top of the footing survived, except for shell lime mortar over the top of the foundation and a single remnant brick, suggesting the wall had been brick-built.

Although later changes in the yard disturbed Phase I evidence, it is clear that the yard gravels were laid after the construction of the dividing wall footings. In the west yard the surface on the southern side of the wall was made to be slightly higher than the northern one. The surface was formed from broken and crushed brick, which, although likely laid when freshly broken, had been worn smooth during the yard's use. The distinct size differences of the brick inclusions within the surface in the yard's northern and southern divisions suggests the yard surfaces, while probably contemporaneous, were laid as two distinct events – possibly by two or more teams of labourers.

Figure 4.39. Section excavated against the dividing wall of the west yard. Note the layer of crushed brick (upper layer) overlying a horizon of bedding sand (light band) and levelling clay. (PAHSMA 2016)

The surface had a distinct profile, following the curvature of the reclamation fills below (Figure 4.39). These bands were at their thickest toward Champ Street retaining wall, thinning as they moved toward the penitentiary. This meant that the yard fell noticeably toward the north, where it sloped toward the base of the penitentiary, and the west, where it sloped toward the dividing wall between ablutions area and laundry. Such a profile would have facilitated the drainage of water off the yard and into the perimeter drainage.

A number of structures were constructed in the west yard in association with the dividing wall. A back-to-back fireplace was built in the central part of the wall (Figure 4.40), the base of the north fireplace being recessed into the yard's surfacing gravels, with the south fireplace set atop the gravel surface. A timber rectangular shelter covered both fireplaces, the timber uprights supported in chamfered sandstone post sockets (Plate 4.6).

A third fireplace was situated at the eastern end of the west yard, abutting the exterior of the day room footings. It had a different method of construction, formed from three brick alignments, either side of which had

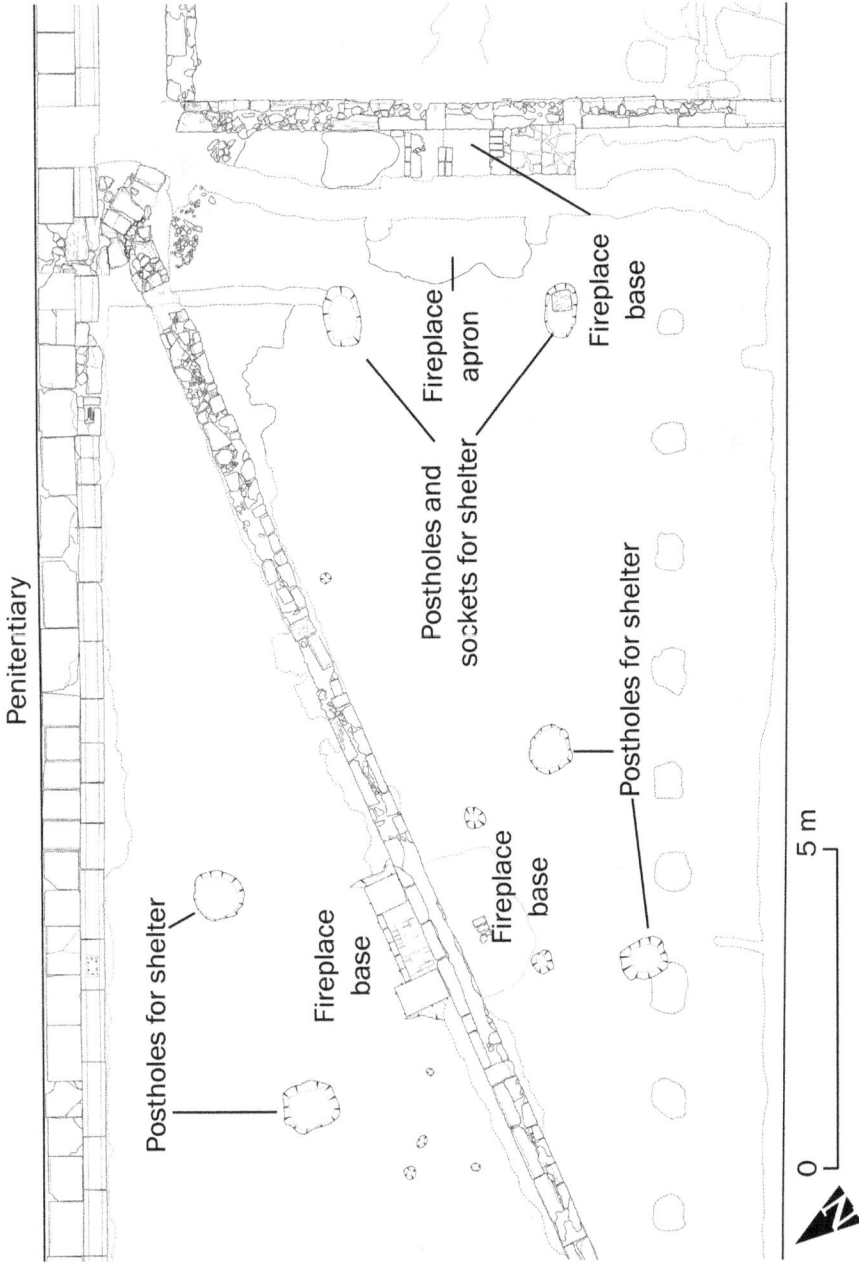

Figure 4.40. Illustration showing the location of the three fireplaces in the west yard.

Figure 4.41. Photograph of the westernmost fireplace, showing the in situ sandstone socket in one of the shelter postholes. (PAHSMA 2016)

been placed sandstone flagging. As with the central fireplaces, the eastern fireplace had had a shelter erected over it, evidenced by two postholes. A sandstone socket was *in situ* within the former cut (Figure 4.41).

The western end of the west yard had been overprinted by the laundry during the Phase II extension (Figure 4.32 and 4.42). The structure had covered a gravel surface with a distinct westward slope, directing water runoff from the yard toward a timber-covered sandstone spoon drain running along the base of the footing between the ablutions and laundry areas (Figure 4.42). The drain directed water northward toward a similar spoon drain running along the northern side of the yard. The drain had been built over during Phase II by the construction of the boiler base and was associated on this northern side with sandstone flagging abutting the penitentiary footing. An iron bracket was set into the wall of the penitentiary (Figure 4.42). Approximately 0.35 metre above the flags, the bracket had once supported timber benching, recorded in the ca. 1856 plan as having lined the edges of the ablutions yard. There were slight wear patterns on the sandstone flagging where continual use of the bench over time had eroded the surface below. Sockets for similar brackets are spaced at regular intervals along the southern

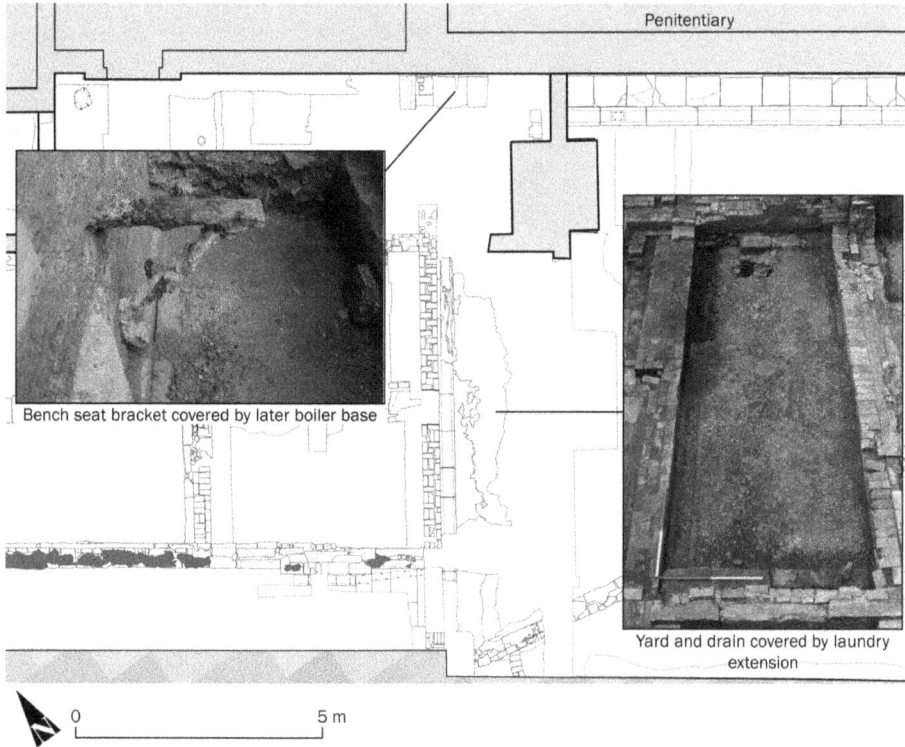

Figure 4.42. Illustration showing the elements covered by the later extension of the laundry into the ablutions area. From left to right: the iron bracket for a bench seat, Phase I ablutions yard gravel surfaces and spoon drain.

wall of the penitentiary and confirm the presence of seating throughout the yard spaces.

A number of different artefact types were compressed into the west yard's crushed brick surface: pieces of writing slate, glass storage bottles, earthenware and architectural components (nails and window glass). However, the largest number of finds were fragments of clay smoking pipes (Figure 4.43). These were scattered across both halves of the yard, with little evident correlation to the yard's architectural features.

The east yard mirrored the arrangement of the western one, although it was smaller: 18 metres (north-west to south-east) by 12 metres. Similar to the western yard, it was divided by a diagonal sandstone footing and set in a shallow foundation cut, with little evident effort to ensure structural stability (Figure 4.44). This was at odds with the deepness of the footing in the west

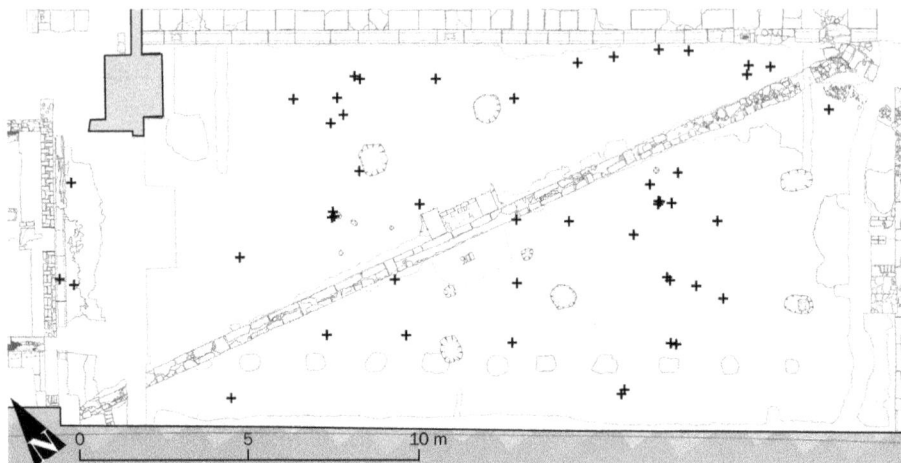

Figure 4.43. Distribution of clay smoking pipe fragments across the west yard (not including sieved finds).

yard. Phase II disturbance meant that less of the footing was present in the east yard, with only two courses remaining *in situ*.

The yard divisions were surfaced with crushed brick, sandstone and dolerite gravel. The composition of this gravel was markedly different to the surface gravel in the west yard, having been greatly disturbed by surfacing works during Phase II. The whole of the yard continued the pronounced south-west to north-east slope of the ablutions area, the yard being level for 8 metres from the base of the Champ Street retaining wall but then markedly falling toward the wall of the penitentiary.

As in the west yard, fireplaces were installed to service both halves of the east yard (Figure 4.45). A brick and sandstone fireplace was constructed abutting the eastern side of the dividing footing. Later Phase II works had severely disturbed the evidence, but two postholes containing extant sandstone sockets denoted the outline of a 3.20 × 2.90 metres structure covering the fireplace.

Another fireplace was also built, abutting the exterior of the central structure's eastern footing. This was constructed from a sandstone foundation, with a brick superstructure (Figure 4.45). A number of sandstone flags were situated around the south-eastern extent of the fireplace, as well as an extensive apron of broken sandstone extending from the base of the fireplace into the

Figure 4.44. Photograph of the footing for the eastern yard's dividing wall. Visible in the section is the reclamation clay below the yard. (PAHSMA 2016)

yard. These features likely related to the fireplace's hard-standing surround. No postholes were evident, suggesting that the fireplace had not been sheltered.

Unlike in the west yard, however, no fireplace was found on the western side of the diagonal wall. Its apparent absence may perhaps be explained by later disturbance, although deep-set features like postholes would likely still have remained in evidence. Although such evidence may have been removed by later activity, its absence is more likely due to the smaller size of the east yard, which would have been adequately served by one fireplace in each yard division.

Just prior to the Intermediate Phase, the west yard received a new surface of coarsely broken dolerite, spread across the yard when the dividing wall and furniture was still in situ (Figure 4.46). There was a density of clay tobacco pipe fragments across the area to an even greater degree than on the compact brick gravel surface it replaced (Figure 4.47). This accumulation of artefacts indicated the surface was exposed for sufficient time for this material to collect prior to it being reconfigured.

This resurfacing event did not markedly alter the layout or function of the yard, although the intensity of use, as evidenced by the clay tobacco pipe assemblage, may have increased. The remnants of post-pipes (the 'shadows' of

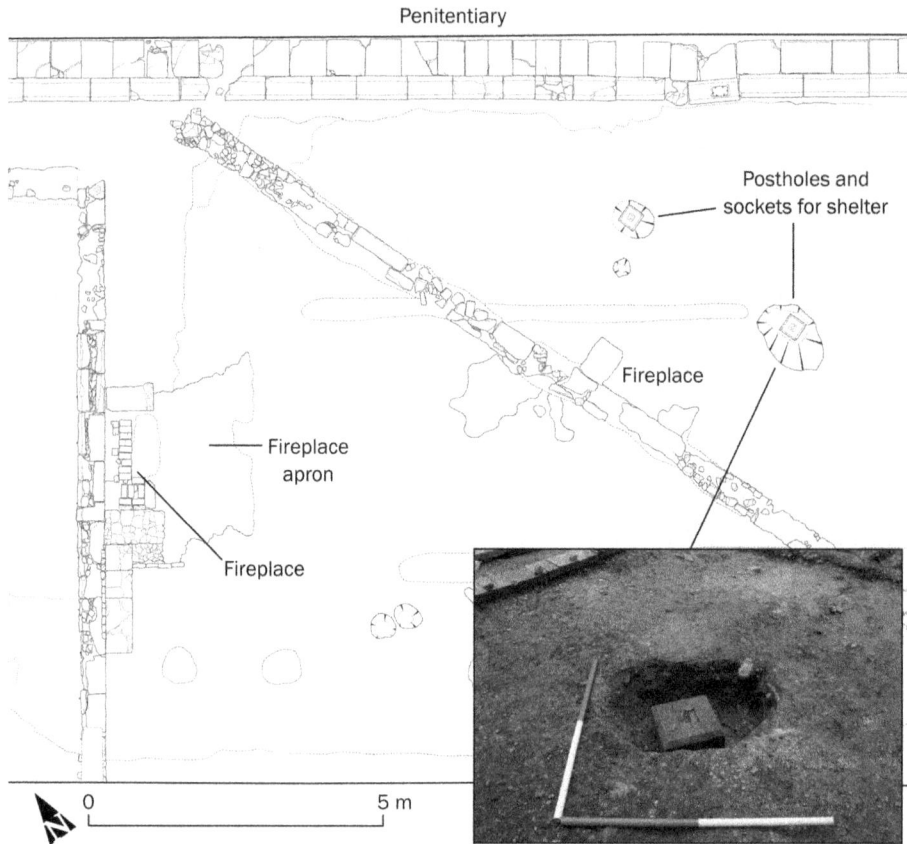

Figure 4.45. Location of fireplaces and associated features in the eastern yard.

the timber supports) through the gravel above the fireplace shelter postholes indicates that the shelters remained *in situ* and active at the time the gravel was laid down. The new surface had also abutted the central fireplaces and had been cut to accommodate a later, minor extension of the northern fireplace.

Penitentiary – Intermediate Phase, ca. 1862

This phase of activity was largely only discernible in the ablutions area, marking its first conversion to a different configuration. At the least, this involved the removal of the dividing walls in both yards, although it may not have resulted in the construction of any additional structures within them. The majority of

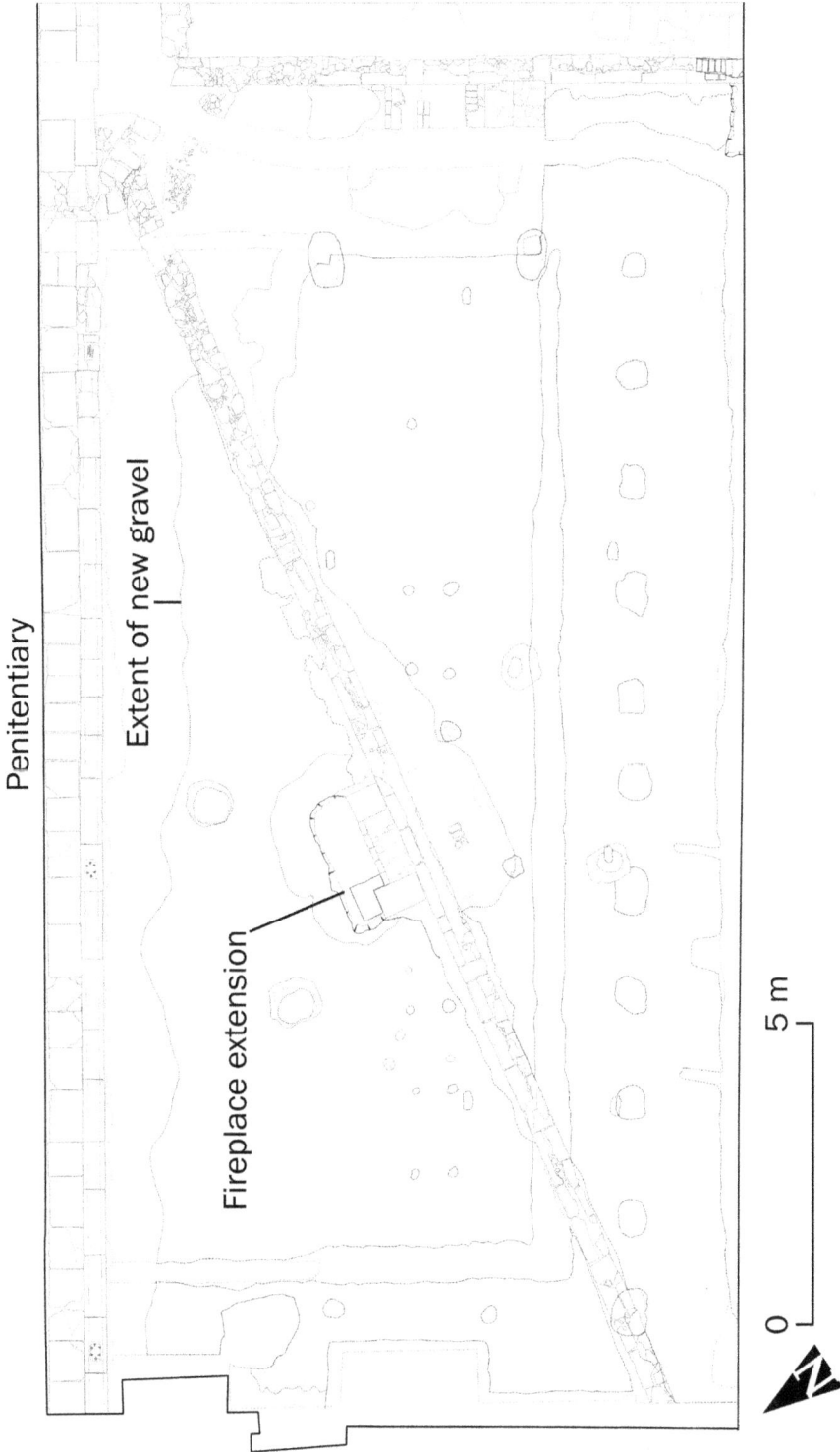

Figure 4.46. Illustration showing the west yard and the extent of the dolerite gravel.

Penitentiary

Extent of new gravel

Fireplace extension

0   5 m

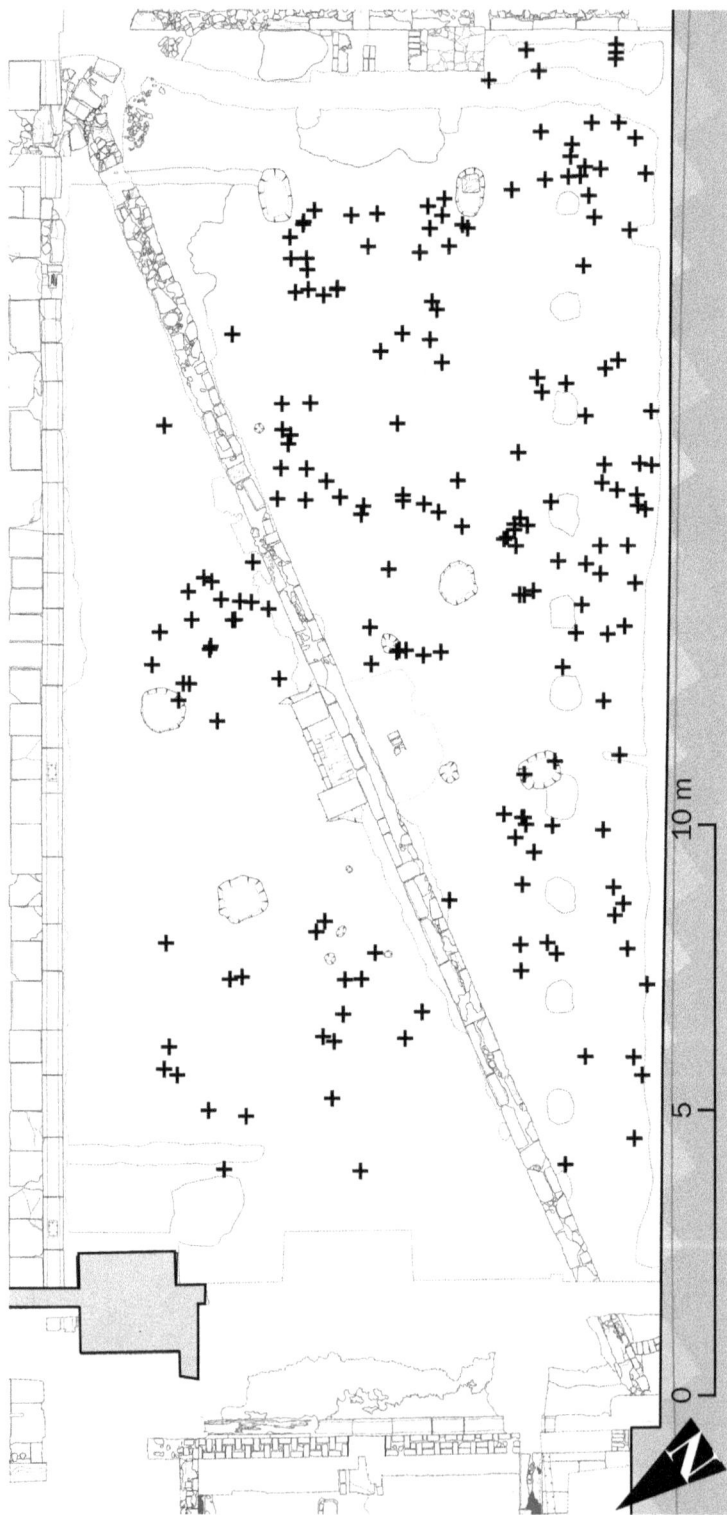

Figure 4.47. Extent and distribution of clay smoking pipe fragments in the west yard, deposited during and after the yard's resurfacing (excluding artefacts recovered from sieving).

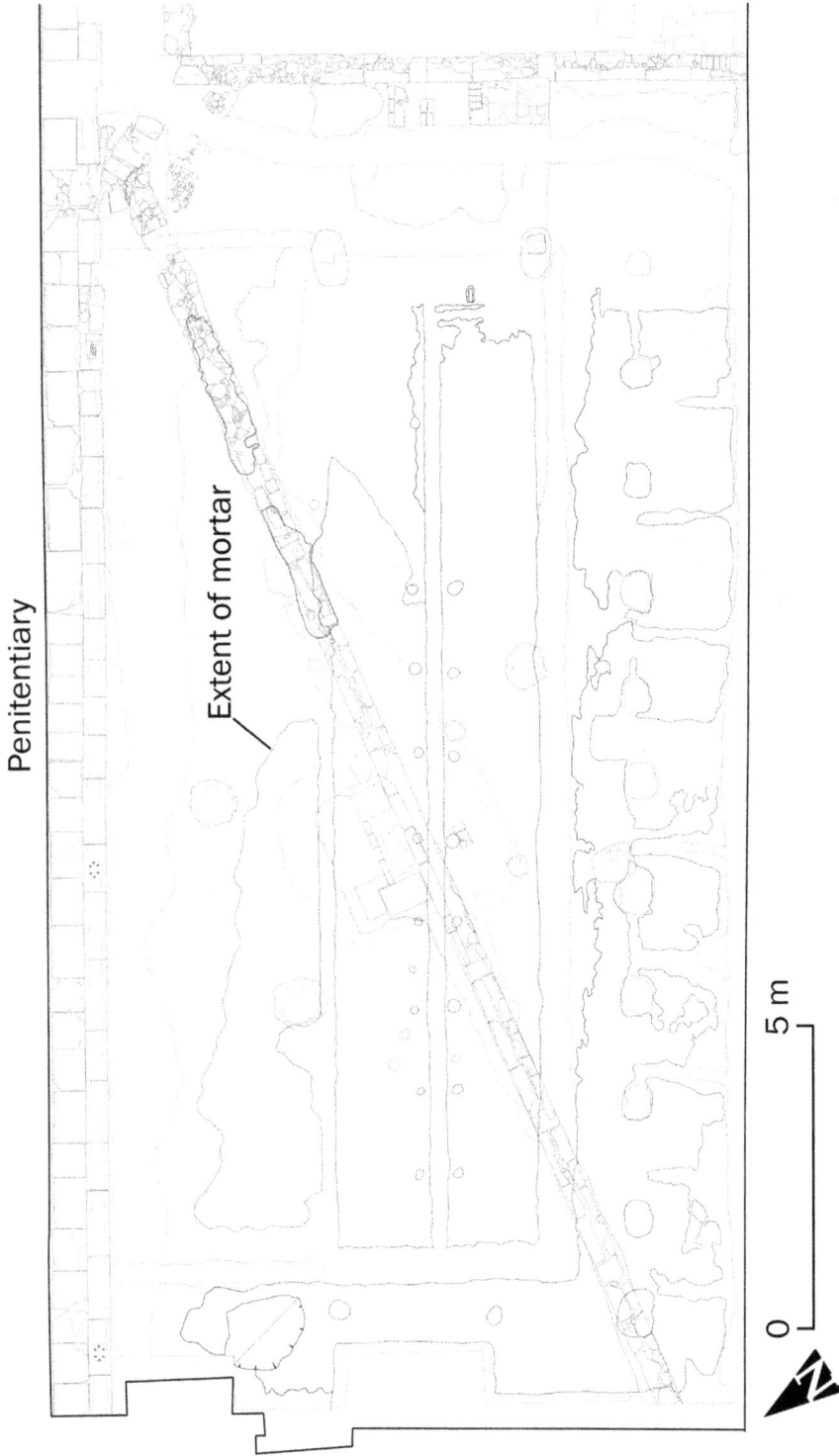

Figure 4.48. Illustration showing the extent of the mortar layer in the west yard of the ablutions area.

Penitentiary

Extent of mortar

0   5 m

Figure 4.49. Compact mortar overlying the first phase gravels in the west yard of the ablutions area. (PAHSMA 2016)

the evidence for this phase was found in the west yard. No features or deposits could be positively linked to this phase in the central structure.

In the west yard this phase resulted in the removal of the upstanding structures and the addition of a third surface. The central back-to-back fireplaces along the dividing wall, as well as the wall itself, were completely levelled, resulting also in disturbance to adjacent surfaces. The location of the two fireplaces was covered by compact deposits of shell lime mortar and brick rubble as a result of salvage and levelling (Figure 4.48). The yard's eastern fireplace (against the central structure) was retained, the chimney stack being retained for use during Phase II.

With the structures levelled, most of the yard was covered by a compact shell lime mortar, siltstone and sandstone gravel composition (Figure 4.49). The compact mortar surface was not present in much of the yard's northern area. It was likely only intended to be laid in the southern extent, corresponding with the flatter area upon which a shelter was later constructed during Phase II. In preparation for the addition of the mortar, the late-Phase I dolerite gravel in the yard was graded with a wide-toothed rake, the resultant striations still visible in the gravel (Figure 4.50).

After the demolition of the diagonal wall and its fireplaces and the laying of the compact mortar surface across most of the west yard, a series of bricks had been cut into the mortar surface (Figure 4.51). They had been arranged in a regular pattern, almost – but not quite – corresponding with the outline of the later Phase II shelter. The truncation of one of these bricks by the shelter does, however, indicate that the two features were not contemporaneous. The bricks were all placed at an even height, suggesting that they may have been used as a building or levelling guide within the yard.

In the east yard of the ablutions area the Intermediate Phase works resulted in a similar demolition of the diagonal yard wall and the removal of the central fireplace. This resulted in disturbance to the original Phase I surface and the deposition of charcoal-rich silts, mortar and sandstone rubble over the location of the footings. There was evidence of a fine dolerite surface laid down over the Phase I brick gravel. A layer of mortar and compact siltstone placed above the dolerite was similar to that encountered in the west yard, with these deposits capping the truncated dividing wall.

The duration of the Intermediate Phase cannot be determined. It may have been an extensive period of use, although this option is considered unlikely as it would have resulted in yards with little or no upstanding furniture – although the central structure may have continued to operate as an amenities block. Instead, this phase more likely represents a short period of activity marking the transition between Phases I and II when only one yard may have been available for convict use while the other was being reconfigured.

Penitentiary – Phase II, ca. 1862–77

The penitentiary's second phase occurred immediately after the events of the Intermediate Phase. Like the previous two phases, the evidence for this period of activity was only recovered from the ablutions and laundry areas. No deposits or features, either in sub-surface or standing fabric, that could be linked to this phase were found within the penitentiary, bakehouse or muster ground.

In the laundry, the former wood store and baths were extended 2.20 metres into the ablutions yard, as part of which a boiler and chimney were added and the internal spaces reconfigured. In the ablutions area, a series of

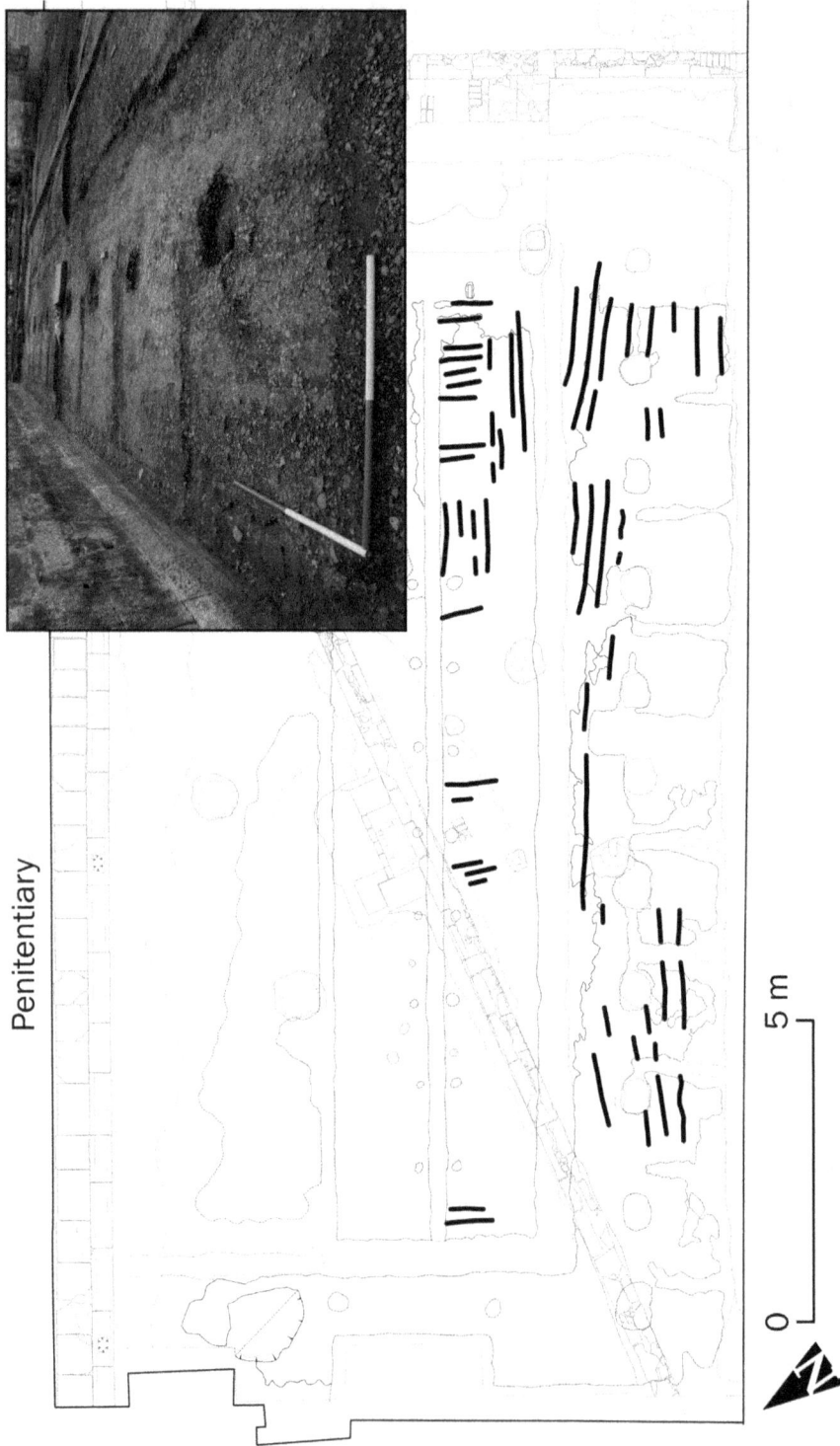

Figure 4.50. Illustration and photograph showing the striations in the gravels below the mortar.

Penitentiary

5 m

0

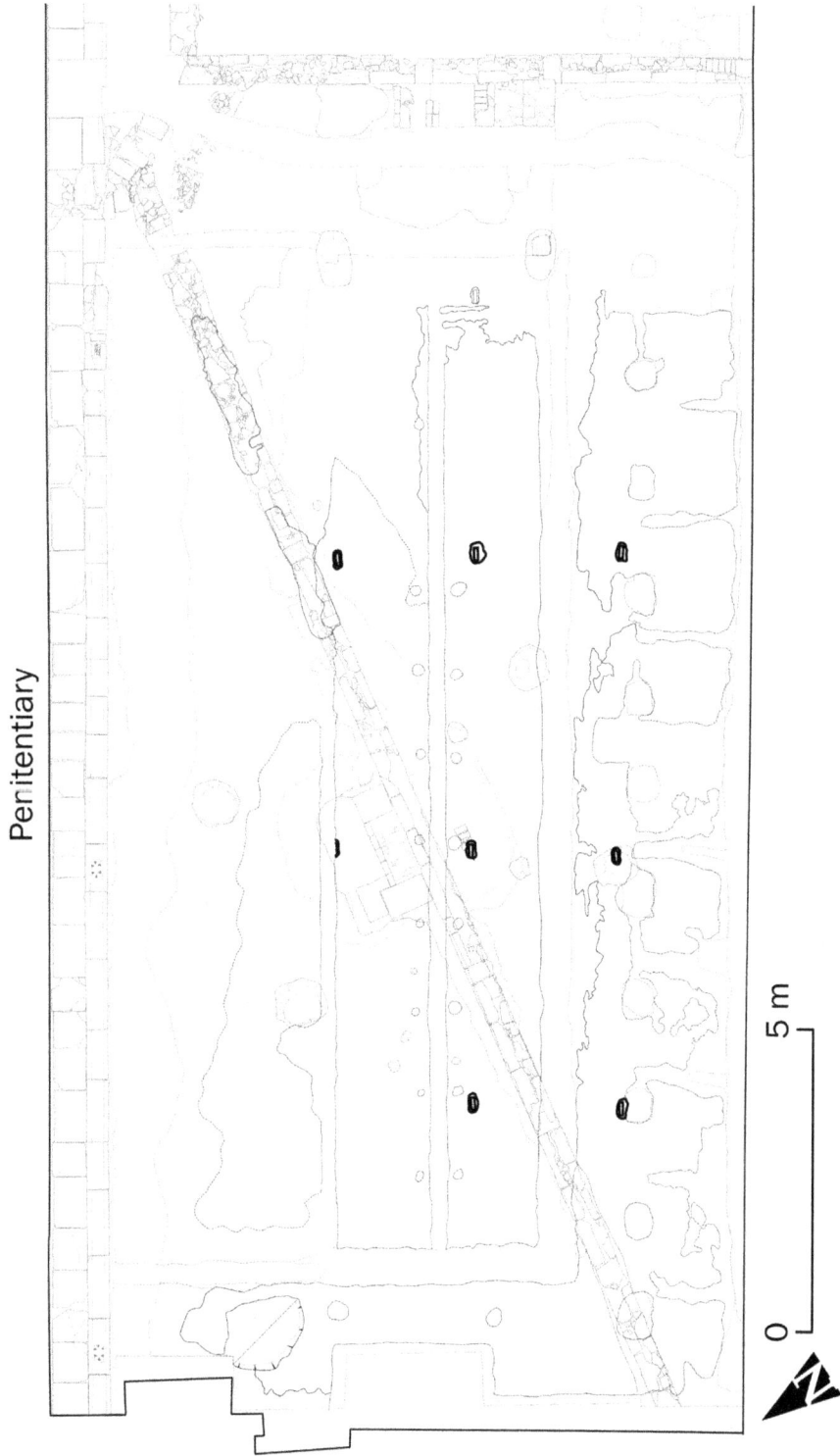

Figure 4.51. Illustration showing the location of the bricks cut into the mortar layer.

Penitentiary

0   5 m

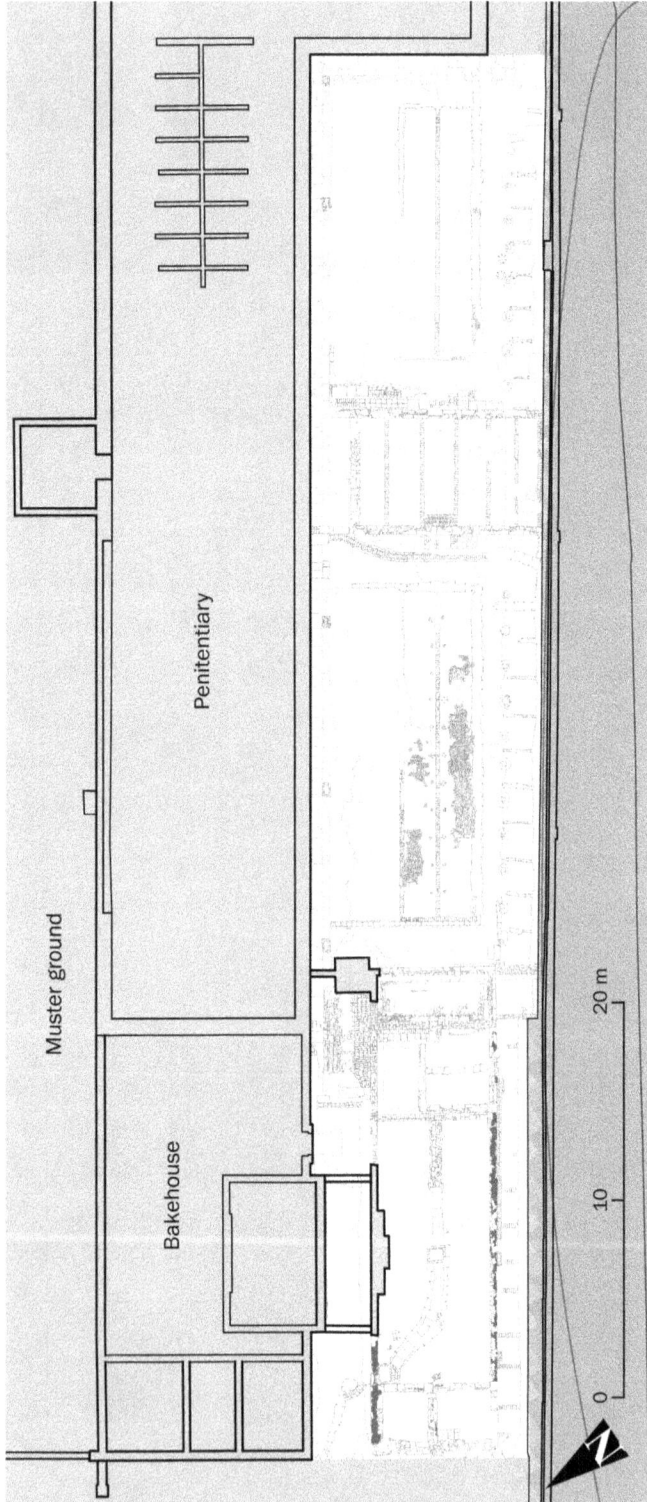

Figure 4.52. Illustrations overlaid on penitentiary plan, showing locations and layouts of ablutions and laundry areas ca. 1862–1877.

Penitentiary

Muster ground

Bakehouse

20 m

10

0

N

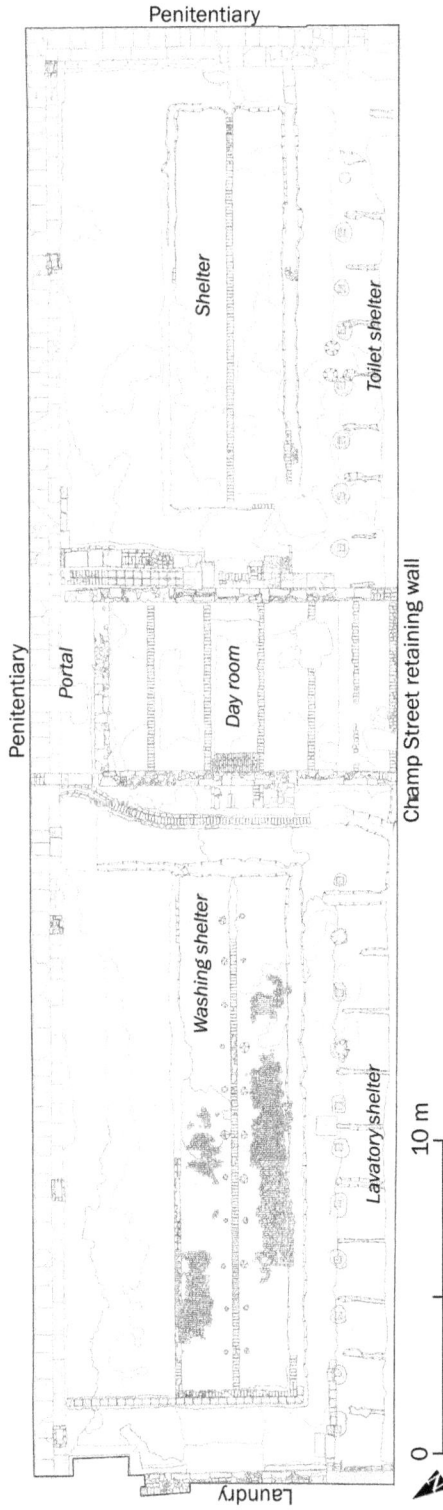

Figure 4.53. Illustration showing the ablutions area during the period ca. 1862–1877.

Figure 4.54. Orthophotograph of the ablutions area during ca. 1862–1877.

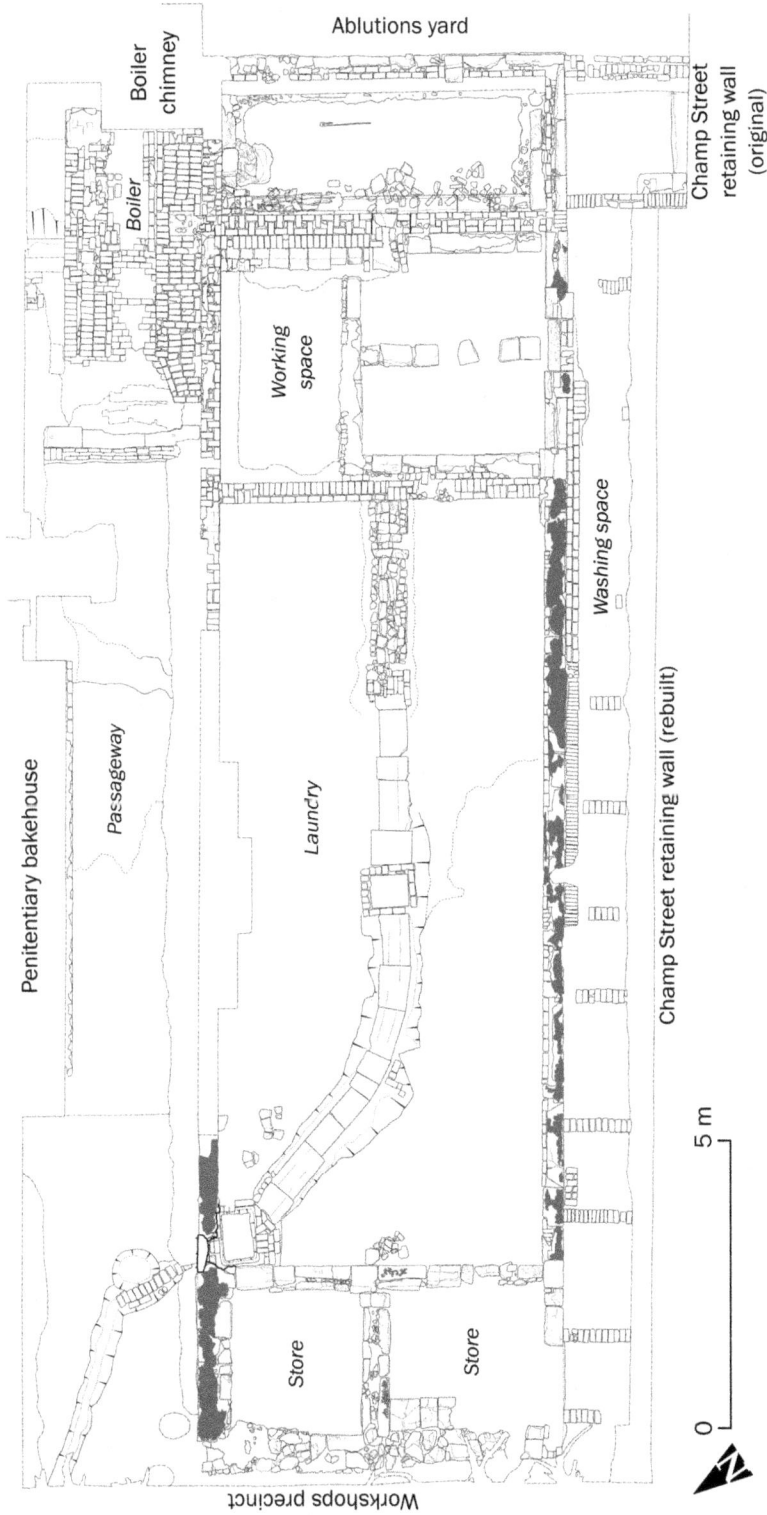

Figure 4.55. Illustration showing the laundry area during the period ca. 1862–1877.

Ablutions yard

Boiler chimney

Boiler

Champ Street retaining wall (original)

Working space

Washing space

Penitentiary bakehouse

Passageway

Laundry

Champ Street retaining wall (rebuilt)

Store

Store

Workshops precinct

5 m

0

N

Figure 4.56. Orthophotograph of the laundry area during ca. 1862–1877.

5 m

0

structures were added to both the east and west yards, comprising centrally placed sheds, and shelters lined along the base of the Champ Street retaining wall. The central structure was converted from an ablutions block into a 'recreational' day room.

The former wood store was converted to house a low-pressure steam boiler and its accompanying chimney. To provide a firm foundation for the boiler, a series of levelling deposits was laid down, covering earlier features of the ablutions yard (Figure 4.57). Some effort was made to retain and cover the yard's earlier spoon drain, indicating an intention to continue to direct water into it during this phase. A rough brick support was constructed under the boiler base and a timber plank placed over the drain. The brick boiler base was built atop this foundation (Figure 4.57). The form of the base suggested that a central iron spherical boiler had been situated over the recessed portion of the base. A number of heat-affected bricks indicated that this recessed portion had once held the firebox, which provided the heat for the boiler.

Associated with the construction of the boiler was the addition of the sandstone and brick footings delineating additional new spaces (Figure 4.58). As part of the construction, waste was deposited across the Phase I ablutions yard surfaces, and a pit sunk to support scaffolding for the boiler chimney's construction. The presence of fine silty deposits containing a high number of artefacts, as well as the brick bearer plates along the interior of the footings, supported the idea the spaces were floored with timber.

In the former bath space, a mixture of rubble, sands and silts indicated a high degree of disturbance from construction work (Figure 4.59). This was supported by a large number of architectural components (like nail fastenings) found within these deposits. A sandstone footing was added to this space, providing support for a timber floor. The presence of silty deposits post-dating the addition of the footing also indicated subfloor deposition and therefore the presence of timber flooring. Such deposits would have built up through use of the space, comprising the accumulated years of sediment and artefacts that fell between the boards. The drain which had run through the space from the ablutions yard was removed and replaced by a new, brick, box drain, running from the space's north eastern corner and out through

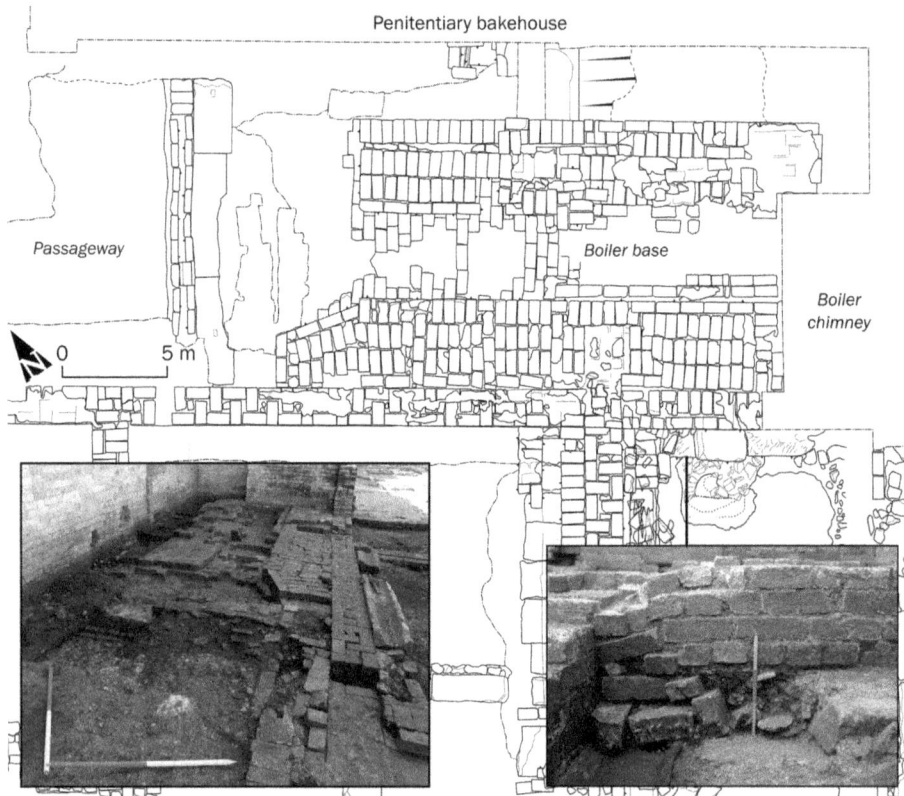

Figure 4.57. Illustration of the boiler base. The photograph on the bottom right shows the height of the base above the ablutions yard surface.

the outlet into the ablutions yard. This was joined at a later stage by a second drain, constructed from clay tiles.

Although the historical evidence does not indicate how the newly enlarged former bath space was used, a mix of artefacts indicated a complex history of use. A large number of clay tobacco pipes were found, suggesting use as a workspace of some kind, within which smoking appears to have been permitted (Figure 4.60). This space is also where the majority of buttons from the laundry area were found, most of them made of bone with three or four sew-through holes (Figure 4.61). Remains of food and beverage containers were found, suggesting that the occupants of this space may have enjoyed a more permissive atmosphere (Figure 4.62). Items such as writing slate and slate pencils, ink bottles and a small quantity of sewing pins also hinted at a mixed use. The latter suggested that the space may have been used for the repair of clothing destined for cleaning in the adjoining laundry room. The predominance of the bone buttons, known

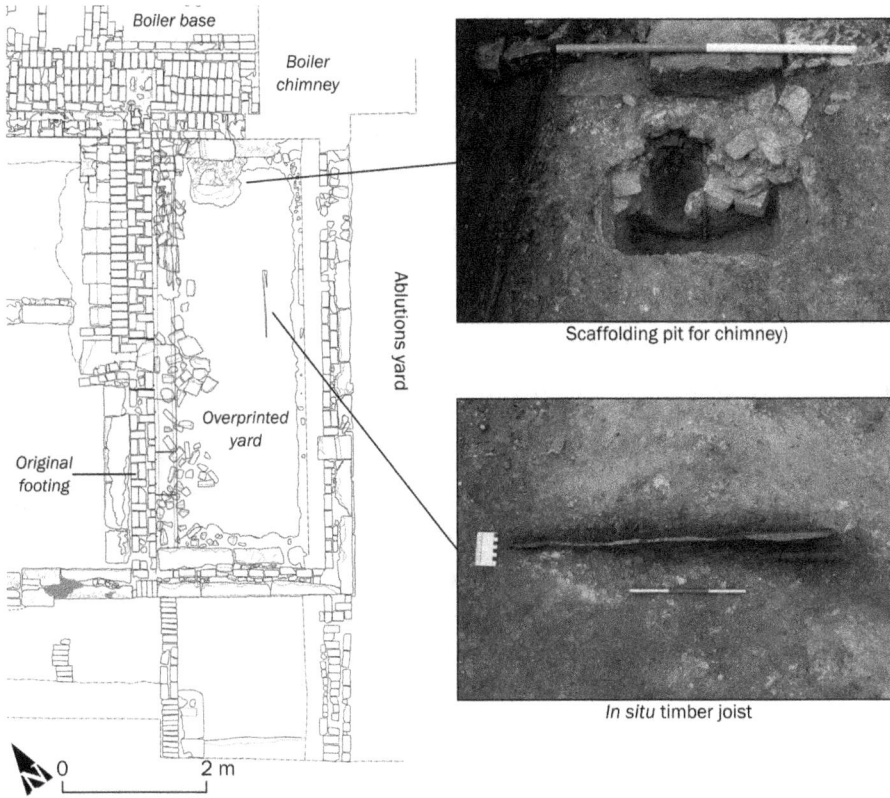

Figure 4.58. Illustration showing the areas added during the laundry extension.

to have been used on convict uniforms, supports this idea. Further discussion of this takes place in 'Private lives in public spaces'.

In the central and western extents of the laundry, the spaces largely retained their earlier configuration. Near the newly installed boiler, a new surface of crushed brick was added, although the compact mortar and brick gravel surface from Phase I was mostly kept. The space between the laundry and bakehouse had a number of new drains installed, including a timber stave drain running into the workshops precinct, and a white resin pipe with lead sheet terminal including the original ferrous nails (Figure 4.63). There is no clear reason why resin was used for this purpose, with no other known examples of its use at Port Arthur. At a later date, a brick box drain was installed along the base of the laundry's northern footing. Both drains led to the sump in the 'laundry' space.

Figure 4.59. Southern portion of 'baths' space. Note the very mixed deposits and the broken pieces of drain tile (right) resulting from the removal of the through drain. (PAHSMA 2016)

There was little evidence that the linen stores in the western extent of the laundry building underwent any change during this phase. Within the central 'laundry' space, sandstone paving was added to the area north of the central drain. This left the remainder of the space surfaced with the Phase I medium of crushed brick. It is possible that the southern half was floored with timber, although the lack of subfloor deposition does not support this. As the sandstone box drain running through the space no longer collected water from the ablutions yard, its eastern end was rebuilt in brick and sandstone, thereby capping it (Figure 4.64).

In the narrow space between the laundry and the Champ Street retaining wall, a rubble and clay deposit was used to fill and level the whole space (Figure 4.65). This overprinted the existing sandstone surface and provided a level deposit upon which to construct a series of brick bearers. These were all set at a similar height and would have supported timber flooring. Shell grit was then spread across the space, potentially with a view to using the shell's calcareous nature to keep the washing area sanitary (although this would have been nullified by the fact it was covered by a timber floor). The former passage between the ablutions area and laundry was discontinued, with the new entrance placed further east. At a later date a spoon drain was constructed along the base of the Champ Street retaining wall.

In the ablutions area during this period, work took place on the construction of new shelter sheds in both yards, the laying of new surfaces across the areas and the repurposing of the central structure from an ablutions shed into a day room.

In the central structure, works began with the addition of six brick alignments running north-west to south-east across the structure's footprint (Figure 4.66). The laying of these resulted in the truncation of the Phase I drainage elements in the southern extent of the area and intrusion into the underlying clay. These brick bearers supported timber bearers, which in turn supported timber joists. A number of remnant timber joists were encountered during the excavation of the overlying demolition debris from the post-abandonment phase.

Commensurate with the structure's remodelling and change of use, the portal space between it and the penitentiary was reconfigured. This resulted in the walls of the portal area being straightened, removing the splayed configuration that had accommodated the termini of the yard dividing walls. New drainage furniture was added externally along the eastern footing of the day room, likely designed to funnel water from a downpipe and into the encircling drainage system. Two new entrances were placed on the east and west sides of the portal space.

Activity within the day room resulted in the construction of two internal fireplaces midway along both the western and eastern walls. Both likely tapped into the two fireplaces and chimneys on the exterior of these walls in the yards, which may have been retained during this period. The brick pads of the fireplaces were set higher than the brick flooring supports, indicating that they had once sat flush with the building's timber flooring. The single remaining brick surface associated with the fireplace on the structure's western footing exhibited wear from exposure during use of the building.

The recovered artefacts supported the interpretation that the reconfiguration of the central structure was for its repurposing as a day room. A large number of architectural objects were recovered, including wrought nails, cut nails and prismatic window glass. The latter was also used throughout the penitentiary proper, providing translucency but not

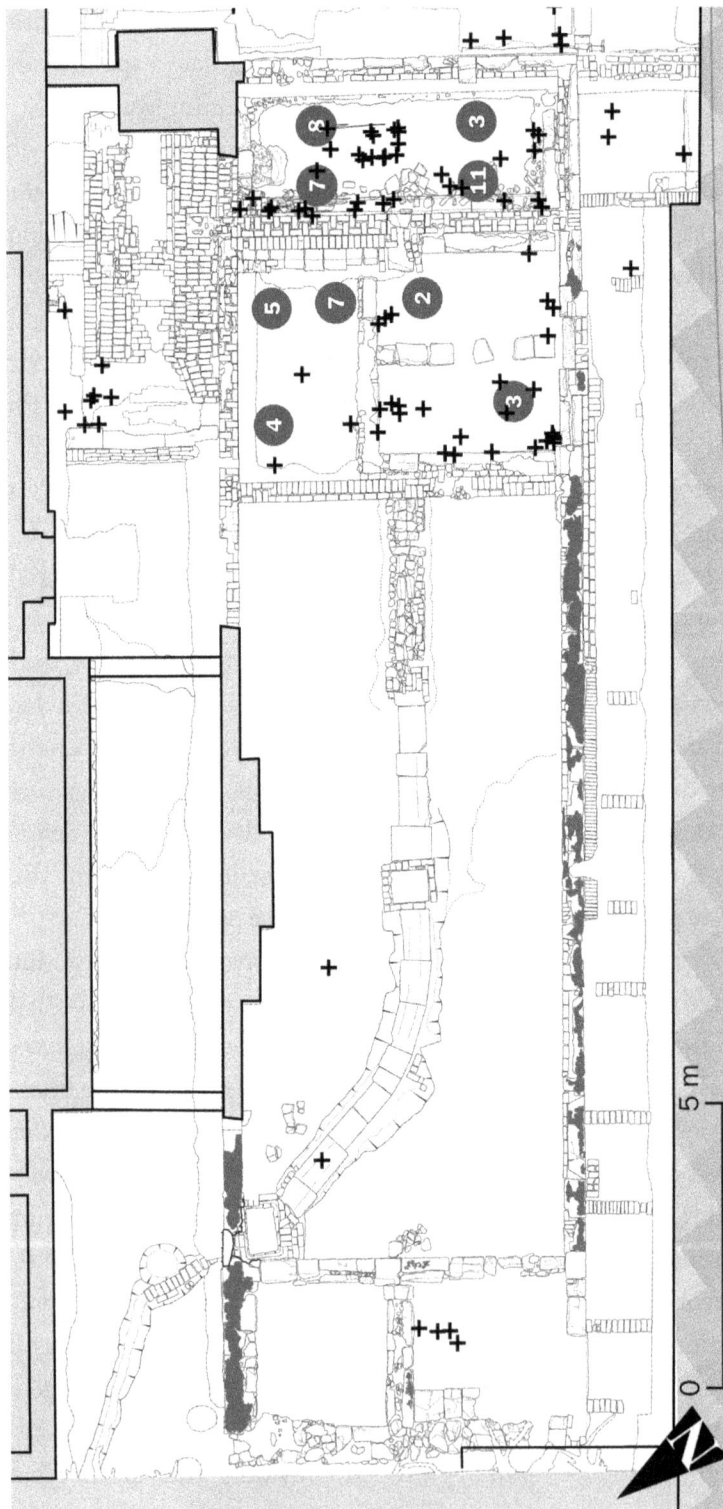

Figure 4.60. Illustration of the laundry showing the distribution of clay smoking pipes from Phase II deposits (circled numbers denote numbers recovered from sieving).

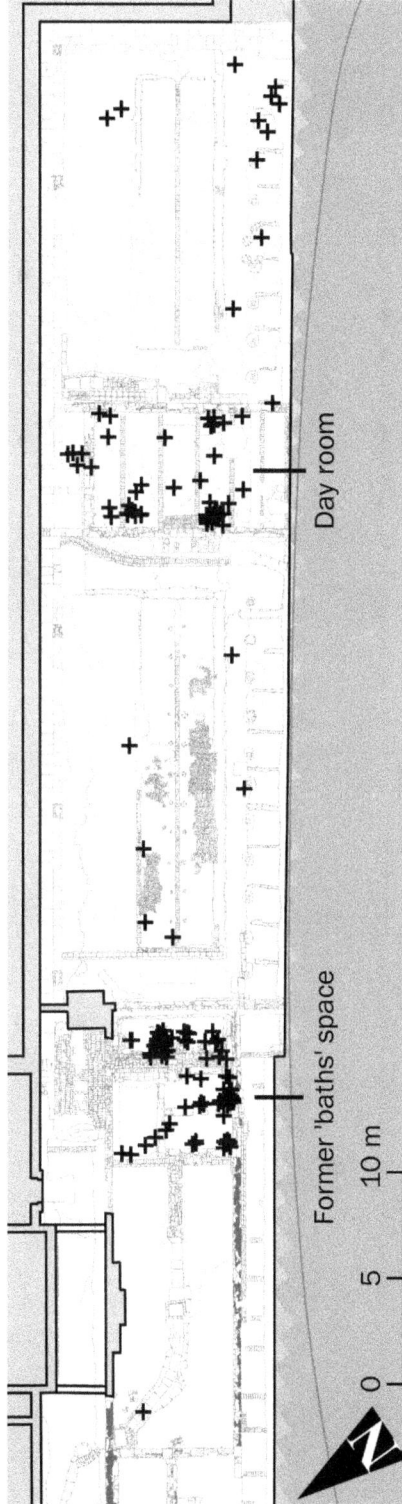

Figure 4.61. Distribution of buttons across the ablutions and laundry area recovered from Phase II deposits. Note the high proportion in the laundry's eastern space.

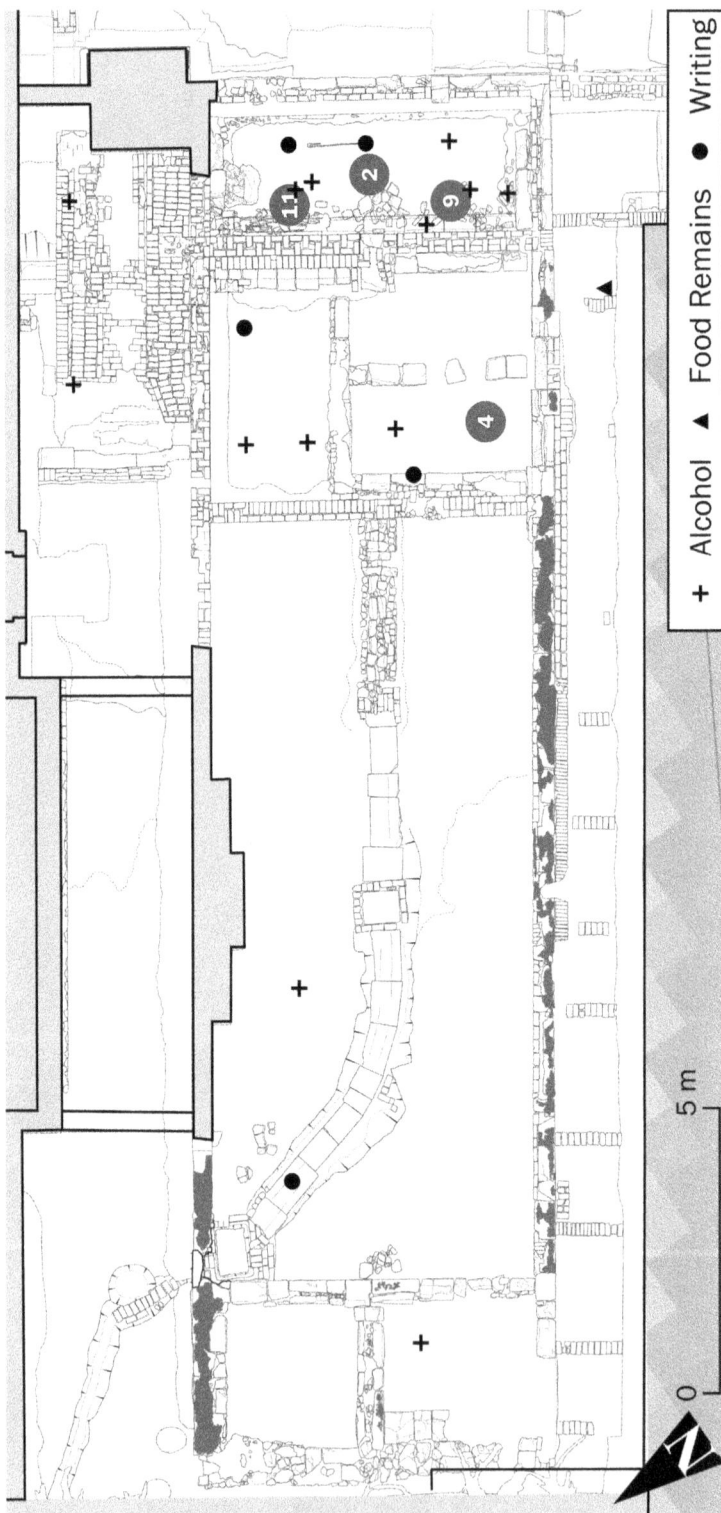

Figure 4.62. Distribution of artefacts related to alcohol, food and writing in the laundry area from Phase II deposits (circled numbers denote numbers recovered from sieving).

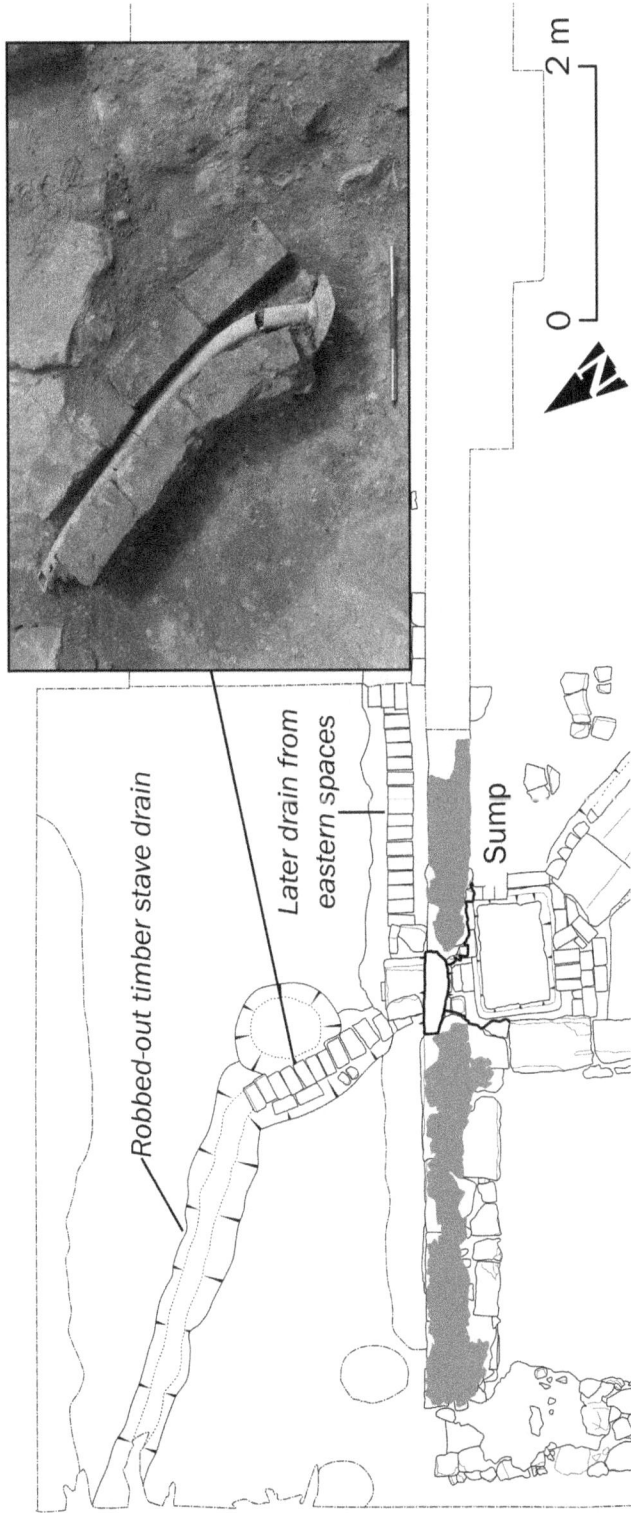

Figure 4.63. Illustration showing the location of the sump and associated drainage. The inset photograph shows the resin pipe in situ.

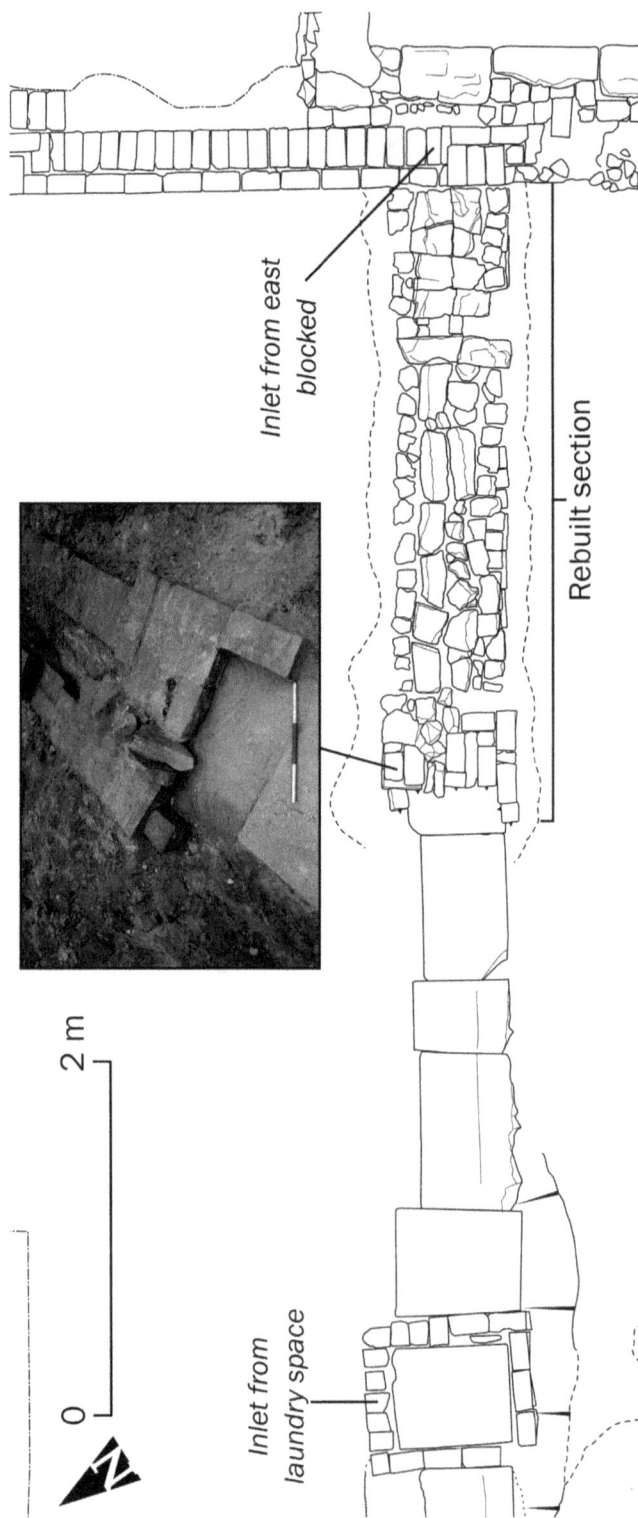

Figure 4.64. Illustration showing the rebuilt section of the central drain.

New entrance to ablutions area

Section through fill, showing early flags beneath

Later drain

Brick bearer

0   5 m

Figure 4.65. Illustration showing the section between Champ Street wall and the laundry.

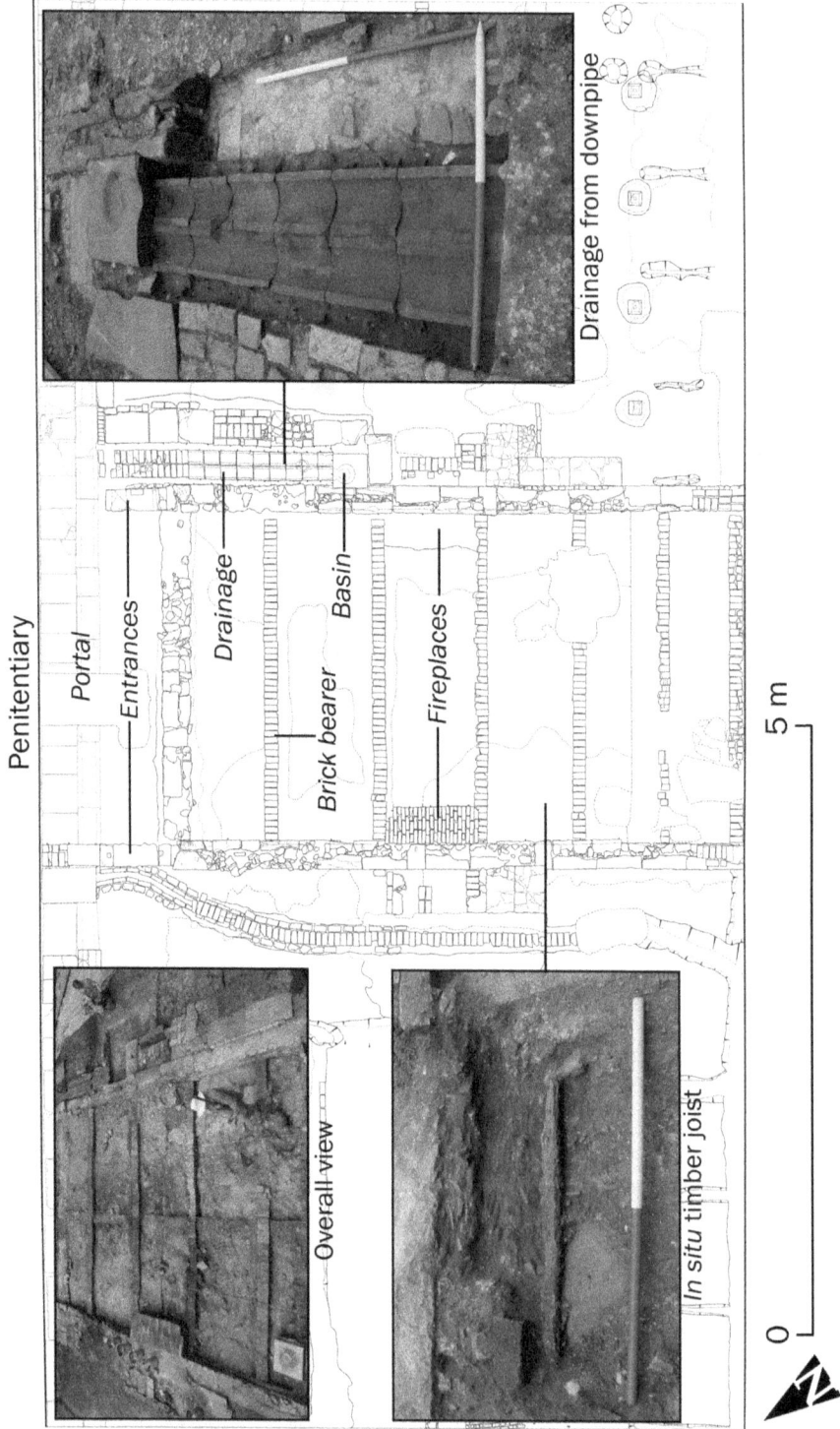

Penitentiary

Portal

Entrances

Drainage

Brick bearer

Basin

Fireplaces

Drainage from downpipe

Overall view

In situ timber joist

0   5 m

Figure 4.66. Illustration showing the day room space and the changes to the area during this phase.

transparency. The presence of clerical equipment (writing slate, slate and graphite pencils, and a stoneware ink bottle), personal items (spectacle glass and frames; a fragment of a fob watch), food containers, utensils and remains, and recreational items (smoking pipes, marbles, tokens) likely also reflect the use of the space as a recreation area.

As during Phase I, the east and west yards were reconfigured in a similar manner, with a freestanding shelter added to both. The archaeological evidence supported the ca. 1863 historic plan: that the west yard was converted to a washing area and the east outfitted with 'water closets' and urinals. In the former, the shelter was built with a brick footing, the structure measuring 16.7 metres (north-west to south-east) by 4 metres (Figure 4.67). The footings formed a foundation for the timber plates of the superstructure, with a row of centrally placed bricks providing additional support.

The interior of the structure had been paved with edge-laid whole and half-bricks, raised up to the level of the surrounding footing by the importation of clay, silt and rubble. This created a hard-wearing and waterproof surface, suggesting that the shelter had served as a washing area for the prisoners. This was further supported by the presence of the postholes down the centre of the shelter, which marked the likely presence of uprights supporting wash troughs. A fragment of earthenware lavatory basin recovered from disturbed fills associated with the shelter's brick surface also indicated the presence of wash furniture. Wastewater from the roof of the shelter was directed into drains, which fed into those along the southern wall of the penitentiary.

A large number of clay tobacco pipe fragments were recovered from the area corresponding with the shelter (Figure 4.68). Pipe fragments scattered to the north and south of the shelter across Phase II gravels indicated that use during this phase had also resulted in the deposition of this type of artefact. These artefacts had either remained *in situ* on the gravel surface or had moved downhill from the area of the shelter.

A shelter measuring 19 metres (south-east to north-west) by 1.9 metres was added to the southern edge of the yard (Figure 4.69). This structure was covered by a skillion roof attached to the Champ Street retaining wall, with its frontage supported by 12 timber uprights set into chamfered sandstone sockets sunk into the Phase I yard surfaces. The ca. 1863 historical plan suggests that these uprights supported a latticework screen. The shelter was floored with timber set on a series of bearers, below which ran an open spoon drain, which passed along the wall, then under the yard's eastern extent to empty into the encircling spoon drain. No archaeological evidence for the drain's purpose was found. However, the ca. 1863 plan indicates that the shelter covered a row of lavatory basins; it is likely that the drain took waste water from these.

A freestanding shelter had similarly been constructed in the east yard. Measuring 13 metres (north-west to south-east) by 4 metres, it was set on brick footings excavated into the former yard surfaces (Figure 4.70). A spoon drain ran along the southern edge of the footing, with runoff directed into the encircling drain on the eastern side of the yard. Unlike the western shelter, there was no evidence that it had been paved with brick. Instead, a deposit of coarsely broken dolerite may have served as the shelter's surface. Alternatively, the central line of bricks may have provided support for a timber floor. No evidence of furniture was found within the shelter, which may have simply provided a covered area for prisoners waiting to use the toilet facilities.

Historical evidence suggests that the toilets were located under a shelter constructed along the south of the yard (Figure 4.71). As in the west yard, the roof had been attached to the Champ Street retaining wall with bolts, supported along the front by a series of timber uprights set into chamfered sandstone sockets. A latticework screen had likely been supported by these uprights and a series of bearers supported timber flooring. No plumbing evidence for the 'water closets' or urinals that were once in the shelter was found, with the covered spoon drain running along the south of the yard relating only to the earlier phase of use. There was no evidence that any attempt was made to funnel waste into this existing subsurface drain. This supports the historical evidence that the toilet amenities were self-contained, requiring periodic emptying and cleaning.[27] That the term 'water closet' was used does indicate that water was used for flushing, and this is supported by the presence of linear cuts on Champ Street retaining wall that likely held overground piping. Concentrations of artefacts were encountered in

---

27 'Interrogatories ... Penal Settlement, Pauper and Lunatics' Depot, Port Arthur, Tasman's Peninsula, 15 November 1865, CO 280/369, reel no.1966–67, p. 87.

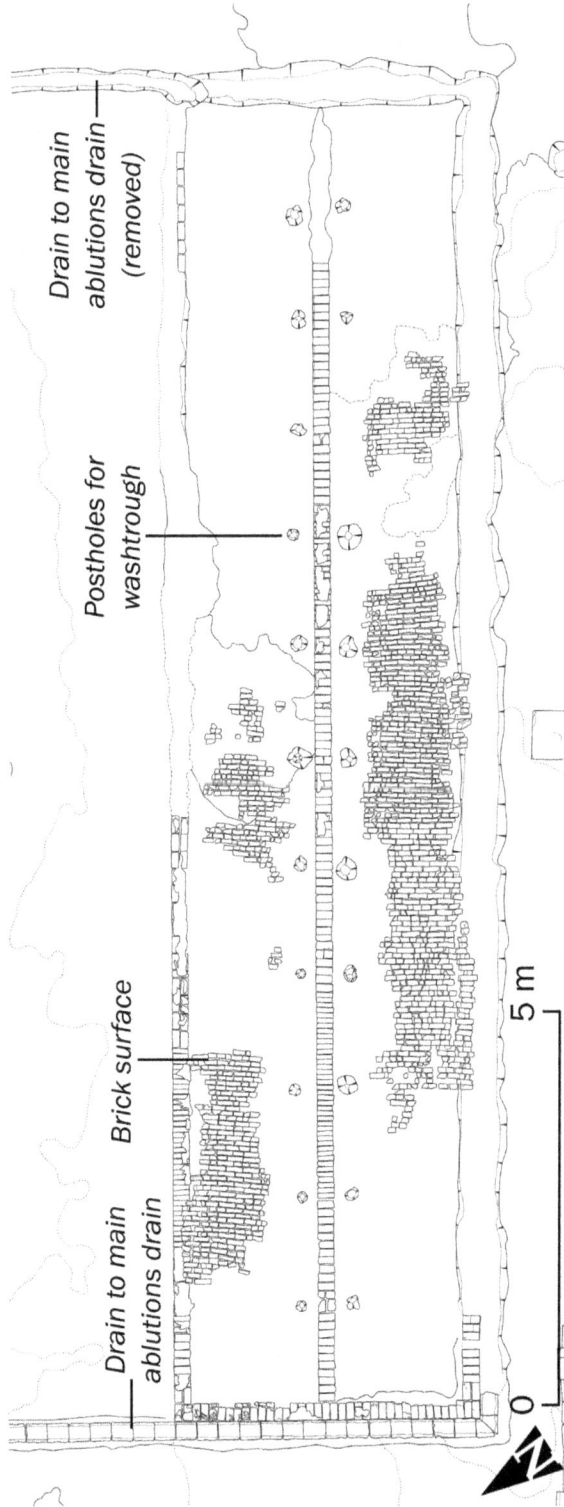

Drain to main
ablutions drain
(removed)

Postholes for
washtrough

Brick surface

Drain to main
ablutions drain

5 m

0

Figure 4.67. Illustration showing the shelter in the west yard.

Figure 4.68. Distribution of clay smoking pipes in the west yard from Phase II deposits (circled numbers denote numbers recovered from sieving).

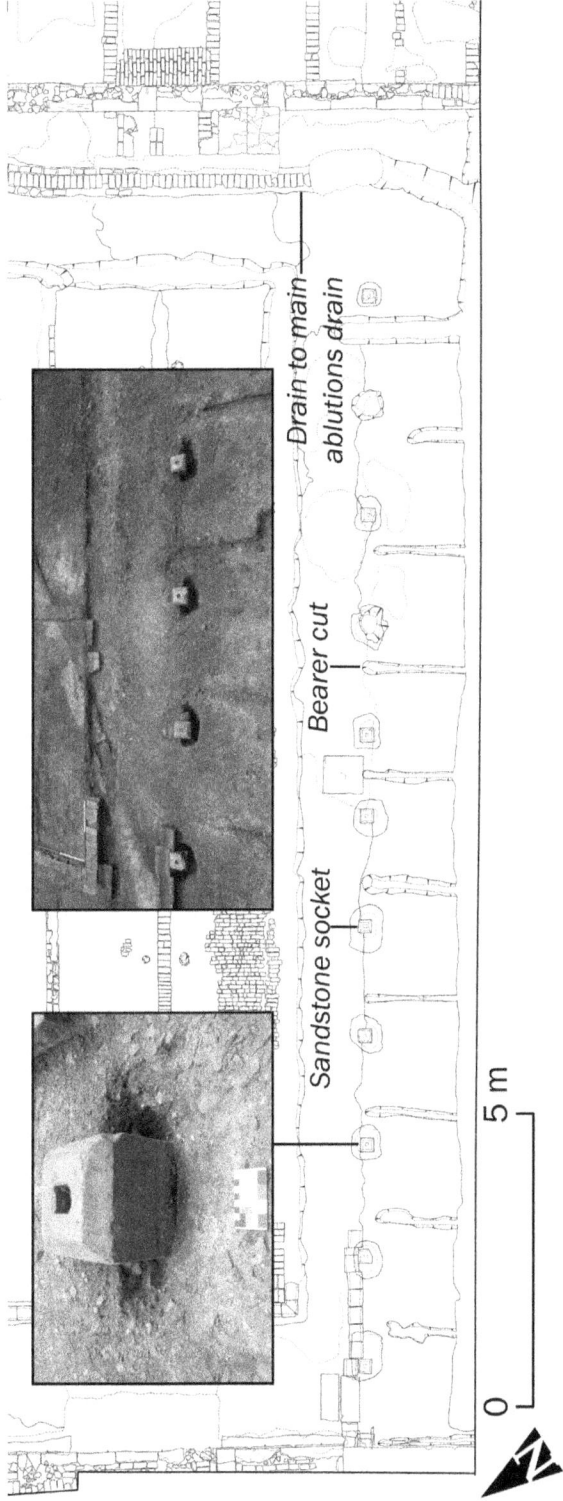

Figure 4.69. Illustration showing southern shelter in the west yard.

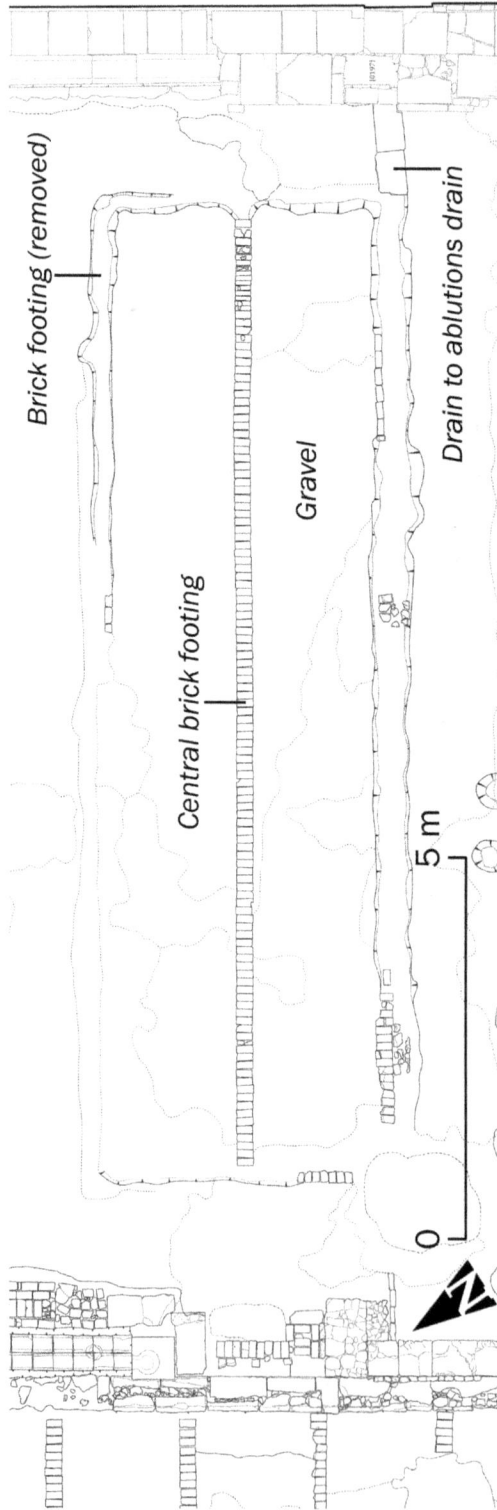

Figure 4.70. Illustration showing footings of central shelter in the east yard.

Brick footing (removed)

Drain to ablutions drain

Gravel

Central brick footing

5 m

0

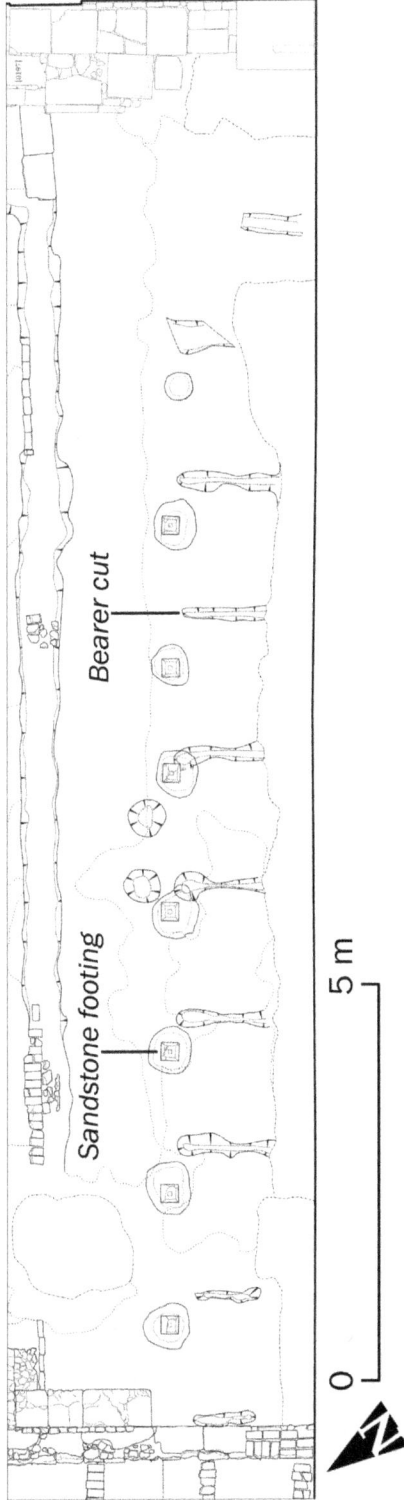

Figure 4.71. Illustration showing southern shelter in the east yard.

the yard. In particular, items including buttons and clay tobacco pipes were scattered around the location of shelters (Figure 4.72).

The construction of the shelters in both yards was accompanied by the addition of new surfacing gravels. Much looser than the compact brick gravel of Phase I, this mixture of siltstone, dolerite and sandstone gravel covered most of the open spaces, with broken dolerite predominant in the covered areas. The addition of the gravels raised the heights of both yards, making more pronounced the curve of the yard toward the rear of the penitentiary building. This would have increased the rate of rainwater flow off the yard, exacerbating the erosion of gravel from the yards' northern extent. Both the eastern and western yard surfaces' top-dressing gravel and levelling deposits also contained a number of tokens, manufactured from lead, copper alloy and ceramic (Figure 4.73). These are discussed in the chapter 'Private lives in public spaces'.

In the west yard there was some later Phase II activity that resulted in the modification of existing features (Figure 4.74). The portion of brick footing added between the ablutions and laundry areas potentially marked the blocking of the access between the back of the laundry and the ablutions yard. Modifications also took place to the subsurface drain running across the yard's eastern extent, with a portion of the drain re-laid and two openings to potentially facilitate the drainage of runoff from the day-room roof.

Post-abandonment summary

The penitentiary precinct was impacted in various ways after the closure of the penal station in 1877. Excavation within the penitentiary revealed burnt deposits and collapse, a result of the 1897 bushfire that destroyed the penitentiary building. As would be expected, the effects of fire, structural collapse and partial demolition resulted in the deposition of large quantities of structural artefacts, most commonly nails, bolts, iron strapping, and prismatic window glass. Over time, the encircling wall of the muster ground was lost and the ground left exposed, causing it to lose much of its surfacing gravel. Use of the area as a caravan park and tennis court in the twentieth century saw the deposition of fine-crushed dolerite across the area.

Within the laundry area, the salvaging of the masonry and timber elements of the building down to ground surface resulted in a high level of disturbance to existing features and deposits, the deposition of masonry debris and the accumulation of silts from exposure. Silts and rubble were deposited as walls were removed and timber elements salvaged. Invasive cuts were made where footings were taken out. Sandstone flagging and timber flooring were lifted and the deposits below were mixed together. In the former laundry space, much of the sandstone of the central drain was removed and the cavity filled with silts and demolition debris. The boiler house, as well as the boiler itself, were removed at this time. This resulted in the deposition of a large amount of brick and mortar debris across the space, as well as the removal of Phase II drainage elements. An accumulation of silt across spaces of the laundry indicated the area had been exposed to the elements for some time after the initial salvaging activity, with the presence of heat-affected deposits the result of the 1897 bushfire .

Similar activity occurred in the ablutions area. Within the day-room space, timber flooring elements were initially salvaged, resulting in the trampling and mixing of the exposed subfloor deposits. This accounted for the very disturbed nature of the deposits identified as part of Phase I and Phase II use. With the flooring removed, work probably began on salvaging the walls and the fireplaces for recycling into other uses. This resulted in the deposition of a large amount of shell lime mortar, plaster and brick rubble, both within the day-room space and in the adjacent yards.

In the west yard, the structures had been demolished/salvaged, resulting in rubble across the original footprints. After the timber frame of the central shelter had been removed, the brick footings had been partially robbed-out and its brick surface partly salvaged. Original bedding/levelling deposits for the surface were also disturbed or removed. The timber flooring, walling and roofing of the southern shelter had also been salvaged. This exposed the Intermediate Phase surfacing below the timber floor and caused a subsequent intermixing with the rubble deposits which accrued along the base of Champ Street wall.

The gravel surfaces of Phase I and Phase II were not badly affected by post-1877 activity, although some mixed deposits did result. In the yard's north-eastern corner, flagging associated with the portal space was part-salvaged, resulting in the exposure of earlier elements and the accumulation of further rubble and silt deposits. In the northern extent of the yard, a layer

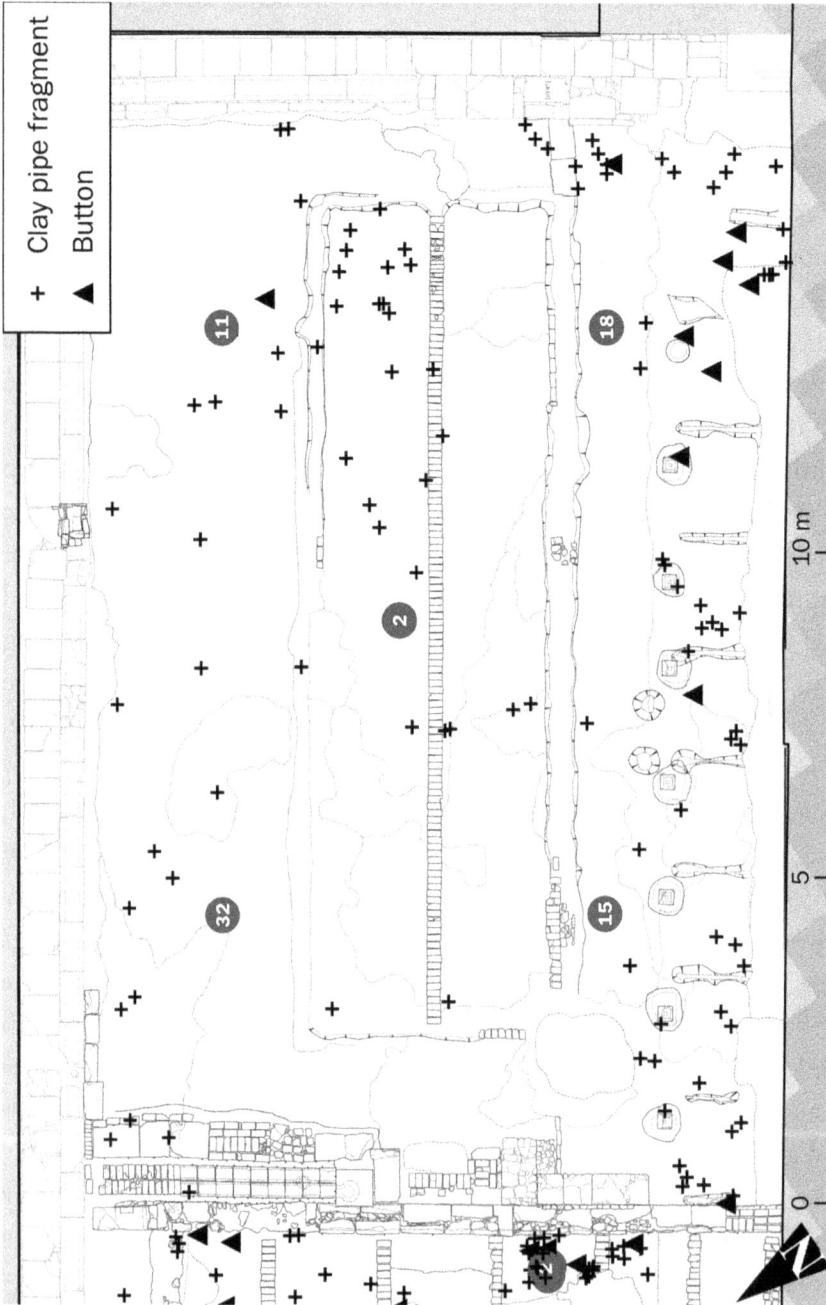

Figure 4.72. Distribution of clay smoking pipes and buttons in the east yard from Phase II deposits (circled numbers denote numbers recovered from sieving).

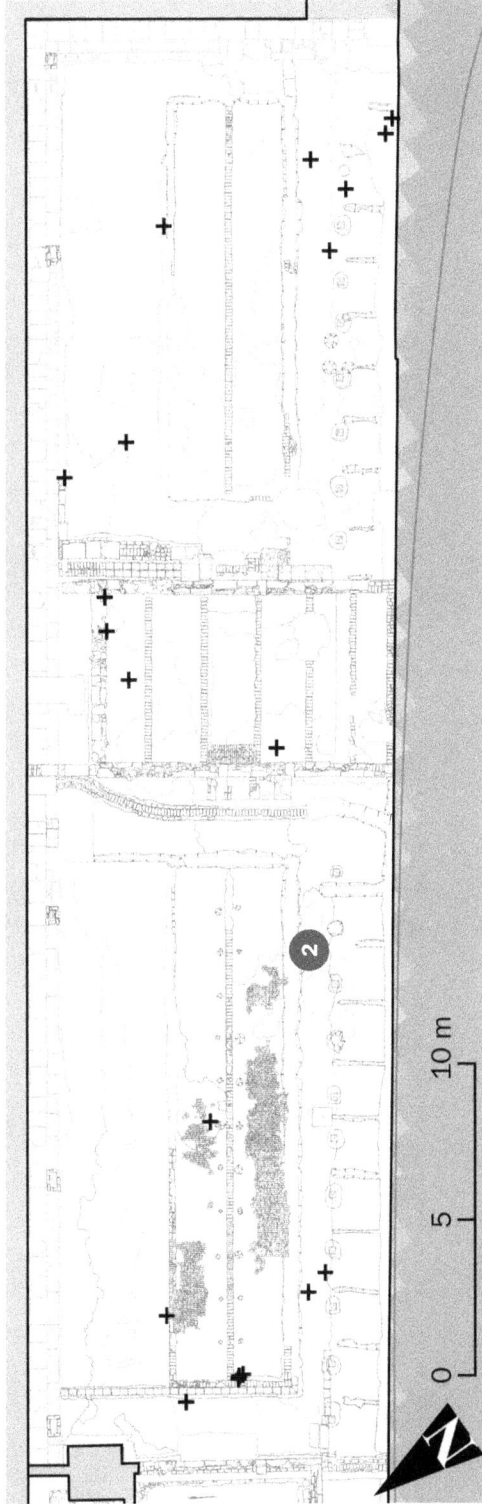

Figure 4.73. Distribution of tokens recovered from Phase II deposits across the ablutions area (circled numbers denote numbers recovered from sieving).

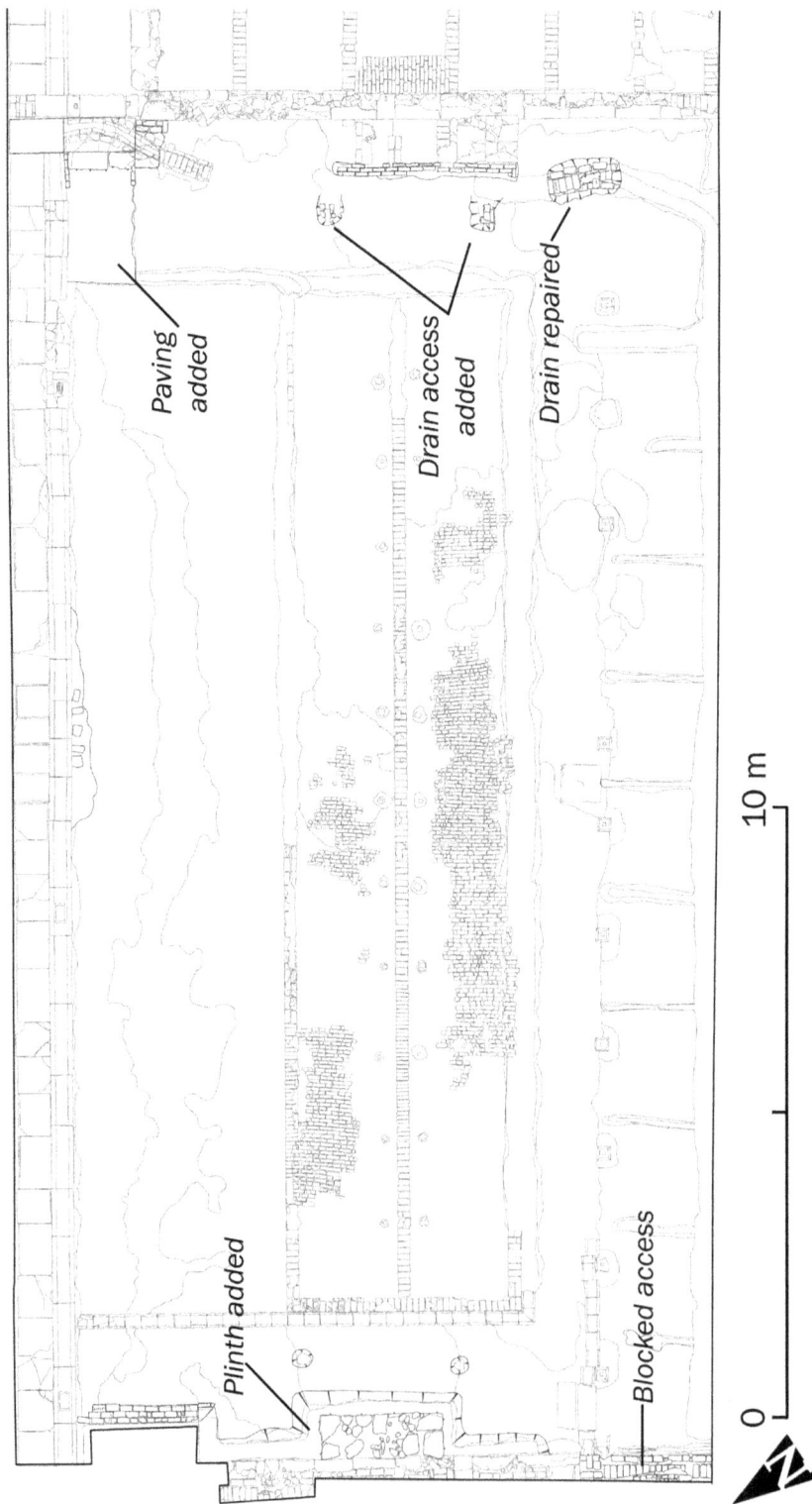

Figure 4.74. Illustration showing late changes to the west yard.

Paving added

Drain access added

Drain repaired

Plinth added

Blocked access

10 m

0

of brick rubble had accumulated where masonry had fallen from the walls of the penitentiary. This deposit was also present across the day-room space and sections of fallen walling also lay on the muster yard surface.

In the east yard, the removal of the timberwork and masonry footings of the central and southern shelters resulted in the deposition of brick, mortar and gravels around the location of the robbed-out footings, with an extended layer of mixed rubble situated along the base of the Champ Street retaining wall. Extensive amounts of disturbance, likely a combination of salvage activity and erosional processes, also occurred around the northern, eastern and western peripheries of the yard. In the yard's east, the layer of flagging running along the periphery was partly salvaged. In places the yard was scoured down to expose deposits from early occupation phases. The footings of the fireplace in the west of the yard were covered by demolition debris from the day room, indicating that this had been salvaged/demolished prior to the commencement of work on the day room. The demolition of the day room resulted in the deposition of mortar, plaster and brick debris across portions of the east yard.

All the areas were exposed for an extended period after a period of salvage and bushfire. Vegetation grew and silts accumulated, particularly where depressions existed after the removal of buildings. However, post-1897 intrusive activity into the sub-surface fabric was slight, going a long way towards explaining the excellent survival of many convict-period features and deposits in these areas. Set against the backdrop of the ivy-laden walls of the penitentiary, this epitome of romantic abandonment would not change again until the development of tourism and formal heritage management in the early 20th century (Figure 4.75).

Figure 4.75. Photograph of the early stages of the excavation showing the shallow nature of the archaeological deposits (note the level of the grass on the right). (PAHSMA 2016)

CONCLUSION:
ONE BUILDING, MANY STORIES

Since the close of the 19th century, Port Arthur has been a hub for tourism. At the beginning, it was those curious to see a part of Tasmania that had been restricted to them for so long. Their recollections and photographs provide us with immediate insight into a place defined by the void left when convicts and administrators were removed. This void was soon filled by those who sought to make a new life amid the relics of the convict past.

The penitentiary has always stood at the heart of this activity. Whether occupied, derelict, bushfire-riven or conserved and interpreted, the structure has remained the focal point of Port Arthur for over 150 years. It is a dominant feature in the landscape: at once a monument to control and coercion and a symbol of engineering knowledge – and perhaps folly. The upstanding brick and sandstone walls of the building, as well as the archaeological remnants of parade ground, watchmen's quarters, workshops, ablutions and laundry areas, have the capacity to tell much of the penal settlement's story: labour, incarceration, supervision, health and welfare.

The archaeological investigations discussed in this book have gone a long way toward helping us understand the full story of the penitentiary precinct. Without the knowledge derived from the investigations, the penitentiary is an imposing structure sitting isolated in a sea of grass, conveying little of the busy industrial nature of its beginnings, nor the retrofitted make-do of the 1850s conversion. Through the program of archaeological investigation that has spanned the period since 1976, we were able to recreate the changing configurations of buildings and ideas, in the process re-engaging with our understandings of its places and spaces.

One of the key stories, largely hidden to us until now, was how the administrators of Port Arthur and the convict labourers co-opted and, perhaps, coerced the landscape to suit their ends. Contemporary illustrations hint at how land and vegetation patterns were reshaped as the settlement grew from its September 1830 beginnings. Archaeological excavations showed how the landscape was reshaped to make room for buildings and workspaces. As the land was changed, its component rock and earth – even the very trees cut down to make way for settlement – were placed back into the harbour to make new space for building.

Archaeological excavations brought us face to face with hidden histories of the mill and granary. We had never really asked why this building was built at Port Arthur in the first place – why a penal station was home to such an incongruous project. Querying the fabric of the building caused us to query the archive, unearthing the records for the correspondence and reports of those responsible for the decisions. In the end, it was economy that tipped the balance, leading to the three-year investment in labour and material. This was a building that straddled the old shoreline and imposed its own, with convicts once again tasked with moving the earth to make new land. Long and complex construction timetables were matched by equally impressive earthworks, as a massive waterfront terrace was filled and cut from the former waterfront.

Through the archaeological investigations we cast new light on the process of conversion and the occupation of the penitentiary from 1854. What had before been an undifferentiated period defined by incarceration, the excavation of ablutions and laundry showed to be more complex. This was a space that evolved in response to the changing circumstances of Port Arthur.

It is clear that the authorities were responsive to how this space worked, redesigning it when it failed to facilitate the efficient implementation of their imposed daily regimes and/or when its deleterious health effects became evident. In the ablutions area, exercise yards and a poorly designed ablutions block gave way to a space designed to better meet the needs of the convict population. The structure of the laundry simultaneously evolved, although it never ceased being a focus of service-related labour.

We were afforded insight into the lives and routines of the prisoners who created and used the spaces of the penitentiary precinct. Brick and stone spoke of the effort required to form this place, their tool-marked or thumb-printed faces evidence of the unfree labour which had shaped them. Dolerite, hand-broken by convicts undergoing punishment, told of the grinding labour that could be part of the prisoner's day-to-day experience. Sandstone – quarried, carted and shaped by convict labour – spoke of the multi-skilled nature of the labour: the hard graft of quarrying by hand, through to the careful shaping of monumental and ornamental stone.

Through the artefacts we were able to examine the changing nature of Port Arthur and its impact upon incarcerated lives. The density of clay tobacco pipes in the ablutions area indicated a changing regulatory environment from the 1850s, as restrictions on tobacco markedly decreased and the pipe became a common object. No longer did its possession signify an individual in favour. Rather, the absence of a pipe marked an individual's undergoing sanction.

The archaeological investigations found clear evidence of illicit activity. Scattered across the ablutions area and from all phases of deposits, roughly made metal and ceramic tokens provide a glimpse of the penitentiary's unregulated side. Whether used for gaming or gambling, all forms of such activity were banned by the settlement regulations, with the charge sheets of Port Arthur providing some examples of where prisoners failed to cover their tracks. The presence of a button, marked in the same patterns as these tokens, perhaps hints at the ways convicts were able to hide their illegal activity in plain sight. Although less definitive, the presence of alcohol within the penitentiary precinct similarly points to the less licit side of convict life.

This book has used the archaeological and historical record to recreate and repopulate the historical environment of the Port Arthur penal station between 1830 and 1877. We have used the penitentiary precinct to ask questions about the evolution of the station: how landscape and the built environment were modified in response to the aims of administrators both near and far. The penitentiary has provided the lens through which we have examined the pivotal role of economy and coerced labour in the convict system. In the conversion of flour mill and granary to penitentiary we have charted the evolution of systems of incarceration in the British Empire. Through the puzzle of the artefacts, we have asked questions about the convict experience. Today, the Port Arthur penitentiary stands as a monument to the vast complexity inherent in Australia's experience of convict transportation.

ABOUT THE AUTHORS

Dr Richard Tuffin is a historical archaeologist currently working as a Postdoctoral Research Fellow at the University of New England. In addition to directing the 2016 Port Arthur archaeological investigations, he has worked as a research and commercial archaeologist in Australia, the Pacific and the UK.

Dr David Roe is archaeology manager at the Port Arthur Historic Site Management Authority. Over the past 45 years he has worked in archaeological research, heritage management and teaching in the UK and Europe, Solomon Islands, Vanuatu and Australia.

Sylvana Szydzik is an archaeologist with 13 years of experience in contemporary heritage conservation and management practices in Australia. She currently works as a Conservation Project Officer at the Port Arthur Historic Site Management Authority, where she is involved in archaeological projects ranging from excavation and survey to collections research.

Dr Jeanne Harris has 35 years' experience in cultural heritage and resources management in the USA and Australia. She is the owner of Urban Analysts, a consultancy specialising in the analysis of historical artefacts.

Ashley Matic was excavation director at Port Arthur during the two seasons of archaeological investigation undertaken in 2013. He has worked as an archaeological consultant and is currently part of the Historic Unrecovered War Casualties team in the History and Heritage Branch of the Royal Australian Air Force.

REFERENCES

Anderson, Clare. 'Transnational Histories of Penal Transportation: Punishment, Labour and Governance in the British Imperial World, 1788–1939.' *Australian Historical Studies* 47, No. 3 (2016): 381–97. https://doi.org/10.1080/1031461X.2016.1203962.

Archaeology at the Cabildo. Louisiana, Louisiana State Museum, n.d.

Atkinson, Alan. 'Writing About Convicts: Our Escape from the One Big Gaol.' *Tasmanian Historical Studies* 6, No. 2 (1999): 17–27.

Bairstow, Damaris, and Martin Davies. *Coal Mines Historic Site Survey: Preliminary Report.* Occasional Paper No. 15. Hobart: Department of Lands, Parks and Wildlife, 1987.

Barnes, R.D., G. Lume, J. Scott, and L. Burke-Smith. *Stabilisation of an Icon: The Penitentiary Precinct Conservation Project, Port Arthur, Tasmania, Australia.* Port Arthur: Port Arthur Historic Site Management Authority, n.d.

Bavin, Louise. 'Punishment, Prisons and Reform: Incarceration in Western Australia in the Nineteenth Century. Special Issue: Historical Refractions, Edited by Charlie Fox.' *Studies in Western Australian History*, No. 14 (1993): 121–48.

Birmingham, Judy, Ian Jack, and Dennis Jeans. *Industrial Archaeology in Australia: Rural Industry.* Victoria: Heinemann Publishers, 1983.

Brand, Ian. *The Convict Probation System: Van Diemen's Land 1839–1854.* Hobart: Blubber Head Press, 1990.

———. *The Port Arthur Coal Mines: 1833–1877.* Launceston: Regal Publications, 1993.

Brodie, Allan, Jane Croom, and James O Davies. *Behind Bars: The Hidden Architecture of England's Prisons.* Swindon: English Heritage, 1999.

Burn, David. *An Excursion to Port Arthur in 1842.* Edited by J.W. Beattie. Hobart: J.W. Beattie, 1850.

Casella, Eleanor. *Archaeology of the Ross Female Factory: Female Incarceration in Van Diemen's Land, Australia.* Records of the Queen Victoria Museum. Launceston: Queen Victoria Museum and Art Gallery, 2002.

———. 'Horizons Beyond the Perimeter Wall: Relational Materiality, Institutional Confinement, and the Archaeology of Being Global.' *Historical Archaeology* 50, No. 3 (2016): 127–43. https://doi.org/10.1007/BF03377338.

Clark, Julia, ed. *The Career of William Thompson, Convict.* Port Arthur: Port Arthur Historic Site Management Authority, 2009.

Colley, Sarah, and Martin Gibbs. 'NSW Archaeology Online: Grey Literature Archive.' In *Archaeology of Sydney Research Group*. Sydney: Sydney eScholarship, 2011. http://nswaol.library.usyd.edu.au.

Connah, Graham. 'The Lake Innes Estate: Privilege and Servitude in Nineteenth-Century Australia.' *World Archaeology* 33, No. 1 (2001): 137–54. https://doi.org/10.1080/00438240120047672.

———. 'Pattern and Purpose in Historical Archaeology.' *Australasian Historical Archaeology* 16 (1998): 3–7. http://www.jstor.org/stable/29544409.

Cotter, John L., Daniel G. Roberts, and Michael Parrington. *The Buried Past: An Archaeological History of Philadelphia*. Philadelphia: University of Pennsylvania Press, 1993.

Crawford, William. *Report of William Crawford, Esq., on the Penitentiaries of the United States, Addressed to His Majesty's Principal Secretary of State for the Home Department*. House of Commons. London, 1834. https://hdl.handle.net/2027/umn.31951002343340d.

Crook, Penny, and Tim Murray. *An Archaeology of Institutional Refuge: The Material Culture of the Hyde Park Barracks, Sydney, 1848–1886*. Sydney: Historic Houses Trust of New South Wales, 2006.

Cunzo, Lu Ann De. 'Reform, Respite, Ritual: An Archaeology of Institutions; the Magdalen Society of Philadelphia, 1800–1850.' *Historical Archaeology* 29, No. 3 (1995): 1–168.

D'Gluyas, Caitlin, Martin Gibbs, Chloe Hamilton, and David Roe. 'Everyday Artefacts: Subsistence and Quality of Life at the Prisoner Barracks, Port Arthur, Tasmania.' *Archaeology in Oceania* 50 (2015): 130–37. https://doi.org/10.1002/arco.5072.

Dane, Alexandra, and Richard Morrison. *Clay Pipes from Port Arthur 1830–1877: A Descriptive Account of the Clay Pipes from Maureen Byrne's 1977–78 Excavations at Port Arthur, Southeast Tasmania*. Canberra: Australian National University, 1979.

Davies, Peter, Penny Crook, and Tim Murray. *An Archaeology of Institutional Confinement: The Hyde Park Barracks, 1848–1886*. Sydney: Sydney University Press, 2013.

Edmonds, Penelope, and Hamish Maxwell-Stewart. '"The Whip Is a Very Contagious Kind of Thing": Flogging and Humanitarian Reform in Penal Australia.' *Journal of Colonialism and Colonial History* 17, No. 1 (2016). https://doi.org/10.1353/cch.2016.0006.

Evans, Robin. *The Fabrication of Virtue: English Prison Architecture, 1750–1840*. Cambridge, New York, Melbourne: Cambridge University Press, 1982.

Ford, Lisa, and David Andrew Roberts. 'New South Wales Penal Settlements and the Transformation of Secondary Punishment in the Nineteenth-Century British Empire.' *Journal of Colonialism and Colonial History* 15, No. 3 (2014). https://doi.org/10.1353/cch.2014.0038.

Foxhall, Katherine. 'From Convicts to Colonists: The Health of Prisoners and the Voyage to Australia, 1823–53.' *The Journal of Imperial And Commonwealth History* 39, No. 1 (2011): 1–19. https://doi.org/10.1080/03086534.2011.543793.

Fredericksen, Clayton. 'Confinement by Isolation: Convict Mechanics and Labour at Fort Dundas, Melville Island.' *Australasian Historical Archaeology* 19 (2001): 48–59.

Gannon, Megan 'Starving Felons, and Other Lessons from Prison Archaeology', 19 May 2015, *Atlas Obscura*, https://www.atlasobscura.com/articles/old-newgateprison.

Garman, James. *Detention Castles of Stone and Steel: Landscape, Labor, and the Urban Penitentiary*. Knoxville: University of Tennessee Press, 2005.

George, Sam. 'Unbuttoned: Archaeological Perspectives on Convicts and Whalers' Clothing in Nineteenth Century Tasmania.' Honours Thesis, LaTrobe University, 1999.

Gibbs, Martin. 'The Convict System of New South Wales: A Review of Archaeological Research since 2001.' *Archaeology in Oceania* 47, No. 2 (2012): 78–83. https://doi.org/10.1002/j.1834-4453.2012.tb00119.x.

———. 'The Enigma of William Jackman, "the Australian Captive": Fictional Account or the True Story of a 19th Century Castaway in Western Australia.' *The Great Circle* 24, No. 2 (2002): 3–21.

Godfrey, Barry. 'Prison Versus Western Australia: Which Worked Best, the Australian Penal Colony or the English Convict Prison System?' *The British Journal of Criminology* 59, No. 5 (2019): 1139–60. https://doi.org/10.1093/bjc/azz012. https://doi.org/10.1093/bjc/azz012.

Gojak, Denis. 'Convict Archaeology in New South Wales: An Overview of the Investigation, Analysis and Conservation of Convict Heritage Sites.' *Australasian Historical Archaeology* 19 (2001): 73–83.

Gojak, Denis, and Iain Stuart. 'The Potential for the Archaeological Study of Clay Tobacco Pipes from Australian Sites.' *Australasian Historical Archaeology* 17 (1999): 38–49.

Hall, Basil. *Travels in North America in the Years 1827 and 1828.* 3 Vols. Vol. 1, Edinburgh: Cadell and Co., 1830.

Hewitt, Geoff. 'Defiance of Authority at Melbourne Gaol: Clay Tobacco Pipes Reworked, Curated and Then Discarded in Haste?' *Australasian Historical Archaeology* 37 (2019): 87–90.

Hewitt, Geoff, and Richard Wright. 'Identification and Historical Truth: The Russell Street Police Garage Burials.' *Australasian Historical Archaeology* 22 (2004): 57–70.

Hinde, Richard S.E. 'Sir Walter Crofton and the Reform of the Irish Convict System, 1854 61 – I.' *Irish Jurist* 12, No. 1 (1977): 115–47.

———. 'Sir Walter Crofton and the Reform of the Irish Convict System, 1854–61 – Ii.' *Irish Jurist* 12, No. 2 (1977): 295–338.

Inwood, Kris, and Hamish Maxwell-Stewart. 'Introduction: Health, Human Capital, and Early Economic Development in Australia and New Zealand.' *Australian Economic History Review* 55, No. 2 (2015): 105–11. https://doi.org/10.1111/aehr.12072.

Jack, Ian. 'Historical Archaeology, Heritage and the University of Sydney.' *Australasian Historical Archaeology* 24 (2006): 19–24.

Jackman, Greg. *Penitentiary/Flourmill Archaeological Interpretation – Preliminary Notes.* Port Arthur: Port Arthur Historic Site Management Authority, 2009.

Karskens, Grace. 'The Convict Road Station Site at Wisemans Ferry: An Historical and Archaeological Investigation.' *Australian Journal of Historical Archaeology* 2 (1984): 17–26.

———. 'Defiance, Deference and Diligence: Three Views of Convicts in New South Wales Road Gangs.' *Australian Journal of Historical Archaeology* 4 (1986): 17–28.

———. *Inside the Rocks: The Archaeology of a Neighbourhood.* Alexandria, New South Wales: Hale & Iremonger Pty Ltd, 1999.

Kercher, B. 'Perish or Prosper: The Law and Convict Transportation in the British Empire, 1700–1850.' *Law and History Review* 21, No. 3 (2003): 527–84. https://doi.org/10.2307/3595119.

Kerr, James S. *Design for Convicts: An Account of Design for Convict Establishments in the Australian Colonies During the Transportation Era.* Sydney: Library of Australian History, 1984.

Lawrence, Susan, and Peter Davies. 'Convict Origins.' In *An Archaeology of Australia since 1788.* Contributions to Global Historical Archaeology. Springer Science+Business Media, 2011. https://doi.org/10.1007/978-1-4419-7485-3.

Lenik, Stephan. 'Mission Plantations, Space, and Social Control: Jesuits as Planters in French Caribbean Colonies and Frontiers.' *Journal of Social Archaeology* 12, No. 1 (2012): 51–71. https://doi.org/10.1177/1469605311426546.

Lowe, Casey &. *48 Macquarie & 220–230 Church Streets, Parramatta: Archaeological Assessment.* report prepared for Coombes Property Group & Drivas Property Group. Sydney, 2017.

Macfie, Peter. 'Government Sawing Establishments in Van Diemen's Land, 1817–1832.' In *Australia's Ever-Changing Forests V: Proceedings of the Fifth National Conference on Australian Forest History*, edited by John Dargavel, Denise Gaughwin and Brenda Libbis, 105–31. Canberra: Australian National University, 2002.

Marshall, Louis. 'A Benign Institution?: Convict Health, Living Conditions, and Labour Management at Port Arthur Penal Station, 1868–1870.' *Journal of Australian Colonial History* (2016): 65–94.

Matic, A., D. Roe, S. Szydzik, A. Waghorn, N. Corbett, and E.J. Harris, 'Technical Report. Archaeological Investigations and Monitoring: Penitentiary Precinct Conservation Project, 2012–2014', Port Arthur: Port Arthur Historic Site Management Authority, 2019.

Maxwell-Stewart, Hamish. *Closing Hell's Gates: The Death of a Convict Station.* Crows Nest, NSW: Allen & Unwin, 2008.

———. 'The Rise and Fall of John Longworth: Work and Punishment in Early Port Arthur.' *Tasmanian Historical Studies* 6, No. 2 (1999): 96–114.

Maxwell-Stewart, Hamish, and Rebecca Kippen. 'Sickness and Death on Convict Voyages to Australia.' In *Lives in Transition: Longitudinal Analysis from Historical Sources*, edited by Peter Baskerville and Kris Inwood, 43–70. Montreal & Kingston, London, Ithaca: McGill-Queen's University Press, 2015.

Mayhew, H., and J. Binny, *The Criminal Prisons of London*. London, 1868.

McGowan, Angela. *Excavations at Lithend, Port Arthur Historic Site.* Hobart: Port Arthur Conservation and Development Project, 1985.

Mein, Erin. 'Inmate Coping Strategies in Fremantle Prison, Western Australia.' Honours Thesis, University of Western Australia, 2012.

Munro, Doug. 'From Macquarie Harbour to Port Arthur: The Founding of a Penal Settlement.' *Tasmanian Historical Research Association* 36, No. 3 (1989): 113–24.

Murray, Tim. 'Integrating Archaeology and History at the "Commonwealth Block": "Little Lon" and Casselden Place.' *International Journal of Historical Archaeology* 10, No. 4 (2006): 385–403. https://doi.org/10.1007/s10761–006–0020–4.

Nash, Michael. 'Convict Shipbuilding in Tasmania.' *Tasmanian Historical Research Association* 50, No. 2 (2003): 83–106.

Owen, Tim, and Jody Steele. *Port Arthur 2002, Sawpit and Tannery Complex Excavation Report.* Report produced for the Port Arthur Historic Site Management Authority, 2002.

Petrow, Stefan. 'Claims of the Colony: Tasmania's Dispute with Britain over the Port Arthur Penal Establishment 1856–1877.' *Tasmanian Historical Research Association* 44, No. 4 (1997): 221–40.

———. 'Policing in a Penal Colony: Governor Arthur's Police System in Van Diemen's Land, 1826–1836.' *Law and History Review* 18, No. 2 (2000): 351–95. https://doi.org/10.2307/744299.

Preston, Keth. 'Prison Treadmills in Van Diemen's Land: Design, Construction and Operation, 1828 to 1856.' *Tasmanian Historical Research Association* 60, No. 2 (2013): 81–99.

Reader, Rachael. *Archaeological Excavation Report: Land Off Stanley Street, Central Salford: Plots B5/6 (New Bailey Prison)*. Manchester: University of Salford, 2015. http://usir.salford.ac.uk/id/eprint/43925/.

Reid, Kirsty. "'Contumacious, Ungovernable and Incorrigible': Convict Women and Workplace Resistance, Van Diemen's Land, 1820–1839.' In *Representing Convicts: New Perspectives on Convict Forced Labour Migration*, edited by Ian Duffield and James Bradley, 106–23. London and Washington: Leicester University Press, 1997.

Ritchie, John. 'Towards Ending an Unclean Thing: The Molesworth Committee and the Abolition of Transportation to New South Wales, 1837–40.' *Historical Studies* 17, No. 67 (1976): 144–64. https://doi.org/10.1080/10314617608595544.

Robbins, William M. 'The Lumber Yards: A Case Study in the Management of Convict Labour 1788–1832.' *Labour History* 79 (2000): 141–61. https://doi.org/10.2307/27516737.

Roberts, David Andrew. 'Colonial Gulag: The Populating of the Port Macquarie Penal Settlement, 1821–1832.' *History Australia* (2017): 588–606. https://doi.org/10.1080/14490854.2017.1389228.

Roscoe, Katy. 'A Natural Hulk: Australia's Carceral Islands in the Colonial Period, 1788–1901.' *International Review of Social History* 63 (2018): 45–63. https://doi.org/doi:10.1017/S0020859018000214.

Sharples, Chris. *A Coastal Erosion Hazard Assessment for the Port Arthur and Coal Mines Historic Sites, Tasman Peninsula, Tasmania*. Report prepared for Port Arthur Historic Site Management Authority, Tasmania, 2017.

Shaw, A.G.L. *Convicts and the Colonies*. 1971 ed. London: Faber, 1966.

Shayt, David H. 'Stairway to Redemption: America's Encounter with the British Prison Treadmill.' *Technology and Culture* 30, No. 4 (1989): 908–38. https://doi.org/10.2307/3106197.

Smith, Jeremy. 'Losing the Plot: Archaeological Investigations of Prisoner Burials at the Old Melbourne Gaol and Pentridge Prison.' *Provenance: The Journal of Public Record Office Victoria*, No. 10 (2011): 62–72.

Starr, Fiona. 'An Archaeology of Improvisation: Convict Artefacts from Hyde Park Barracks, Sydney, 1819–1848.' *Australasian Historical Archaeology* 33 (2015): 37–54.

Thompson, John. *Probation in Paradise: The Story of Convict Probationers on Tasman's and Forestier's Peninsulas, Van Diemen's Land, 1841–1857*. Hobart: John Thompson, 2007.

Thorp, Wendy. 'Directed for the Public Stock: The Convict Work Gang System and Its Sites.' In *Archaeology and Colonisation: Australia in the World Context*, edited by J. Birmingham, D. Bairstow, and A. Wilson, 109–22. Sydney: The Australian Society for Historical Archaeology Inc., 1987.

Townsend, Norma. 'A "Mere Lottery": The Convict System in New South Wales through the Eyes of the Molesworth Committee.' *Push from the Bush* 21 (1985): 58–86.

Tuffin, Richard. 'The Evolution of Convict Labour Management in Van Diemen's Land: Placing the "Penal Peninsula" in a Colonial Context.' *Tasmanian Historical Research Association* 54, No. 2 (2007): 69–83.

———. 'A Monument to Folly? The Port Arthur Flourmill and Granary.' *Tasmanian Historical Studies* 9 (2004): 124–8.

———. 'Port Arthur Conduct Record Offences, 1830–1868: Collective and Non-Collective Prisoner Offences.' Armidale: University of New England, 2020. https://hdl.handle.net/1959.11/29249.

———. 'The Post Mortem Treatment of Convicts in Van Diemen's Land, 1814–1874.' *Journal of Australian Colonial History* 9 (2007): 99–126.

Tuffin, Richard, and Martin Gibbs. 'The Archaeology of the Convict Probation System: The Labor Landscapes of Port Arthur and the Cascades Probation Station, 1839–55.' *International Journal of Historical Archaeology* 24, No. 3 (2020): 589–617. https://doi.org/10.1007/s10761–019–00523-w.

———. 'Early Port Arthur: Convict Colonization and the Formation of a Penal Station in Van Diemen's Land 1830–35.' *International Journal of Historical Archaeology* 23 (2019): 568–95. https://doi.org/10.1007/S10761–018–0479–9.

———. '"Uninformed and Impractical"? The Convict Probation System and Its Impact Upon the Landscape of 1840s Van Diemen's Land.' *History Australia* 17, no. 1 (2020): 87–114. https://doi.org/10.1080/14490854.2020.1717352.

Tuffin, Richard, Martin Gibbs, David Roberts, Hamish Maxwell-Stewart, David Roe, Jody Steele, and Susan Hood. 'Landscapes of Production and Punishment: Convict Labour in the Australian Context.' *Journal of Social Archaeology* 18, No. 1 (2018): 50–76. https://doi.org/10.1177/1469605317748387.

Tuffin, Richard, Peter Rigozzi, David Roe, and Jody Steele. 'Old V New? Comparing the Use of Traditional Recording Methodologies with Photogrammetry in Archaeological Practice at the Port Arthur Historic Site.' Digital Cultural Heritage: Future Visions, University of Queensland, 2017.

Winter, Sean. *Transforming the Colony: The Archaeology of Convictism in Western Australia.* Newcastle-upon-Tyne: Cambridge Scholars Publishing, 2017.

Winter, Sean, and Tom Whitley. 'The Fremantle Prison Project.' *Australasian Historical Archaeology: Journal of the Australasian Society for Historical Archaeology* 33 (2015): 73–77.

Young, David. *Making Crime Pay: The Evolution of Convict Tourism in Tasmania.* Hobart: Tasmanian Historical Research Association, 1996.

INDEX

Page numbers in *italics* refer to figures. 'Images' refer to photographs of a feature. 'Plans' refer to original drawn plans and to modern drawings or diagrams representing reconstructions of an area.

www.ingramcontent.com/pod-product-compliance
Lightning Source LLC
Chambersburg PA
CBHW080550270326
41929CB00019B/3250